The Gettier Problem

When philosophers try to understand the nature of knowledge, they arguably have to confront the Gettier Problem. This problem, set out in Edmund Gettier's famous paper of 1963, has possibly yet to be solved, and has challenged our best attempts to define what knowledge is. This volume offers an organised sequence of accessible and distinctive chapters explaining the history of debate surrounding Gettier's challenge, and where that debate should take us next. The chapters describe and evaluate a wide range of ideas about knowledge that have been sparked by philosophical engagements with the Gettier problem, including such phenomena as fallibility, reasoning, evidence, reliability, truth-tracking, context, luck, intellectual virtue, wisdom, conceptual analysis, intuition, experimental philosophy, and explication. The result is an authoritative survey of fifty-plus years of epistemological research – along with provocative ideas for future research – into the nature of knowledge.

Stephen Hetherington is Professor of Philosophy at the University of New South Wales, Sydney. His many publications in epistemology include *Knowledge and the Gettier Problem* (2016).

Classic Philosophical Arguments

Over the centuries, a number of individual arguments have formed a crucial part of philosophical enquiry. The volumes in this series examine these arguments, looking at the ramifications and applications which they have come to have, the challenges which they have encountered, and the ways in which they have stood the test of time.

Titles in the series

The Prisoner's Dilemma
Edited by Martin Peterson

The Original Position
Edited by Timothy Hinton

The Brain in a Vat
Edited by Sanford C. Goldberg

Pascal's Wager
Edited by Paul Bartha and Lawrence Pasternack

The Gettier Problem
Edited by Stephen Hetherington

The Gettier Problem

Edited by

Stephen Hetherington
University of New South Wales, Sydney

CAMBRIDGE
UNIVERSITY PRESS

CAMBRIDGE
UNIVERSITY PRESS

University Printing House, Cambridge CB2 8BS, United Kingdom

One Liberty Plaza, 20th Floor, New York, NY 10006, USA

477 Williamstown Road, Port Melbourne, VIC 3207, Australia

314–321, 3rd Floor, Plot 3, Splendor Forum, Jasola District Centre,
New Delhi – 110025, India

79 Anson Road, #06–04/06, Singapore 079906

Cambridge University Press is part of the University of Cambridge.

It furthers the University's mission by disseminating knowledge in the pursuit of
education, learning, and research at the highest international levels of excellence.

www.cambridge.org
Information on this title: www.cambridge.org/9781107178847
DOI: 10.1017/9781316827413

© Stephen Hetherington 2019

First published 2019

Printed and bound in Great Britain by Clays Ltd, Elcograf S.p.A.

A catalogue record for this publication is available from the British Library.

ISBN 978-1-107-17884-7 Hardback
ISBN 978-1-316-63110-2 Paperback

Contents

List of Contributors   *page* vii

Preface   ix

Introduction: Meet the Gettier Problem   1
Stephen Hetherington

1. The Gettier Problem and Fallibilism   11
Charity Anderson

2. Epistemic Closure and Post-Gettier Epistemology of Reasoning   27
Claudio de Almeida

3. Gettier Cases and Evidence   48
Clayton Littlejohn

4. The Gettier Problem and Externalism   66
Rodrigo Borges

5. The Gettier Problem and Context   78
Delia Belleri and Annalisa Coliva

6. The Gettier Problem and Epistemic Luck   96
Duncan Pritchard

7. The Sensitivity Response to the Gettier Problem   108
Kelly Becker

8. The Gettier Problem and Intellectual Virtue   125
John Greco

9. Knowledge and Wisdom   144
Ernest Sosa

10. The Gettier Problem and the Program of Analysis   159
Patrick Rysiew

11. Intuition in the Gettier Problem   177
Elijah Chudnoff

12. Experimental Epistemology and "Gettier" Cases   199
John Turri

13. The Gettier Problem's Explicability Problem   218
Stephen Hetherington

Bibliography   235
Index   252

Contributors

Charity Anderson is Assistant Professor of Philosophy at Baylor University, Waco, Texas.

Kelly Becker is Professor of Philosophy at the University of New Mexico.

Delia Belleri is Assistant Professor of Philosophy at the University of Vienna.

Rodrigo Borges is Assistant Professor of Philosophy at Pontifical Catholic University of Rio Grande do Sul (PUCRS) in Porto Alegre, Brazil.

Elijah Chudnoff is Associate Professor of Philosophy at the University of Miami.

Annalisa Coliva is Professor of Philosophy at the University of California, Irvine.

Claudio de Almeida is Professor of Philosophy at Pontifical Catholic University of Rio Grande do Sul (PUCRS), in Porto Alegre, Brazil.

John Greco is Leonard and Elizabeth Eslick Professor of Philosophy at Saint Louis University.

Stephen Hetherington is Professor of Philosophy at the University of New South Wales, Sydney.

Clayton Littlejohn is Reader in Philosophy at King's College London.

Duncan Pritchard is Chancellor's Professor of Philosophy at the University of California, Irvine, and Professor of Philosophy at the University of Edinburgh.

Patrick Rysiew is Professor of Philosophy at the University of Victoria, Canada.

Ernest Sosa is Board of Governors Professor of Philosophy at Rutgers University.

John Turri is Canada Research Chair of Philosophy and Cognitive Science at the University of Waterloo, Canada.

Preface

The Gettier problem is a classic – and continuing – moment within modern philosophy. It began with a punchy question – the title of Edmund Gettier's 1963 paper, "Is justified true belief knowledge?" – and a snappy argument – Gettier's – for a confronting answer. Gettier was asking whether knowledge is wholly definable as a justified true belief; his answer was a decisive "No." In which case, epistemologists were left wondering – really wondering – about what knowledge *is*, if it is not what, according to Gettier, they had taken it to be.

Sparking this epistemological upheaval was no small achievement. To understand how much of an upheaval it was, remember that the initial characterization that philosophers ever offer of epistemology, such as to their introductory students, *is* that it is "theory of knowledge." Epistemologists were therefore hit hard – very hard – by the thought of lacking an agreed definition of what knowledge is. What were they even theorizing *about*? So, it is hardly surprising that Gettier's argument had the initial impact that it did.

Of course, his argument would not have continued making such an impact if epistemologists had swiftly and surely concurred on a reply to that argument – for instance, a reply decreeing what knowledge is, if not simply a justified true belief. But no such consensus arose – at the time, or soon after, or soon after that, or . . .

We are still waiting. We thereby face what soon became known as the Gettier *problem*.

And thus we have this book.

I am very grateful to Hilary Gaskin at Cambridge University Press for inviting me to edit the book, as well as for her subsequent advice and guidance. The Gettier problem is one of the topics that sparked my youthful epistemological instincts. And although I am no longer youthful, the Gettier problem remains with me. I hope that this book can help others to appreciate some of the philosophical complexity and richness that has created and sustained the problem. In surprisingly many respects, it has been a *good* problem for epistemology to have.

Introduction: Meet the Gettier Problem

Stephen Hetherington

I.1 Introduction to an Introduction

How do philosophical movements or eras begin? How do they end? All too often, they fade away with a whisper or two – dying quietly, unnoticed, supplanted through distraction by new ideas or issues or fashions. They might enter the world unobtrusively, too – barely acknowledged, recognized only with hindsight. Not always, though: sometimes, a philosophical movement's or era's end or beginning can be dramatic, even explosive.

That is how post-Gettier epistemology began – with a deafening "kapow!" Epistemology had been proceeding along familiar paths: business as normal. In that spirit, 1962 came and went, as 1961 had done, like 1960 before it, following a calm 1959 . . . .[1] Then 1963 arrived. Fresh issues of that year's array of academic philosophy journals appeared. And then, a few months into the year, without fanfare, one of those journals – *Analysis*, an excellent journal dedicated to publishing concise philosophy papers – gave us just such a paper by Edmund Gettier, a young American philosopher. Epistemology has looked quite different since that June 1963 issue of *Analysis*. Gettier's paper was called "Is justified true belief knowledge?" Having asked the question, he answered it: "No." And decisively so, in the view of epistemologists *en masse* – then and since. The year 1963 was soon recognized by epistemologists as having been a time of transition for them. Pre-Gettier epistemology had ended; post-Gettier epistemology was under way.

It still is. We are the epistemological heirs of that exciting moment. We are post-Gettier epistemologists. Indeed, we are post-Gettier philosophers, given epistemology's historical importance within philosophy – and given how Gettier's argument struck so many as a clearly successful instance

---

[1] For a survey of that stage of epistemology, a survey untouched by the torrent that was about to descend, see Hill (1961).

of philosophical reasoning. Gettier initiated what swiftly became a powerfully influential and wide-reaching wave of epistemological inquiry. That wave is still surging – sometimes gently, at other times loomingly. Not all epistemologists have ridden it, and some fight it even while riding it; many others, though, embrace its flow and power.[2]

More prosaically, Gettier and the impact made by his paper even changed philosophy's everyday lexicon. When someone's name has become as lexically embedded as has happened for Gettier's, this is clearly a mark of professional respect. We now have such philosophically everyday words as "Gettiered," "unGettiered," "Gettierized," "Gettier-proof," and "Gettier cases." Respect, indeed.

1.2 The Gettier Argument

In his paper's two-and-a-half pages, Gettier presented a single succinct argument. It was built around two imagined stories – two counterexamples. These were directed by Gettier against what, he also argued, was a discernible form of thesis that philosophers had adopted when trying to understand the nature of knowledge. This form of thesis was, according to Gettier, a form of definition. He claimed that it was a general form instantiated by various specific attempts to understand what it is for someone to have some knowledge – attempts that had begun in ancient Greek philosophy and continued into the 1960s, when Gettier was writing.[3]

This section will briefly describe the key elements of that picture from Gettier – the kind of knowledge that philosophers had been attempting to define, the general form of definition that they had used, and how the counterexamples were to be brought to bear against that general form of definition.

---

[2] This is a personal note. I was a second-year undergraduate when I first met Gettier's paper. I was introduced to it by William Lycan, then visiting at the University of Sydney from Ohio State University, where his colleagues included George Pappas and Marshall Swain, the editors of a terrific and just-then-appeared collection of papers (1978) on the influence of Gettier's paper within epistemology. The book, like the course, like the issues, felt fresh and energetic. It was one of the two textbooks – the other was Roth and Galis (1970), also excellent, which included Gettier's paper – for the course. This was my most personally exciting undergraduate course. Lycan conveyed so well the sense that these were issues on which real philosophical progress might be made, with new ideas swirling around us, close enough to be touched, and with much precise thinking on display. Gettier's challenge felt very real, very urgent.

[3] He first cited Plato, from the *Meno* and the *Theaetetus*, before mentioning Ayer (1956) and Chisholm (1957).

The kind of knowledge. Gettier was discussing what philosophers refer to as propositional knowledge. This is knowledge that we report or describe by according it a propositional content. For instance, he knows (propositionally) that he is standing in his office: "he is standing in his office" is a proposition with an indicative form, one that claims to report or describe a state of affairs (namely, his standing in his office). When philosophers say that they are telling us about the nature of knowledge, propositional knowledge is usually – for better or for worse – their intended prey.[4]

The form of definition. Philosophers seek understanding, and one of the phenomena of which epistemologists, in particular, seek understanding is knowledge. But not all philosophical understanding, we might feel, needs to be as strict and complete as is conveyed by a *definition*: "virtue = df ...," "evil = df ...," etc. Given philosophy's difficulty, in practice we might well be pleased to attain even some philosophical understanding that is only partial and suggestive, still exploratory and allusive: even that could be a job well done. Nonetheless, if we do find an accurate definition of something that matters to us, we might consider this to be a job *very* well done. The nature of knowledge, like that of virtue, or of evil, say, probably matters to many of us. So, can we understand it insightfully and fully? Can we understand it by defining – accurately – what constitutes having some knowledge?

Gettier claimed at the outset of his paper that he was engaging with a philosophical tradition where, apparently, some of its most prominent practitioners were indeed confident of having achieved a definitional level of understanding of knowledge's nature. Although those philosophers might disagree over details – and Gettier described those differing details for three such philosophers (Plato, A. J. Ayer, and R. M. Chisholm) – they could still be regarded as giving voice, even across the centuries, to a shared underlying form of definition.

What form were those definitions taking? Since Gettier highlighted it – in preparation for launching his counterexamples against it – this form of definition has generally been called the *justified-true-belief* definition of knowledge. It is a general picture of what knowing is (this is why I use the word "form"). Here is its basic idea:

---

[4] This is not universally so. In recent years, especially, there has been much epistemological focus on knowledge-how – knowing how to perform some (kind of) action. See, for example, Ryle (1946; 1949), Stanley and Williamson (2000), and Hetherington (2011a).

One's having some instance of knowledge *is* (by definition) one's having a belief that is true (accurate) and justified (somehow rationally well-supported).

This formula is intended as a definition of its left-hand-side – that is, of *what it is* to have an instance of knowledge. We are being told that – by definition (albeit in general terms) – any instance of knowledge is nothing more and nothing less than a well-justified true belief. Different epistemologists might then offer differing suggestions as to how to make this generic picture more detailed; the general picture remains, though.

The counterexamples. I mentioned that epistemology now includes the concept of a *Gettier case*. That concept is traceable to Gettier's two counterexamples.[5] I also mentioned that he used them in order to question the justified-true-belief definition. But he was not questioning every aspect of that definition. The definition can be treated as a conjunction of two claims – only one of which Gettier was questioning. Here are the two claims:

JTB-Necessity. Being a justified true belief is always needed for being knowledge: each of those three elements – justification, truth, and belief – is always required if an instance of knowledge is to be constituted.

JTB-Sufficiency. Being a justified true belief is always sufficient for being knowledge: the combination of those three elements – justification, truth, and belief – is always enough to constitute an instance of knowledge.

Gettier's counterexamples were intended to reveal the falsity only of the latter thesis – JTB-Sufficiency. Each of his two imagined situations tells a story about a particular person, Smith. Setting aside the colorful details of each case, the following combination of circumstances obtains in each: Smith forms a belief that is true, is justified, yet is not knowledge. At any rate, that is how Gettier interpreted these situations. Nor was he alone in having that reaction. The vast majority of epistemologists – from 1963 to now – have agreed with that sort of interpretation of these and like situations. Epistemology thus formed the concept of a Gettier case – and soon regarded it as a powerful concept. Each such case (we are now routinely told) is a successful counter-example to "the sufficiency half" of the justified-true-belief definition of knowledge.

---

[5] This is not to say that no similar cases had ever appeared previously within philosophy. It was the cases plus the systematic use to which Gettier and others put them that have given us this concept. For some discussion of earlier cases with a similar internal structure, see Shope (1983, pp. 19–21) and Hetherington (2016a, p. 5).

And there have been many such cases, each of them inspired by Gettier. The book's cover hints at one of them – the famous sheep-in-the-field case. This one is from Roderick Chisholm (1966, p. 23n22; 1977, p. 105; 1989, p. 93). It imagines someone's gazing at a field, noticing what looks like a sheep, and forming the belief that there is a sheep in the field. The belief is true, although only because there is a sheep far away in this same field, hidden from this person's view. (What is being seen is a dog that is disguised as a sheep.)

I.3 The Gettier Argument's Apparent Significance

Suppose that Gettier was right in his answer to his article's own titular question: suppose that the justified-true-belief definition is mistaken, because JTB-Sufficiency is mistaken. This looks like a powerful blow to have struck against the justified-true-belief definition of knowledge. Is this also enough to make Gettier's argument significant? That might depend on how important is it to see the falsity of that definition (if indeed it is false). Might it depend, too, on what might be revealed about epistemology, or even about philosophy more broadly, by seeing the definition's falsity in the particular *way* in which Gettier revealed its falsity (if indeed he did)?

The justified-true-belief definition did strike epistemologists as having been an important philosophical insight – albeit one that suddenly, just like that, Gettier had refuted. At least part of that importance was historical; or so Gettier apparently thought. As Section I.2 noted, he began his paper by arguing that instances of this general way of defining knowledge had been with us since Plato – almost the beginning of Western philosophy – and were still with us. Epistemologists in 1963 did not question that view of the historical significance of his argument's target.[6]

There are other potential sources of significance, too. Suppose that Gettier was not reacting against a conception of knowledge that had in fact been guiding all epistemologists for all of those centuries. If so, perhaps he was oversimplifying the history of epistemology in this respect. Is it possible, for instance, that he was discussing only one of *two* forms – broadly characterized – that knowledge might take? Ultimately, philosophy might need to choose between fallibilist and infallibilist conceptions of knowledge; perhaps some of philosophy's historically significant figures adopted

---

[6] But this has subsequently been questioned. For example, see Kaplan (1985), Dutant (2015), and Le Morvan (2016).

infallibilist conceptions of knowledge. Seemingly, though, Gettier's argument was only about fallibilist conceptions of it. (He introduces his argument by *saying* that the sort of justification that he will be discussing leaves open the possibility that the belief being justified is false, even while being justified. That is a fallibilist way of thinking about knowledge's justification component.) This might undermine the *historical* reach of Gettier's argument.

Still, the argument could remain conceptually important, particularly if independent reasoning tells us that some sort of fallibilist conception of knowledge is what we should be adopting. For then we could regard Gettier as having shown, dramatically and decisively, that we need to say more, if we are to understand fallible knowledge (and thereby knowledge at all), than that a belief is knowledge if and only if it is true and fallibly justified. This could be a spur to further fallibilist thinking about knowledge's nature.

Philosophers also saw significance in Gettier's argument precisely because it seemed to show that real philosophical insight – a real result, even if a critical or destructive one, about how to define knowledge – could be attained; and it could be attained simply yet decisively. This was methodologically inspiring for those who might otherwise feel that philosophy is never a way to gain real results, real insights. Thanks to Gettier, maybe there can be real philosophical progress, achievable purely by thinking!

I.4 The Gettier Problem

Even so, philosophers soon viewed Gettier as having given to epistemology what they called the Gettier *problem*. It is useful to distinguish between two ways of interpreting this idea. We can talk of the *in-principle* Gettier problem and of the *in-practice* Gettier problem.

The in-principle Gettier problem. This was the intellectual puzzle, the philosophical conundrum, posed by Gettier. Could it be solved? The usual formulation of it was along these questioning lines:

> How should knowledge be defined, if not merely as justified true belief? What more is needed, if a belief – presumably a true and justified one – is to be knowledge, given that Gettier cases reveal the insufficiency, for describing something as knowledge, of describing it merely as a belief that is true and justified?

The challenge of answering these questions is the Gettier problem, under-stood purely as an intellectual challenge.[7]

The in-practice Gettier problem. The intellectual challenge posed by the in-principle Gettier problem soon proved to be, as a matter of professional practice among epistemologists, exceedingly difficult to meet. One epistemol-ogist after another would claim to have solved the Gettier problem (the in-principle problem). Some such claims would attract support; never enough support, though, to convince epistemologists as a group. And this was a problem of its own – a professional problem, a collectively lived problem of philosophers devoting much time to trying to solve the in-principle Gettier problem while never agreeing on success being achieved. "Why cannot we agree on how to solve the Gettier problem?" That question was ever present. The result is that, by now, we have long had the in-practice Gettier problem.[8] Individual Gettier cases have often seemed to offer clear indicators of something going awry within them; and hence of what to fix within them if knowledge was to have been present within the particular case's circum-stances; hence, too, of what knowledge even is. The in-practice problem, however, is that all of these proposed solutions have continued being suscep-tible to Gettier cases – that is, to further instances of the (in-principle) Gettier problem. The (in-practice) Gettier problem thus grew and grew. It is still growing.

1.5 Post-Gettier Epistemology

The in-practice Gettier problem is therefore still with us: rampant disagree-ment persists among epistemologists as to how to solve the in-principle Gettier problem. Is that also a worrying state of affairs? Should epistemolo-gists be perturbed, for example, at the possibility of there being something problematic about the practice of epistemology itself? Is the Gettier problem's in-practice version an indication of a wider problem – about epistemology as a whole, about epistemology's potential ever to solve its own (in-principle) problems?

Not all epistemologists are worried. Many are encouraged by the range of independently interesting epistemic concepts and theses – about knowledge, but also about associated phenomena, such as belief and justification – that seem to have emerged from epistemology's post-Gettier efforts. Post-Gettier

---

[7] The justified-true-belief definition was sometimes called "JTB" for short. Correlatively, the in-principle Gettier problem was sometimes referred to as the quest to ascertain the correct "JTB+."

[8] Lycan (2006) refers to it as "the Gettier Problem problem."

epistemology has struck many as being quite fruitful – in a range of ways, regardless of whether it has reached an in-practice solution to the in-principle Gettier problem.

The independently interesting ideas to emerge from post-Gettier epistemology have also included potential morals about epistemology as a whole – meta-epistemological thoughts. We might wonder about the methodology on display in Gettier's argument – the use of imagined or intuited counterexamples to a definition that aspires to being a full understanding of some phenomenon such as knowledge. Should we always seek a definition, when seeking philosophical understanding? What alternatives are there? How reliable are intuitions about how to "read" particular cases (either real or imagined)? Are such intuitions decisive? If not, how strongly should they guide our thinking? And so on.

1.6 This Book's Structure

This book is organized to reflect (i) the intellectual structuring of the in-principle Gettier problem – how Gettier's article introduced its two counterexamples – and (ii) the post-Gettier professional realities that have constituted both the optimistic and the possibly worrying elements of the in-practice Gettier problem. Accordingly, the book has the following three parts (only informally, I should add).

As this introduction has explained, Gettier's paper began by situating its target (the justified-true-belief definition of knowledge), and thereby the paper itself, within what it claimed is a clear historical tradition. Gettier then began his argument by highlighting two key epistemic principles, describing each as vital to the counterexamples that he was about to describe. Chapters 1 (Charity Anderson) and 2 (Claudio de Almeida) are therefore about those principles – respectively, *fallibilism about knowledge's justificatory component* and *justificatory closure* (Gettier 1963, p. 121):

> First, in that sense of "justified" in which S's being justified in believing P is a necessary condition of S's knowing that P, it is possible for a person to be justified in believing a proposition that is in fact false. Secondly, for any proposition P, if S is justified in believing P, and P entails Q, and S deduces Q from P and accepts Q as a result of this deduction, then S is justified in believing Q.

Each of those pivotal principles has attracted much attention. Partly, this is because, once noticed, they have been deemed to possess independent epistemological interest. But the attention paid to them is also due to their having helped to generate the internal details of Gettier's two cases – and thereby the in-principle Gettier problem.

What I think of as the book's second part is on various epistemic concepts upon which, *especially* because of Gettier's challenge, epistemologists have focused. Like those two key epistemic principles of Gettier's, mentioned a moment ago, these concepts have been widely regarded within epistemology as independently interesting. But they have indeed been part of the in-practice Gettier problem's taking shape since 1963. As Section I.5 mentioned, once epistemologists began trying to understand Gettier cases with the goal of reaching an improved definition of knowledge, a diversity of seemingly associated epistemic concepts were introduced, highlighted, sharpened, sometimes discarded, often revived, etc. So, Chapters 3 through 8 are about what have probably been the most epistemologically discussed and influential of those concepts:

Chapter 3 (Clayton Littlejohn): Gettier and evidence (including disjunctivism);
Chapter 4 (Rodrigo Borges): Gettier and externalism;
Chapter 5 (Delia Belleri and Annalisa Coliva): Gettier and context (including contextualism and contrastivism);
Chapter 6 (Duncan Pritchard): Gettier and luck (including epistemic safety);
Chapter 7 (Kelly Becker): Gettier and epistemic sensitivity;
Chapter 8 (John Greco): Gettier and cognitive virtues;
Chapter 9 (Ernest Sosa): Gettier and epistemic wisdom (a synoptic vision of what we might learn from post-Gettier epistemology, by an epistemologist who was involved in such epistemology from the outset).

Finally, the book's third part discusses some fundamental *methodological* questions. Gettier posed such an apparently powerful challenge to what would otherwise, it seems, have felt like such an unassailable definition of knowledge that questions were bound to arise about what it was about epistemological thinking that had – mistakenly, it suddenly seemed to epistemologists – made that definition appear so impregnable. Thanks to Gettier, should new forms of epistemological thinking be envisaged? In short, some potentially significant methodological questions have been posed within – and about – post-Gettier epistemology:

Chapter 10 (Patrick Rysiew): Gettier and conceptual analysis (including the rise of knowledge-first epistemology, due mainly to Williamson [2000]);

Chapter 11 (Elijah Chudnoff): Gettier and intuition (including the rise of experimental philosophy, due especially to Weinberg, Nichols, and Stich [2001]);

Chapter 12 (John Turri): Gettier and experimental philosophy, in more detail (given how closely its origins were tied to talk about Gettier cases);

Chapter 13 (Stephen Hetherington): Gettier and explicability (whether any Gettier case can be understood so as to support the usual interpretation of its central belief as failing to be knowledge).[9]

It is unquestionable that the Gettier problem has been a philosophically rich field of study, as this book demonstrates. What is the Gettier problem's future? Will it be solved? (Has it already been solved?) Will it continue being so epistemologically influential? What would *post*-post-Gettier epistemology be like? Tantalizing questions, all.

---

[9] For fuller introductions to the nature and history of the Gettier problem, see Shope (1983), Lycan (2006), and Hetherington (2011b; 2016a, ch. 1; 2016b).

1   The Gettier Problem and Fallibilism

Charity Anderson

1.1 Introduction

In his seminal article, Gettier (1963) established that justified true belief (JTB) is not sufficient for knowledge. He did so in the context of two conditions: first, that a belief can be justified and false; second, that justification is closed under deductive entailment. This chapter focuses on the first of these two commitments: that justification and truth can come apart. There is widespread support for the idea that it is possible for one to have justification for a proposition – even justification of knowledge-level strength – and yet believe falsely. Call this thesis JF. JF is commonly taken to be a presupposition of the Gettier problem. Some further insist that JF is a constraint on a satisfactory solution to the Gettier problem. Putative responses to the problem that do not respect this constraint, it is said, run the risk of *avoiding* rather than solving the problem.[1]

The relationship between justification and truth presented in JF has been thought to be a commitment of *fallibilism*. Thus, JF is characterized as a fallibilist constraint. In this chapter, I aim to shed light on the role of fallibilism within the Gettier problem and potential solutions. I investigate the kind of constraints that could reasonably be placed on an acceptable solution and, in particular, the extent to which a fallibilist constraint ought to be placed on a satisfactory solution. Finally, I reconsider the narrative concerning the relationship between JF and fallibilism about knowledge.

The chapter is divided into two sections. Section 1.2 considers the scope of the fallibilist constraint. As it appears in Gettier's article, the fallibilist constraint applies specifically to the justification condition on

I am grateful to John Hawthorne, Alexander Pruss, and Jeffrey Russell for helpful conversation on the issues in this paper, and to Andrew Moon for comments on a draft.
[1] See Zagzebski (1994) and Hetherington (2012; 2016a).

knowledge – where justification is thought of as one among three necessary and jointly sufficient conditions on knowledge (together with truth and belief). Gettier's counterexample revealed the need to add a fourth condition to the traditional analysis of knowledge.[2] It is an open question whether we ought to extend a fallibilist constraint to the elusive fourth condition. That is, it is an open question whether the fourth condition must be such that, when it obtains, the belief can be false. (I'll follow standard usage in thinking of the fourth condition as the "gap filler": that which, when added to JTB, results in a combination that suffices for knowledge.)[3] I examine two ways to think about the scope of the fallibilist constraint. The first extends fallibilism to the fourth condition. Together with extension of a closure principle, these constraints deliver the result that the Gettier problem is unsolvable. A second, more promising option limits the scope of the fallibilist constraint to the justification condition, without extending it to the fourth condition. This option moves us in the direction of a solution, but one which, ultimately, some may find unsatisfying – because it is thought to be "infallibilist" in some objectionable sense. In the course of discussion, I will examine a test case arising in recent literature, with the goal of clarifying the source of this recent dispute.

Section 1.3 examines attempts to make the option of a factive fourth condition acceptable for fallibilists. I argue that such a picture can fall within the family of fallibilist views of knowledge. While JF is rightly considered a "fallibilist" assumption within the Gettier problem, fallibilists about knowledge are not committed to adding only nonfactive conditions to the JTB account. This results in further options for fallibilist responses to the Gettier problem.[4] It is not the case that only an infallibilist picture of knowledge eliminates the Gettier problem.

---

[2] Either that or we must reconceive of the justification component; hereafter I will focus on the option of adding a fourth condition, although I acknowledge that reinventing justification is also an option that some have taken. I expect that reconceiving of justification is not among the options that my intended interlocutors would find appealing, as this option will more likely be taken to be "infallibilist."

[3] A relevant body of literature concerns whether "warrant" entails truth. See especially Merricks (1995), Ryan (1996), and Moon (2013). "Warrant" standardly names the "gap filler" condition(s), and, according to some, may be factorized into multiple conditions. My discussion here will investigate the components as factorized. One advantage of this approach is that it will be easier to see the properties of the various components and to determine which are fallible and which factive. Here I will be specifically interested in the status of the fourth condition, as distinct from a justification component.

[4] See Howard-Snyder et al. (2003) for an alternative fallibilist response.

1.2 Nonfactive Justification

As did many of his contemporaries, Gettier took justification to be a necessary component of knowledge, and was writing in a context where justification was thought to be sufficient, in combination with truth and belief, for knowledge.[5] Gettier (1963, p. 121) expected that his counterexample to the JTB account of knowledge could be applied without loss to accounts which substitute either "having adequate evidence for p" or "having the right to be sure that p is true" for "justification" in the analysis of knowledge. Both the idea that justification is a necessary component of knowledge and the idea that one can have justification for a proposition that is false are strongly plausible theses. (To a large extent, both are still widely accepted, though some have moved away from talking about *justification* altogether, and thus are silent on JF.)[6]

JF is widely accepted for good reason: it is strongly intuitive that we can be justified in believing a proposition that, unbeknownst to us, is false. We sometimes have strong evidence for propositions that are false. For example, suppose that a trustworthy friend tells me that she will be at the party tonight and I believe her. On the basis of her testimony, I am justified in believing that she will be at the party, even if she suddenly becomes ill and remains at home. Similarly, I might have justification to believe something that is highly probable, such as that my ticket will lose the lottery, or that my car has not been stolen in the past half hour, and yet my belief can turn out to be false. The experience of discovering that a belief which one holds for good reason is false is commonplace. Assuming a connection between justification and evidence or between justification and reasons, these kinds of examples underlie motivation for JF.

It is seldom suggested that the best resolution to the Gettier problem is to deny JF. One reason for this is that if JF is false, and we cannot have justification for false beliefs, the number of our beliefs that are justified is radically more limited than we typically suppose. If one also holds, as many do, the idea that there is sameness of justification across good and bad cases, the result is that our knowledge will likewise be more limited. To illustrate this, I'll rely on an evidentialist conception of justification (though other pictures

---

[5] Gettier cites Ayer (1956) and Chisholm (1957) as among those who advocate for the "traditional" JTB view. Some have thought that the JTB account of knowledge was the standard view of knowledge for hundreds of years prior to Gettier – citing support even within Plato's writings. See Dutant (2015) for an alternative to this traditionally accepted narrative.

[6] The notion of *warrant*, in particular, has rivaled *justification* as a replacement concept. Insofar as *justification* is given an internalist reading, it has fallen somewhat out of favor with externalists. But, with the exception of a few extreme externalist pictures (advocates of E = K, the view that one's evidence consists of all and only the propositions one knows, in particular), many still find the notion central to theorizing about knowledge.

could be substituted). The evidence we have for many of the propositions that we take ourselves to know is such that the evidence does not guarantee the truth of the propositions. Consider two agents with the same strong evidence for a proposition – one with an unlucky false belief and the other a true belief. (We need not invoke a BIV counterpart to get an example of this kind off the ground; a parked car case will do. Imagine that the relevant proposition is: *my car has not been stolen today*. Imagine also that the first agent's car was stolen five minutes ago, and that the second agent's car remains in the lot where it was parked, despite the relevant circumstances being otherwise similar.) Many find compelling the thought that, if the first agent is not justified in believing *p*, neither is the second. Pairs of cases of this sort are easily generated, and, together with the intuitive judgment about the sameness of justification across cases, they threaten the idea that we have an abundance of widespread ordinary knowledge. On pain of skepticism, we must affirm JF. In this way, JF is thought to be essential to an antiskeptical picture.[7]

A "gap" between justification and truth is also essential to the construction of Gettier cases using Linda Zagzebski's well-known "double-luck" recipe, where the introduction of bad luck is followed by a dose of good luck resulting in a justified true belief, but one which we intuitively judge is not knowledge. (Without JF we would be unable to follow the first step of the "recipe" – that is, imagining an agent with a justified false belief.) Zagzebski articulates the centrality of JF to the Gettier problem as follows: "as long as the concept of knowledge closely connects the justification component and the truth component, but permits *some* degree of independence between them, justified true belief will never be sufficient for knowledge" (1994, p. 69). Zagzebski claims that the lesson of Gettier is that we must either add a fourth component to the JTB analysis or we must reconceive the notion of justification. As long as we do not add a fourth condition that guarantees truth (or reinvent justification such that it is factive), application of the double-luck recipe that Zagzebski articulates will succeed in producing Gettier-style counterexamples.[8]

---

[7] See Hoffmann (1975) for a defense of this point specifically in the context of the Gettier problem. Hoffmann draws on parity reasoning between the "good" and "bad" cases (with respect to sameness of evidence) to argue against Almeder's thesis that evidence entails truth. Hoffman contends that, if Almeder were correct, skepticism would ensue (Almeder 1974).

[8] See Zagzebski (1994, p. 72): "It appears, then, that no account of knowledge as true belief plus something else can withstand Gettier objections as long as there is a small degree of independence between truth and the other conditions of knowledge." It is not clear whether Zagzebski intends to claim that JF ought to be thought of as extended to include any and all conditions added to true belief, or whether she merely is making the observation that, if we extend JF in this way, we will not be able to solve the problem.

Presented in this way, fallibilism appears to be the root cause of the Gettier problem. Holding fallibilism fixed, a solution to the Gettier problem requires that we add a component to the JTB analysis of knowledge. Whether this component must also be nonfactive is an open question. Section 1.3 will discuss the option of a factive fourth condition.

1.2.1 Constraints on a Solution

Gettier's article initiated a search – conceived of as a challenge – to find the elusive fourth condition. It is worth noting, though, that Gettier himself never explicitly states a "challenge." Instead, he makes an observation: justified true belief is insufficient for knowledge. This observation is now nearly unanimously accepted and points to the need for (and marked the start of endless attempts to provide) a further condition on the traditional analysis of knowledge. Of course, some – notably, Timothy Williamson – reject this project of analysis as unfruitful and misguided, but this kind of response is for the most part an outlier position: many have taken the "challenge" over the years.[9] In this section, I will examine what parameters we ought to place on an adequate solution.

Gettier did not himself set down constraints on what could serve as a satisfactory fourth component. Granted, one might suppose that, *in the spirit of* Gettier, we ought to think that his fallibilist constraint on justification – that a belief can be justified and false – should be extended as a constraint on the fourth condition (see Hetherington 2012). But this expectation has unwelcome results. Before we pursue this line of thought, let me address a related matter.

One issue that is somewhat neglected in the literature concerns whether Gettier's other assumption – a closure principle for justification – ought also to be extended so as to apply to the fourth condition. That is, little has been said concerning whether the fourth condition is closed under competent deduction.[10] I will make two points concerning this issue. First, note that the motivation for extending the fallibilist constraint applies equally to extension of a closure principle. At least, if the reason for extending fallibilism is to provide a solution that treats the fourth condition in the same way as Gettier treats the justification condition, this reasoning equally motivates extension of a closure principle.

---

[9] See Shope (1983) and Lycan (2006) for summaries of those attempts.
[10] Merricks (1995) is a noteworthy exception. See also Ryan (1996) and Howard-Snyder et al. (2003).

Second, as Merricks (1995) notes, there is some independent pressure to think that the fourth condition is closed.[11] Suppose that it is not closed: in settings where the fourth condition fails to obtain for the proposition deduced, knowledge will also fail to obtain. In this way, closure failure for the fourth condition will result in closure failure for knowledge.[12] (One might try a gerrymandered approach, where the fourth condition is closed when the initial belief is true, but fails to be closed when the initial belief is false. Or, alternatively, where the fourth condition is closed only when the initial belief is justified. But, as these strategies are *ad hoc*, they are unlikely to be appealing.) Thus, insofar as one finds closure for knowledge attractive, one ought to expect the fourth condition to be closed.[13]

We can now proceed to the central point. If the fourth condition is closed and the fourth condition is fallibilist – that is, the fourth condition can obtain when a belief is false – then the fourth condition will not be able to play the role of "gap filler" in an analysis of knowledge. Any proposed analysis of knowledge whereby knowledge consists of JTB plus a fourth condition, where the justification condition and the fourth condition each respect both constraints under consideration, will be open to Gettierization.[14] Application of the structure of one of Gettier's original counterexamples will make the point evident. In Gettier's second counterexample, an agent forms a justified true belief, *p or q*, that fails to be knowledge because the belief is the result of the agent's reasoning via disjunction introduction that began with a justified false belief. Supposing that the fourth condition is fallibilist and closed under entailment, this process can be replicated by using a belief that meets the fourth condition.[15] Imagine an agent who has a justified false belief that satisfies the fourth condition. We can then construct cases where the agent,

[11] The relevant closure principle will inevitably be more nuanced than the idea gestured at here. Neither knowledge nor justification is, strictly speaking, closed under deduction. Qualifications must be added: for example, that the deduction is competent, that the proposition is deduced from known (or justified) premises, that the premises are not forgotten throughout the process, and so on. See Hawthorne (2004, ch. 1) for helpful discussion. A comprehensive treatment of the nuances is beyond the scope of this paper, but the reader may supply the needed qualifications throughout.

[12] Some are happy to accept this result. Dretske (2005), for example, adopts this strategy: his sensitivity condition is not closed, but he welcomes the result that knowledge is not closed.

[13] Nevertheless, some have objected to this type of argument. See Ryan (1996) and Howard-Snyder et al. (2003) for relevant discussion.

[14] The result can be obtained with a weaker principle than deductive closure. Closure under disjunction introduction suffices to deliver the unwelcome result.

[15] Merricks (1995) makes this structural point concerning "warrant." It is worth considering how the argument will apply to a factorized analysis, as I do here, where we consider the fourth condition as distinct from justification.

relying on disjunction introduction, forms a justified true belief that meets the fourth condition, but where the belief fails to be known.

The lesson is that to insist that any "extra" conditions on knowledge – conditions in addition to justification, truth, and belief – respect both of the constraints that Gettier places on justification (a fallibilist constraint and closure) is to set up the problem in such a way that, in principle, it cannot be solved.[16]

(A similar process delivers the result that the fourth condition must entail justification. Suppose that it does not: then we may construct cases as follows. An agent has a justified false belief that p, and an unjustified true belief that q that satisfies the fourth condition. If both justification and the fourth condition are closed, then the agent may deduce p or q and the belief will be justified, true, and meet the fourth condition, but will be unknown. Hence, if the fourth condition is closed and does not entail justification, it will not play the role of "gap filler.")[17,18]

It is clear that we cannot extend both constraints to the fourth condition (unless, of course, we are willing to rest content with an unsolvable problem). Initial investigation suggests that we have reason to extend closure and to loosen our fallibilist grip – at least for those who find closure for knowledge attractive. For now, I merely note that, as constraints on an adequate solution, together these deliver the unfortunate result of ruling out "solving" the problem. In Section 1.3, I will attempt to make the option of an "infallibilist" fourth condition palatable for fallibilists about knowledge.

1.2.2 "Manifest Failure" and Infallibilism

It will be instructive, at this point, to explore a dispute arising in recent literature. The dispute illustrates the specific issue under discussion – namely,

---

[16] Hetherington (2012; 2016a) insists that a "solution" to the Gettier problem requires that all additional conditions are fallibilist.

[17] One might think that the most plausible conclusion to draw is that closure must be rejected. But notice that rejection of closure in full generality will not suffice to avoid the result. What is needed is not merely the claim that the fourth condition is not closed in every instance of competent deduction; rather, it is that there is no case of the kind described where the fourth condition transmits via competent disjunction introduction. This will be significantly more difficult to motivate than mere rejection of fully general closure, and is likely to look implausibly gerrymandered.

[18] It is likely to be objected that if the fourth condition entails both truth and justification, it also entails knowledge and thus leads to a failed project – where the aim of the project is to provide an analysis of knowledge in terms that are each necessary but none of which are individually sufficient for knowledge. Although this may strike some as an unsatisfying result, I suggest that such an "analysis" of knowledge would nevertheless provide us with an informative identity.

whether fallibilism ought to be extended to the fourth condition. I will first survey the details of the dispute and then draw on the above remarks to attempt to resolve the disagreement.

Turri (2011) suggests a solution to the Gettier problem. His proposal develops Sosa's general framework (2007a), whereby knowledge is a performance that exhibits an "AAA" structure. According to Sosa, knowledge that *p* involves the following: one's belief that *p* must be accurate (true), adroit (display intellectual competence), and apt (true *because* competent). Turri agrees that knowledge requires these conditions, but maintains that they are together insufficient for knowledge. To demonstrate that the AAA structure is insufficient, Turri presents a case where a subject's belief is true because competent but where the truth of the belief is nevertheless a result of a deviant causal chain. His counterexample is structurally similar to the case of the *epistemic guardian angel*.[19] In short, the case is one where a guardian angel admires a subject for being competent and therefore decides to rearrange the world, as needed, to ensure that the subject's beliefs are true. The relevant feature of this kind of counterexample is that the agent's belief is true *because of* the agent's competence, but we tend to judge that knowledge is absent. To avoid this difficulty, Turri's proposed solution expands on Sosa's account as follows: knowledge requires not merely *apt* belief (true *because* competent) but also *adept* belief – true belief that *manifests* a competence. Not all outcomes that occur because of a competence are outcomes that manifest that competence. To illustrate the difference, Turri draws on the idea of fragility. Suppose that two glasses are falling off a table. We can imagine different outcomes for each glass: the first glass shatters on the floor; the second glass is caught before it hits the floor. The glass that breaks when it hits the floor *manifests* fragility, but the glass that is caught before it hits the floor does not manifest fragility – even though it is caught *because* it is fragile. According to Turri, Gettier subjects do not manifest a competence when they believe the truth. If we add *adeptness* to Sosa's account of knowledge, Turri claims, the Gettier problem is solved.

It will be helpful to consider briefly how Turri's account handles fake-barn cases. Rather than commit to one solution, Turri sketches a few options, all of which are consistent with his account. Turri himself boldly reports that he lacks the requisite intuition regarding fake-barn cases, and so his preferred option is to deny that fake-barn cases are in fact Gettier cases; nevertheless, he provides several options to accommodate the intuition. In the familiar

---

[19] Greco (1999) presents this case as a difficulty for simple reliabilism.

fake-barn case, an agent – call him Henry – uses his eyesight to form a true belief that *there is a barn*. Unfortunately, his environment is such that he easily could have formed a false belief – due to the many nearby barn façades. To respect the received intuition – that Henry does not know that *there is a barn* – one option for Turri's account is to claim that although Henry's competence is manifested, it could easily have failed to be manifested, and this feature of Henry's epistemic position is relevant in a knowledge-depriving way. Henry would have formed a false belief had he looked at a nearby façade, and in that case his competence would not have been manifested: successful manifestation of a competence occurs only in cases of knowledge. Note that this strategy makes manifestation of a competence insufficient to play the role of the missing Gettier condition; on this picture, knowledge requires *safe* manifestation of a competence. (This is obviously not as elegant a solution as Turri's original proposal alone.)

Another option for explaining the intuition that Henry does not know is to maintain that the manifestation of a competence is environment-sensitive. One might simply deny that Henry has a competence to identify barns when he is in barn façade country. Clearly, if Henry does not possess the requisite competence, he cannot manifest the competence. (Of course, in these kinds of case the agent might think that he is manifesting a competence, even when he is not, but this is merely a result of the fact that the manifestation of a competence fails to be luminous: an agent is not always in a position to know when he manifests a competence.)[20]

Hetherington (2012) objects that Turri's proposal does not qualify as a solution, because it does not maintain the gap between justification and truth that Gettier assumes. Therefore, Hetherington claims, Turri's alleged solution fails to even interact or engage with the problem. Specifically, Hetherington maintains that Turri does not respect the fallibilist constraint: his objection is that Turri's "solution" is "covertly infallibilist" and so is irrelevant to the challenge of the Gettier problem. At the center of his concern is the idea that Gettier's challenge was posed within a fallibilist conception of knowledge, and so should be answered in that spirit.

Let's consider whether Turri in fact violates the methodological parameters of the problem. Turri's fourth condition does indeed eliminate any gap between manifestation of competence and truth: one cannot

---

[20] See Turri (2012a) for additional possible explanations of the absence of knowledge in this kind of Gettier-style case.

manifest a competence and have a false belief. But his account builds on Sosa's AAA analysis, which includes a justification-like component which is nonfactive – a belief can be adroit and false. Thus, Turri's solution technically respects JF.[21] Consider an account of knowledge as justified true belief plus a fourth condition where the fourth condition is factive and where justification (or whatever plays the justification role) is non-factive. An account of this type respects Gettier's *actual* constraint: insofar as the account maintains a "gap" between justification and truth, JF is maintained.[22]

We have seen that we are faced with a choice: either the fourth condition ensures truth or it does not. If it does not, and the fourth condition is closed under known entailment, the account will be Gettierizable. If it does ensure truth, the potential for a solution is at least a possibility. I suggest that, on these grounds, we are hard-pressed to insist that Turri's solution – or any solution that fails to extend fallibilism to the fourth condition – be ruled out for this reason alone.

As our discussion has noted, it is not obvious that Gettier himself envisioned the extension of fallibilism and closure to the fourth condition as a constraint on a solution. Moreover, it is implausible that Gettier intended his problem to be constrained in such a way that it is in principle unsolvable. And even if that were his intention, it would be foolish to play by those rules once we see the impossibility of succeeding. I suggest that we are better off thinking of Gettier's article as presenting a puzzle with various options for responding, even if no option is fully satisfying. The strategy that I have explored here – an "infallibilist" fourth condition – opens the door to various solutions to the Gettier problem. Perhaps not everyone will be content to call this kind of reply a "solution," but this option strikes me as preferable to an in-principle unsolvable problem. In the next section, I will argue that a factive fourth condition does not, in fact, lead to infallibilism about knowledge.

---

[21] Another option is that manifestation of competence is not an added fourth condition, but instead a way of "reinventing" justification. If this is how Turri intends it, then he rejects a key assumption on which Gettier relies. In the next section I'll argue that even though this kind of account rejects JF, it is still compatible with fallibilism about knowledge.

[22] One might worry that "manifestation of a competence" or any other fourth condition that entails truth is no more basic than knowing. If our goal is to analyze knowledge, one way in which this strategy might fail is by providing a component whose extension overlaps exactly with knowledge. We might question whether such an analysis is doing the work that we wanted it to do for us. See Kearns (2007) for a defense of the significance of this type of analysis.

1.3 Fallibilism and Factivity

Suppose that you are a committed fallibilist. What, minimally, is required to be included in the family of views called "fallibilism about knowledge"? Here I suggest that views according to which knowledge involves JTB plus a factive condition, but a factive condition which is not luminous, can plausibly be characterized as fallibilist.[23] The case that I present is stipulative: suppose that infallibilism is the view that knowledge requires a condition that is both factive and luminous.[24] (Following Williamson, I will understand "luminous" as follows: a condition C is *luminous* for S if, whenever C obtains, S is in a position to know that it obtains.)[25] Fallibilism, in turn, will be the theory that knowledge does not require such a condition. I'll call these views infallibilism* and fallibilism*, respectively. On this way of thinking, fallibilism* is compatible with a factive fourth condition, so long as the condition is not luminous.

In favor of this stipulative picture, I will show that that fallibilism* is not encumbered by the same ill-favored consequences in which infallibilism is taken to result: most importantly, fallibilism* does not result in skepticism. (Avoidance of skepticism is, again and again, appealed to as the central motivation for fallibilism.)[26] Fallibilism* does not place overly demanding standards on knowing. It is consistent with the fact that we often make mistakes – even in cases where we think that we know. We have already observed that fallibilism* offers us a path to a solution to the Gettier problem. In this section, we will see that it has other advantages.

Here is one further preliminary clarification. As I use the terms here, both fallibilism about knowledge and infallibilism about knowledge are theses about the nature of knowledge – that is, they are views about what knowledge

---

[23] One might be tempted to think that a view that affirms JF is sufficient for fallibilism about knowledge, but note that, by that reasoning, Turri's account – and any account that affirms JF but involves a factive fourth condition – will clearly fall into the fallibilist camp.

[24] There is not space here to argue for this view, though I have done so elsewhere (Anderson, manuscript). The salient point of my argument is that factivity without luminosity provides us with, at best, a "cheap" kind of infallibilism. Williamson's knowledge-first picture – which has been called "infallibilist" by some – falls into this camp. Many common tests for infallibilism – skepticism, Cartesian standards, and so on – deliver the result that views of this kind fall on the fallibilist side.

[25] Infallible knowledge might additionally require that the absence of the condition be luminous to the agent – that is, it may require that when C is absent, S is in a position to know that C is absent – but luminosity as stated above will suffice for our purposes here.

[26] See Cohen (1988) and Lewis (1996) for a sample. The idea that infallibilism leads to skepticism is so entrenched in the literature that it is almost a datum.

requires. They are not statements about the extent of our knowledge. Thus, the way I am using the terms, it is open to one to be a fallibilist about knowledge and yet maintain that we have some infallible knowledge. This picture is one whereby knowledge does not *require* demanding standards, but leaves open whether we meet those standards for some items of knowledge (such as knowledge that 2 + 2 = 4). By contrast, it is not an option to be an infallibilist about knowledge but maintain that some of our knowledge does not meet those demanding standards.

Recently, fallibilism about knowledge has enjoyed near-unanimous acceptance in contemporary epistemology. But many representative statements of fallibilism are subject to a problem: on the assumption that fallibilism and infallibilism about knowledge are exhaustive options, many statements of fallibilism in the literature offer a corresponding picture of infallibilism that is inadequate. One could have a fantastic epistemic position – entailing evidence, for example – but have no idea that one has this evidence. Thus, there is a clear sense in which one fails to have the best epistemic position that one could have: on the assumption that one sometimes has entailing evidence and sometimes does not, but one cannot tell when one has it and when one fails to have it, one will be subject to all sorts of error, and unable to avoid the uncertainty and inclinations to hedge that often accompany agents who make such errors.[27] While surely it would be advantageous, in one sense, to have entailing evidence, to possess it without being aware that one possesses it will not result in the kind of secure epistemic position that we often associate with infallibilism.

A further and more troubling problem results from the fact that, given some of the prominent glosses of fallibilism, there are "cheap" ways to possess infallible knowledge.[28] For example, E = K – the view that one's evidence consists of all and only the propositions that one knows – results in an agent's trivially possessing entailing evidence for each and every proposition that the agent knows. Although, by some lights, this picture will count as infallibilist, however trivial, since neither knowledge nor evidence is luminous, it will not suffice for infallibilism* (Williamson 2000).

It will be helpful to consider in more detail some of the common motivations for fallibilism. Among the most prominent reasons for

---

[27] As a matter of fact, in my view, a full picture of infallibilism will involve more than this, but this minimalist picture will suffice for what I want to argue here.

[28] See Anderson (manuscript) for a more comprehensive treatment of this issue and an argument that Cartesian infallibilism is more difficult to attain than common statements of fallibilism suggest.

adopting fallibilism is the widely accepted idea that infallibilism leads to skepticism. Infallibilism places overly demanding conditions on knowledge – conditions that we meet for too few, if any, propositions. Since most contemporary epistemologists are antiskeptics, given this narrative, fallibilism is the only available option.

Another thought that inspires fallibilism is the fact that we make mistakes. Our faculties are reliable enough to deliver knowledge in a wide variety of situations, but they are not perfectly reliable: sometimes we mess up even when our faculties are working properly and we are in a suitable environment for their use. Yet we have knowledge. Fallibilists about knowledge often aim to describe a theory of knowledge that captures, or is in response to, these central observations.

With this in mind, we can see that a factive fourth condition does not lead to an infallibilism about knowledge that fits with these motivations. A factive fourth condition on knowledge does not lead to skepticism. If satisfaction of the fourth condition needed to be internally accessible, then skepticism might threaten. But the account under investigation includes no such stipulation, and in fact prohibits it. A factive fourth condition is also compatible with the observation concerning our making mistakes. Our faculties can be less than perfectly reliable even if there is no gap between the fourth condition and truth. As long as the fourth condition is externalist, so that we are not always in a position to tell when it holds, the fourth condition can guarantee truth without a commitment to infallibilism about knowledge.

A further advantage of the picture of fallibilism* is that it is compatible with a factive fourth condition and thereby results in a fallibilist picture of knowledge that can solve the Gettier problem. A final advantage is that if one's analysis of knowledge is such that knowledge requires a fourth condition that is factive and fails to be luminous, but which is distinct from the justification condition (which is not factive), then fallibilism* is compatible with JF. Thus, fallibilists* need not give up the intuitive thought mentioned at the start of the chapter – that justification is the same across good and bad cases.

These points will be most easily demonstrated by drawing on Turri's account as an example. It is important to recall that, on his view, manifesting a competence is not something accessible to the agent. One cannot tell by mere reflection alone (and one is not always in a position to know) whether one manifests a competence when one believes p or whether one merely appears to manifest a competence. The presence and absence of manifestation is not luminous to the agent. So, even though Turri's fourth condition is factive, on my view his account falls within the family of fallibilist views since it does not place a condition on knowledge that is both luminous and factive.[29]

It is instructive to consider how a view with a factive fourth condition might diagnose two different types of Gettier-style cases. Consider first a standard Gettier case involving inference from false belief. Suppose that Smith justifiably believes *JONES* (Jones will get the job and Jones has ten coins in his pocket), and infers *POCKET* (the man who will get the job has ten coins in his pocket). If the fourth condition is closed and factive, then the explanation for why Smith does not know *POCKET* is that the first proposition, *JONES*, which is false, is such that the fourth condition does not obtain with respect to it. Of course, Smith won't be able to tell that the fourth condition fails to obtain with respect to his belief that *JONES*. But since, on our current proposal, the fourth condition is factive, it will not obtain when the proposition is false.[30]

Consider next a second type of Gettier-style case, which depends not on inference from a false belief, but rather on an unfriendly environment. Henry is in fake-barn country looking at a barn. His belief BARN, *that's a barn*, is true, but easily could have been false. On the assumption that we aim to respect the standard intuition – that Henry's belief that BARN is unknown – an explanation is needed as to why he fails to know.

At this point, it will be helpful to bear in mind that I have not argued that a factive fourth condition is sufficient in itself to solve the Gettier problem. I have argued here that a factive fourth condition is necessary to solve the problem, but it remains to be seen whether the fourth condition must involve more than factivity. (Perhaps, as Turri mentions, there are additional constraints, such as safety or an appropriate environment.) My aim here has been to show that views with a factive fourth condition ought to be evaluated in terms of how they fare with respect to solving the problem, rather than being ruled out in advance for being infallibilist.

Return again to Hetherington's critique of Turri. We are now in a better position to assess whether Turri's solution violates the spirit of Gettier's problem by adopting infallibilism. The motivations for infallibilism discussed here suggest that it does not. Suppose that knowledge requires true belief that

---

[29] This point applies more broadly to any view that shares this feature with Turri's account – including those that have been called "warrant infallibilism." Thanks to Andrew Moon here.

[30] One might worry that this type of account makes the truth condition superfluous. I expect we can be persuaded to take on this consequence once we appreciate that there is no way to avoid the result.

manifests a competence. This does not lead to skepticism, and it is consistent with the fact that we sometimes make mistakes even when we think we know. Turri's solution does not place overly demanding requirements on knowledge. Arguably, his proposal falls into the family of views that I have argued here belong to fallibilism* about knowledge.

The dissatisfaction with, and worries about, infallibilism are not applicable to Turri's solution.[31] This lesson applies more generally: a nonluminous "infallibilist" fourth condition does not land us in skepticism, is compatible with the general imperfection of our faculties, and does not place overly demanding standards on knowledge. Recall that one motivation for JF was that we wanted knowledge-level justification to be the kind of thing that we have often and for many propositions. The type of manifestation of a competence that Turri suggests is required for knowledge is an ordinary, everyday sort of manifestation. It is ordinary in that it does not require a kind of ability beyond what is possessed by an average person, and it is everyday in the sense that it affirms the idea that most of us have a vast amount of knowledge that we gain on a daily basis in normal circumstances. It does not require Cartesian certainty, or a modal success-rate above our usual abilities. Thus, I suggest that, although it includes a factive fourth condition, Turri's solution does not count as infallibilist. While conceding that Turri is not fallibilist by the lights of some statements of fallibilism in the literature, his solution is nevertheless fallibilist in a substantive way. In light of this, I think that we would be misguided to reject his solution – and relevantly similar solutions – simply because they do not align with certain common notions of fallibilism.

Might a solution of this type solve the Gettier problem? Undoubtedly, some will decry such a solution as not playing by the rules. But, as I have tried to argue here, while this kind of strategy does not provide us with an analysis of knowledge according to which all conditions (excluding truth) are nonfactive, it clears the way for a solution – and it does so without landing us in skepticism, the long-feared result of infallibilism. Without adoption of fallibilism*, the possibilities for a fallibilist theory of knowledge to avoid the Gettier problem look grim.

Reluctance to embrace this type of strategy in response to the Gettier problem seems to rest on a misconception concerning the scope of fallibilism.

---

[31] Of course, we might find Turri's account unsatisfactory for other reasons. Greco (2012), for example, notes that he finds the account unhelpful because it fails to provide a principled explanation for certain contrast cases – a failure that arises precisely because agents are not in a position to know when they manifest a competence and when they fail to do so.

Perhaps we are too committed to the unsolvability of the problem to be open to this route. The Gettier problem has been with us for many years: its presence pervades introductory textbooks, and any account of the recent history of epistemology will inevitably include this formidable puzzle. This alone provides reason to resist what might be thought of as too "easy" a response. But a solution of the type that Turri offers (and it is not the only fallibilist option involving a factive fourth condition) shows us that, as we move away from a fallibilist picture of knowledge to a fallibilist* picture, the Gettier problem's threat weakens its grip; hence, even fallibilists may find solutions.

If what I have argued is correct, Gettier's article is no less significant: his observation – that justified true belief is insufficient for knowledge – was correct. Perhaps, however, we are in danger of overlooking the full significance of his article. Even after more than fifty years, we have yet to fully exhaust the insights to be drawn from his observation.

2 Epistemic Closure and Post-Gettier Epistemology of Reasoning

Claudio de Almeida

2.1 Introduction: To Expose Parochialism in the Epistemology of Reasoning

This is a tale of parochial responses to philosophical hardship.[1] The form of parochialism discussed here began to take shape when Gettier called our attention to an assumption that had *tacitly* been adopted at the dawn of logic by Aristotle and his contemporaries. Then, in the wake of Gettier's impact, Dretske made one of the most impressive evolutionary moves in all of epistemology: He implanted in our collective psyche the suspicion that that fundamental assumption is false.[2] You may know a thing or two about how Gettier and Dretske, as a duo, changed the epistemology of reasoning if you have read so much as a couple of encyclopedia/dictionary entries on what occupies us when we theorize about how reasoning extends our stock of knowledge. And you would be right if you thought that, after thousands of published pages on what we've come to know as the "epistemic closure issue," it is surprising to find so much discrepancy in the ways that authors have presented the problem. You would have expected to see expert consensus on what the problem is exactly when we discuss "epistemic closure." What follows will, I hope, show that epistemologists could have become more precise when characterizing the problems and the theoretical options falling under the rubric "epistemic closure," if we only had managed to lessen our parochial proclivities. The ensuing discussion schematically lays out the issues and the options, some of them new to the discussion. (It will inevitably

I'm indebted to Risto Hilpinen and John Turri for helpful comments on drafts of this chapter, and to the editor, Stephen, for inordinate amounts of patience and encouragement.

[1] I trust it will be clear that I mean no disrespect when characterizing some of the views discussed here as "parochial." (My targets are some of the most venerable authors we have known, no less.) It should become clear that the adjective is technically irreplaceable in this context.

[2] See Gettier (1963) and Dretske (1970; 2014).

be fast-paced while traversing more familiar territory, as space is saved for the potentially more surprising aspects of our problems.)

2.2 Closure of What Under What?

"The closure mess" is how Kvanvig (2005) once described some formulations of so-called "epistemic closure principles" that we find in the literature.[3] The mess is not much less messy today, but I believe we can move toward giving it a good scrub. Here is a brief report on what so riled Kvanvig, including some of the fuel added to the messy stuff since he issued his wake-up call.

Gettier made us acknowledge that we expect belief formed as a conclusion of valid (deductive) reasoning from justified beliefs to be justified. This suggests that *justification is closed under valid reasoning* (or valid "inference"), as captured by this close paraphrase of Gettier's formulation:

JCVR. For any agent S and beliefs p and q, if S holds a justified belief that p and forms the belief that q as a result of reasoning validly to q from p, then S holds a justified belief that q.[4]

Dretske (1970), who had nothing to say against JCVR and thought, quite generally, that the closure issue was the issue of whether "the epistemic worth of a proposition is hereditary under entailment" (1970, p. 34), propelled our thoughts further down this path, from merely acknowledging JCVR to a discussion of whether something like JCVR is (a) true and (b) has a true analogue for knowledge. We then had a new problem: If knowledge is not only justified true belief, the claim that both truth and justification are transmitted from premises to conclusion in valid reasoning might be insufficient to explain inferential knowledge thus acquired. Dretske's own JCVR-analogue for knowledge doesn't quite do what he suggested it would do. He asked us to ponder this principle of closure under *known* entailment:

CKE. If S knows that p, and knows that p entails q, then S knows that q.

There are two fairly obvious problems with CKE. First, it is objectionably *elitist*. How many people who perform valid reasoning from what they know

---

[3] He elaborates on the problem in Kvanvig (2006).
[4] I drop the quantifiers from now on where they are obvious, and keep the schemata as uncluttered as possible. I'll also steer clear of the debate over multi-versus-single-premise closure, since that wouldn't help to clarify the main issues involving epistemic closure.

have the concept of entailment? Not too many.[5] Second, one may know that *p* and that *p* entails *q*, and yet fail to form the belief that *q*. Dretske describes scenarios where one may be tempted to withhold belief in a proposition that one sees logically follows from what s/he takes him/herself to know. Recall the zebra scene (1970, p. 39): A nonphilosophical person may think it natural to resist the belief that what she's looking at is not a mule in a perfect zebra disguise while insisting that she knows both that the animal is a zebra and that its being a zebra entails that the animal is not a perfectly disguised mule. She may simply laugh off the mule hypothesis as ridiculous, or comical, and think that the issue thereby goes away, thus remaining oblivious to the threat of inconsistency. But the motivation to identify a JCVR-analogue for knowledge remains, and it has easily been found:

KCVR. If S knows that *p* and forms the belief that *q* as a result of reasoning validly to *q* from *p*, then S knows that *q*.[6]

Here, we reach a more interesting aspect of the closure debate. We can clearly see that neither JCVR nor KCVR is a principle according to which Dretske's object, "the epistemic worth" of a proposition, is closed under *entailment*. Both principles concern valid deduction. And we could have been told in much clearer terms than we find in the literature that neither is a *fundamental* closure principle. Both give us the opportunity to ask: In virtue of what is either justification or knowledge closed under valid deduction? The pursuit of this line of inquiry immediately shows that there is no tenable principle of knowledge-closure under entailment. The reason for it is well-known: valid deduction works only if you *perform it*. Still, surely some of a proposition's "epistemic worth" for you is independent of the contingent fact that you fail to enjoy your epistemic wealth. Think about it in this way: Even if you never spend a dime, you may still be a millionaire. But the problem here is whether you are epistemically well-endowed, not whether you spend your fortune. This leads us to the fact that many seem happy to call the following principle – the principle that *something in knowledge* is made available for the acquisition of new knowledge through valid reasoning – a "closure principle."

---

[5] Would putting this in (object-language) terms of conditional knowledge – as in " . . . and knows that if p then q . . . " – dispose of the elitism objection? Apparently not, since the agent must still perceive the relation between antecedent and consequent as compelling her to believe the consequent, given belief in the antecedent, *on pain of irrationality*. I thank Risto Hilpinen for discussion on which this note is based.

[6] Hawthorne (2004; 2014) adds a clause that has been endorsed by Luper (2016) and Pritchard (2016a), among others. No discussion of it is essential to what follows.

SIK. If S knows that *p*, and *p* entails *q*, then S *is in a position to know that q.*

However, as Kvanvig urges, this is stretching the concept of closure to break-ing point, since here the property mentioned in the antecedent (knowing that *p*) is not what is thought to be transmitted by entailment. Moreover, SIK is appallingly obscure. "What," we might reasonably ask, "is it to be *in a position to know*, given entailment?"

There is a Dretskean reply to the above question. Both Dretske (2014) and his critic Hawthorne (2014) seem ready to acknowledge that the good thing made available, in valid reasoning, from old knowledge to new knowledge is something that supervenes on our having *good evidence* for drawing a given conclusion. We are used to calling that praiseworthy status "epistemic justification" (of the kind relevant to *inferential* knowledge; none of this endorses *evidentialism* in epistemology). So we should ask them why they have failed to explicitly discuss *justification-closure,* the following genuine closure principle:

JC. If S is justified in believing that *p* (i.e. has a justification for believing that *p*), and *p* entails *q*, then S is justified in believing that *q*.

Some, such as Hawthorne (2014), have avoided acknowledging JC as part of a policy of remaining tight-lipped about anything justification-related when discussing closure principles. But, sometimes, reasons are offered for antipa-thy against the notion. David and Warfield, for instance, while acknowledging the obscurity of versions of SIK, explain their focus on such knowledge-based principles as follows (2008, p. 141):

> We focus on closure principles involving knowledge because most dis-cussions of closure-based skepticism turn on closure principles involving knowledge, and also because we like knowledge [*sic*] and want to think about knowledge and knowledge-skepticism. Also, we tend to think that knowledge is somewhat easier to handle than notions like justification or rationality.

Well, don't we all like knowledge? But can there be progress in efforts to clarify the motivation for SIK that avoids all talk of justification, "entitle-ment," or "rationality"?

We find similarly insouciant satisfaction with mere avoidance of justifica-tion-talk in the words of another philosopher who worries about epistemic closure, Becker. While warning the true-blue Goldmanian reliabilist against a "justificationist trap" set by Goldman, Becker notes (2007, pp. 34–5):

it is not clear that justification [on Goldman's construal] is required for knowledge ... [I]f we ... require justification, ... suitably refined, for knowledge, many of the hard-fought gains of reliabilism will be lost ... [T]his is to fall into the justificationist trap. Reliabilists should get out of the business of justification and stick to the central issue: knowledge ... Of course, some belief-truth link is essential to an account of knowledge ... To that end, we need to change the name of the game from justification to the more general concept of warrant.

Isn't this perilously close to waging war against a *word*? Justification is as permissive a concept as we need it to be, as post-Goldman epistemology so clearly shows.

Ideologically motivated aversion to justification-talk has produced massive distortion in the literature on epistemic closure. We find an interesting manifestation of the phenomenon in Luper's *Stanford Encyclopedia of Philosophy* entry on "Epistemic Closure." He introduces the issue with this question: "Precisely what is meant by the claim that knowledge is closed under entailment?" (2016, sec. 1). He then displays the following "straight principle" as material for discussion: "SP: If person S knows p, and p entails q, then S knows q"; and comments on SP as follows (2016, sec. 1): "The straight principle needs qualifying, but this should not concern us so long as the qualifications are natural given the idea we are trying to capture, namely, that we can extend our knowledge by recognizing, and accepting thereby, things that follow from something that we know."

As we have seen when considering justification-aversion in the works of three philosophers above (not counting "knowledge-firsters" such as Hawthorne), there is nothing uncontroversial about the qualifications that seep into a discussion of Luper's "straight principle," beginning with this: Knowledge is not closed under entailment. Period. The fact is never explicitly acknowledged by Luper in his *Stanford Encyclopedia* piece.[7] The question with which he introduces the view that knowledge is closed under *competent deduction* is misleading. It should actually lead us back to the issue of why the SIK principle is obscure. But the issue is hidden from view in so many sources in the closure debate, Luper's work included.

Only one epistemic property can plausibly be thought to be closed under entailment: epistemic justification – more precisely, "propositional justification," as we often call it, following Firth (1978), or "epistemic

---

[7] He does acknowledge, in a *single paragraph* added to the 2016 version of the entry, that JC seems unimpeachable.

entitlement," or "epistemic rationality." So, our discussion will hence-forth be concerned with the tenability of JC, the principle undergirding any claim according to which competent deduction infallibly transmits knowledge from premises to conclusion, regardless of whether some of those writing on the issue are willing to acknowledge the fact that no explanation of one's being *in a position to know* will result from justifi-cation-aversion.

One last point should be addressed before we reach the heart of this debate. One of those who have led the way to an understanding that JC is *the* closure principle to occupy us when we meet threats to epistemic closure (including threats to either KCVR or JCVR), Klein, suggests that JC may face two relatively minor objections that can be met only if we impose two restrictions on JC (2002, p. 342): "We can stipulate," according to him, "that [(a)] the domain of the propositions in the generalization of [JC] includes only con-tingent propositions that [(b)] are within S's capacity to grasp and that the entailment is 'obvious' to S."

Restriction (a) will be addressed in Sections 2.3–2.5. How about restric-tion (b)? Should we think of epistemic entitlement as reaching only to propositions that we can understand and entailment relations that we can grasp? I can't see why this kind of restriction is thought to be so appealing. Suppose you are now epistemically entitled to believe that *p*. By (unrestricted) JC, we should think that there is a proposition of immense complexity that is entailed by *p* but that you cannot now grasp, given your present intellectual resources. (Think, for instance, of a proposition including fifteen conditionals.) Given your incapacity to grasp that immensely complex logical consequence of *p*, you can't "see" that it is a consequence of *p*. But we should think that you might eventually (conceivably) *evolve*, shouldn't we? On Klein's view, when/if you become capable of "seeing" the entailment and "grasping" that consequence of *p*, the restriction will not apply. You will then be epistemically entitled to believe that consequence of *p*. Why should we think that epistemic *entitle-ment* (i.e. epistemic *permission*) is correlated with *cognitive evolution*? No good answer to this question seems forthcoming from those endorsing the Kleinian restriction. I suggest that you should forget the restriction. It peddles an anthropologized notion of epistemic entitlement, the motiva-tion for which is mysterious.

So, we reach a central question in the epistemology of reasoning: Are there credible threats to JC? What follows is a glimpse of the extreme measures to which JC-advocates have resorted.

2.3 Closure and Parochialism in Philosophical Logic

There is a very bold JC-protecting move in philosophical logic. We've known it by the label "relevance logic" – or "relevant logic," as some of its proponents call it, to emphasize the boldness by turning the epithet into a battle cry. As exciting as it undoubtedly is for the ingenuity that has been put into it, the project of relevance logic is a very parochial enterprise, for ignoring its own JC-protecting vocation. This is not the place for a sweeping examination of the project, but we have the space to pinpoint the source of its parochialism.

Relevance logic derives intuitive appeal from the claim that some classical inference rules sanction fallacious reasoning – specifically, cases of non sequitur. The complaint is an old one, and prima facie appealing. To invoke the preferred example, *ex falso quodlibet*, it is safe to say that you will have no inclination to derive a desired conclusion from arbitrary premises that you see are jointly inconsistent (if only because you would not, and should not, believe the premises).[8] More generally, you will have no inclination to draw a conclusion from premises that you believe are completely irrelevant to the concluding claim. This is all well and good by any standards for sound reasoning. Deviations *in reasoning* are clearly pathological. But look carefully at what relevance logicians make of this platitude. Here's how two influential relevantists, Mares and Meyer, put it (2001, p. 280):

> Entailment ... is the relation that holds between the *premises* of a valid argument and its *conclusion*. Yet modern logic, which at least since DeMorgan and Peirce has prided itself on taking relations seriously, failed to do so with respect to the central notion of *logical consequence* that is its business to analyze.

In keeping with that kind of ambitious language, elsewhere Mares undertakes to remind us that "[n]on-sequiturs are bad" (2005, p. 609), and notes: "The classical notion of validity does not agree with our pre-logical intuitions about where the division between good arguments and *non-sequiturs* should be" (2005, p. 609; see also Mares 2004, pp. 3–4). Likewise, while addressing the view that the truth-conditions of the indicative natural-language "if" coincide with the classical view of "⊃," Read claims that "it has long been recognized that

---

[8] Deleting "arbitrary" from this sentence would blur the intuitive appeal to a pretheoretical notion of relevance. Moreover, as the parenthetical remark suggests, any generic epistemological injunction against inconsistency as a doxastic practice would explain why you're exposed to censure if your premises contain (or imply) contradictories.

treating 'if' as material, or truth-functional, validates clearly invalid arguments" (1988, p. 23). Why is it taking us so long to learn the lesson that the indicative "if" is not material, given that its nontruth-functionality, according to Read (1988, p. 189), "has been shown repeatedly over the last eighty or more years" – that is, repeatedly in the last one hundred years, with Read's own important contribution to the lesson factored in by now? The more obvious explanation is that perhaps (relevantist enthusiasm notwithstanding) no such thing has yet clearly been shown to general satisfaction.

Be that as it may, only a fool would think that the rift between relevantists and classicists is the yield of a simple-minded error by one party to the dispute. But this is consistent with thinking that, somewhere along the way, oversimplification has crept into our understanding of these issues. Here's one potential *locus* of oversimplification: a narrow-minded appeal to the notion of a non sequitur when the relevantist brings a charge of inadequacy against the classical account of validity (and logical consequence). The relevantist complaint is that non sequiturs are sanctioned by an account of validity whose sole objective is to secure truth-preservation. The point of appealing to non sequiturs is to get us to understand that truth-preservation is not sufficient for valid reasoning. But the answer to the following question is, throughout relevantist theorizing, left implicit at best: Why is a non sequitur bad, really? You don't go far enough in attempting to answer the question if you simply say that a non sequitur is a piece of deductive reasoning in which the premises fail to be relevant to the conclusion, or fail to *relevantly guarantee* the truth of the conclusion (in the sense of being evidentially essential to the conclusion). A satisfying reply would hold that, in a case of reasoning properly described as a non sequitur, something of *epistemic value* other than truth, either knowledge or justification, fails to be transmitted from premises to conclusion. We all agree that relevance is at most an instrumental value. We should think that relevance is a necessary condition of justification-transmission, and, if justification is necessary for knowledge and there is knowledge at the starting point, valid reasoning gives us knowledge at the destination (or at least never leads to ignorance, if we are reasoning circularly).[9]

Although not typically explicit in relevantist literature when the motivation for the project is explained, the epistemological demand should be met with

---

[9] Most of us would also claim that *only if* the premises are cases of knowledge will knowledge be the output in sound reasoning. But I have argued in detail against that claim (2017).

an approving yawn from relevantists. So, we should think that the problem becomes that of how some classically valid argument forms may fail to transmit the valuable epistemic quantity (or fail to preserve it) from premises to conclusions by displaying *relevance deficit*. Is that an accurate report on relevantist motivation?

As it turns out, not exactly. Relevantists are quick to admit that not every form of classically sanctioned non sequitur is a case of relevance deficit by any pretheoretical notion of relevance. The broader theme of non sequitur-avoidance generalizes to the claim that classical rules are not infallibly *truth-preserving*, with cases of relevance deficit subsumed under an unqualified charge of failure in truth-preservation. But, when we look at the troublesome inferences, it is clear that the charge that truth-preservation fails could be replaced by the charge that justification-transmission fails, since every reason to think that a reasoner has moved from true premises to a false conclusion in valid reasoning is a reason to think that her premises don't justify her conclusion.[10] As long as truth and justification are distinguished, these are distinct charges. And the difference is dramatically important in a dispute over finding the most compelling explanation for the relevant cases of non sequitur (as we shall see).

Looking at the classicism/relevantism dispute from that perspective, relevantist talk of non sequiturs seems parochial, in that it fails to highlight an obvious feature of non sequiturs: in every non sequitur, the premises jointly fail to justify the conclusion. So, why wouldn't relevantist concern with non sequiturs be an opportunity to denounce classical logic for failing to protect JC? No answer is forthcoming from relevantists.[11] Consider the following cases of apparent JC-failure, all of which are of relevantist concern, none of which is an obvious case of relevance deficit, but all of which might (parochially) be regarded as cases of invalidity.

Napoleon.[12] While preparing a talk on Napoleon, you double-check your sources and conclude that you can safely claim that (~*p*) *Napoleon was not Italian (not Genoese)*. You expect trouble at the talk, because Napoleon

---

[10] A true proposition describing evidential insufficiency in a non sequitur is what epistemologists call an "undercutting defeater." See de Almeida (2017) for details.

[11] As in Burgess (2005), here, too, the term "relevantism" should apply to a broad range of critics for whom there are cases of non sequitur sanctioned by classical logic, even though some of these authors have little else in common with card-carrying relevance logicians. In addition to those non-card-carrying "collaborators" whom Burgess mentions, I'd add Stalnaker (1975), McGee (1985), Adams (1988), Woods (1997), Bennett (2003), and Sanford (2003).

[12] The case is originally from de Almeida (forthcoming a).

was born in Corsica, and you have a colleague who insists that Corsica belonged to Italy (to Genoa) when Napoleon was born.[13] It didn't. It had just been acquired by France. In any case, what most matters to your talk is that you have knowledge-level justification for believing (and claiming) that (*q*) *Napoleon was ruthless.* You're about to leave for your talk when a paralyzing thought crosses your mind. That Corsica-obsessed colleague of yours will certainly find a way to give you a hard time at the talk. Given that you're entitled to believe ~*p* and ~*p* classically entails *p* ⊃ ~*q*, then, according to your epistemology teacher, you're entitled to believe that *if Napoleon was Italian, he was not ruthless.* And you're now wondering how you can convince your audience that your claim about Napoleon's character can't possibly depend on when the Treaty of Versailles was signed![14]

JFK. Suppose new evidence puts all conspiracy theories to rest and establishes that John Kennedy was, indeed, killed by the shots fired at him in Dallas (and not, say, because he was poisoned on his way to the hospital), and the new evidence also establishes that only Oswald could have fired the fatal shots. We're now justified in believing that, *if someone fatally shot Kennedy in Dallas, Oswald was the shooter.* But we're not justified in believing, by Contraposition, that *if Oswald didn't fatally shoot Kennedy in Dallas, no one else did.*[15]

Reagan. Just before the 1980 US presidential election, you noticed that, according to the credible opinion polls, Republican Reagan was way ahead of Democrat Carter, the second-place candidate in the race. This justified your belief that *a Republican will win the election.* You also knew that there was another Republican in the race, Anderson. This justified your belief that, *if a Republican wins the election and Reagan loses, then Anderson wins.* But you also knew that Anderson was a distant third-place candidate.

---

[13] Assume that Napoleon's birthdate is not disputed by the troublemaker.

[14] Note that *you* would naturally be thinking of the problematic conditional in subjunctive terms – *if Napoleon were Italian* . . ., or *if Napoleon had been Italian* . . . But you obviously can't refuse to engage with one who puts that hypothesis in *weaker terms* – *if Napoleon was Italian* . . . – in order to challenge your claim that Napoleon was ruthless. Woods (1997, pp. 53–4): "Even in a context in which it is a presupposition accepted by speaker and hearer that I have not been misinformed, I can hardly decline to accept 'If Mary has left-wing views, I have been totally misinformed.'" And he adds: "in such a case I should *not* say, 'If Mary had had left-wing views, I would have been totally misinformed.'"

[15] This is a version of a case suggested by Sanford (2003, p. 227), who appropriated Adams' famous JFK example to make a point about indicative conditionals. A similar case is offered in Jackson (1987).

So, you were not justified in believing, by Exportation and *modus ponens*, that, *if it's not Reagan who wins, it's Anderson*.[16]

The Mayor. You believe, on excellent evidence, that *the mayor is a model citizen*. According to your epistemology teacher, justification is infallibly transmitted by classical entailment. So, if the teacher is right, you are justified in believing, on the basis of your admiration for the mayor, that *the mayor is either a model citizen or Tony Soprano's secret accomplice in an extortion scheme*. But you can't understand how either the belief that *the mayor is a model citizen* or the evidence for believing that he is that kind of citizen could justify the disjunctive proposition. You just can't shake the feeling that a disjunction presents us with *live possibilities*; but your evidence rules out the hypothesis that the mayor is a criminal.[17]

Here are some quick remarks on these cases of apparent JC-failure. The Napoleon case involves one of the (improperly so-called) "paradoxes of implication." It's one of the reasons why we have relevance logic. My point here is simply that, if the relevantist is not seeking to block the apparent absurdity that ensues from holding JC in conjunction with classical entailment (and classical truth-conditions for indicative conditionals), we need an explanation for relevantist outrage in response to cases such as this. But pro-JC needs are not even acknowledged by relevantists. They keep their allegiance to JC at a subconscious level. Classical entailment/semantics alone is supposed to shoulder the blame for said absurdities.

The same can be said about Contraposition, as in the JFK case. The classical truth-conditions for the conditional must take the blame, according to Contraposition detractors, for what stands out as a case of JC-failure, if the classical rule is exempted from blame. So, the *tacit* relevantist claim is that JC should be left alone. Relevantists write as if classical entailment is *obviously* the culprit.

The case against *modus ponens* is of obvious concern to classicists who identify the natural-language "if" with "⊃" and rely on a distinction between truth and assertibility – as in Jackson (1987) and Sorensen (1988). Relevantist complaints regarding the material conditional are *easily* seen as at least *legitimate*.

The rule of Addition is a well-known villain, as the discomfort in the Mayor case shows. Does it deserve its reputation? We'll look into this shortly. In any

---

[16] The case comes from McGee (1985, p. 462).   [17] The example comes from de Almeida (2017).

case, my point is not adjudicating the classicism/relevantism dispute. It's simply that JC-denial is not even on the philosophical logician's radar, as s/he makes some of the most dramatic claims we have seen in philosophy since time immemorial. (Recall Mares' perceived need to remind us that non sequiturs are bad!)

2.4 Closure and Parochialism in Epistemology

Most of those who argue for JC in epistemology do so indirectly, by arguing against the epistemological views (most notably, Dretske's and Nozick's) on which closure fails. There are degrees of indirection, however. The least indirect pro-JC claims may take, for instance, the form of BonJour's (1987) claim, according to which having closure failure as a consequence of your epistemology amounts to a *reductio* of your epistemology. This is closure-dogmatism on steroids. More indirect pro-JC moves find independent evidence against epistemologies on which closure fails. For instance, Sosa (1999b) and Luper (2003; 2016) claim that those inclined to accept Nozickian epistemology should be more attracted to their own versions of truth-tracking epistemology, partly because these protect closure principles. I won't discuss indirect pro-JC moves in what follows. I will, instead, briefly comment on the two most ambitious direct pro-JC theoretical moves we have known in epistemological ranks. These JC-defenders seek to show that anti-JC impulses stem from a failure to notice certain easy-to-miss epistemic phenomena. One of these pro-JC moves is a clear case of parochialism. The other is a form of closure-dogmatism – if we're really keen on distinguishing between dogmatism and parochialism.

Klein's 1981 pro-JC move is impressively effective against Dretske-style counterexamples to JC.[18] It arises from the observation that Dretske-style counterexamples to justification closure derive their impact from confusion between JC and the following, stronger principle that I have labeled "evidential closure," which, adapted to our purposes, might be expressed as follows:

Evidential closure (EC). If S is justified in believing that *p* (i.e. has a justification for believing that *p*) on the basis of body of evidence *e*, and *p* entails *q*, then S is justified in believing that *q on e*.

---

[18] This is an edited version of a paragraph in de Almeida (forthcoming a).

The distinction helps to dispose of Dretske-style counterexamples. Once at the zoo under normal conditions, the evidence you have for believing you're looking at zebras may be deemed inadequate for you to believe you're not looking at perfectly disguised mules – in a way that poses no obvious threat to JC. The case derives its anticlosure impact from the feeling that you need stronger evidence in order to rule out the disguised-mule hypothesis. But that leaves the door open for the (Moorean) claim that you are epistemically entitled to believe that those animals are not disguised mules, on the basis of a belief that you are, by hypothesis, already entitled to hold *on a different basis* – namely, the belief that the animals are zebras (and that no zebra is a mule).[19]

The success of Klein's 1981 proclosure counterattack remains the basis for his later *Stanford Encyclopedia of Philosophy* (2015) claim that the old move, with assistance from a critique of Nozick's anti-JC move, should ward off any threats to JC. But the latter-day claim should strike us as optimistic in view of counterexamples that seem immune to the therapeutic effect of the distinction between EC and JC, such as those presented in Section 2.3. Therein lies the parochial aspect of Klein's defense of JC.

Classicists such as Klein can escape parochialism and fall prey to justification-dogmatism. That seems to have been the fate of a proposal put forward by Sorensen (1988) and endorsed by Hawthorne (2004). Theirs is not a clearly parochial view. It can be applied to a very broad range of cases of apparent JC-failure – maybe to all of them.

Sorensen's proposal calls for recognition of what he has labeled "junk knowledge." However, none of what he says about the notion pertains exclusively to knowledge. He might as well have spoken about "junk justification." But it might be confusing if I discussed the Sorensenian view as one regarding "junk justification" (a term that no one currently uses). With that in mind, I defer to his terminological preference in what follows.

Here's the Sorensenian view of junk knowledge. Contrary to what relevantists and like-minded logicians would claim, in the troublesome cases highlighted in Section 2.3, classical validity is not refuted by the purported counterexamples: the believer does have knowledge of the conclusion, given knowledge of the premises. The impression that classical semantics somehow perversely sanctions non sequiturs arises from

---

[19] In de Almeida (forthcoming b), I offer an introduction to Mooreanism that highlights a problematic aspect of the view.

inattention to the fact that "much of what we know is subterranean" (Sorensen 1988, p. 454): that is, there is such a thing as *junk knowledge*, "knowledge from which we cannot draw familiar inferences that would expand what we know" (1988, p. 433). The emphasis is on failure to *expand* one's stock of knowledge by validly drawing what looks like a false conclusion from cases of knowledge that the believer cannot manifest without creating misleading evidence to interlocutors – evidence that invites the performance of the troublesome inferences. In each such case, the conclusion "is an item in [the believer's] corpus of knowledge despite its worthlessness" (1988, p. 446).

Applying the proposal to our cases, in the Mayor case you do know that *the mayor is either a model citizen or Tony Soprano's secret accomplice in an extortion scheme*, since the disjunction is validly drawn from your knowledge that *the mayor is a model citizen*. But if you were to manifest that junk disjunctive knowledge in an act of assertion, your interlocutor would be invited to assume that, if you came across evidence that the mayor is a less-than-model citizen – as you would, for instance, if you learned that she has an unpaid parking ticket – you would be prepared to conclude, by Disjunctive Syllogism, that she is Soprano's secret agent at City Hall. But you wouldn't use the disjunction in Disjunctive Syllogism. Your knowledge of the 'Soprano disjunction' is epistemic junk (according to Sorensen). Or consider McGee's (1985) purported counterexample to *modus ponens*. Although the premises are cases of knowledge for you, manifesting that knowledge invites your audience to draw that apparently false conclusion. But that's because, in asserting the premises, you fail to indicate that your knowledge of the conditional (*if a Republican wins the election and Reagan loses, then it will be Anderson who wins*) is wholly dependent on your belief that Reagan is the Republican who will win; it has nothing to do with believing that Anderson has a fighting chance. So, by manifesting your junk conditional knowledge, you're perpetrating a "conversational misdeed." Resistance to *modus ponens* is a product of such a kind of uncooperative behavior (whereby you dump your junk knowledge on interlocutors). Likewise in our Napoleon case: your Corsica-obsessed colleague might try to derail your talk by revealing your junk conditional knowledge (of the form "$\sim p \supset (p \supset \sim q)$," by Conditional Proof), thus forcing you to address an absurd hypothesis about Napoleon's character. And, in the JFK case, your knowledge of Oswald's guilt is not perspicuously revealed by your junk conditional knowledge, since there you should make the stronger assertion you're entitled to make: that is, you should assert the consequent (*Oswald fatally shot Kennedy*). If you cooperatively asserted the consequent, you would be protecting your inter-locutor from the temptation to perform Contraposition on your junk conditional knowledge.

How comprehensive is the junk-knowledge proposal as a JC-protecting move? Can it account for the kind of skeptical threat about which Klein worries? Maybe. Although Sorensen does not consider skeptical scenarios such as Detske's zebra case, we are tempted to explain the phenomenon, in Sorensenian terms, by saying that you have junk knowledge that *if you are looking at zebras, then you're not looking at disguised mules*. But, once your junk conditional knowledge is exposed, you may balk at the prospect of using it in *modus ponens* (which hints at JC-denial). Our attention then shifts to where it belongs – to whether an interlocutor should prevail with her reasons for peddling a skeptical argument, according to which you resist *modus ponens* because you're not justified in believing the antecedent (that those are zebras).

Note that nothing in the junk-knowledge theory hinges on whether the believer performs the classically valid inference in any of the troublesome cases. Presumably, the believer is *epistemically entitled* to perform it. For Sorensen, enemies of the view that the indicative natural-language "if" *just is* the horseshoe ("⊃") have been misled by inattention to the junk-knowledge phenomenon.

In view of the stealthy way by which epistemic junk is supposed to creep into episodes of reasoning, what is to keep us from regarding the junk-knowledge hypothesis as an *ad hoc* classicist move? According to Sorensen, noticing that *junk knowledge is a special case of unassertible knowledge*. He rightly notes that "[e]pistemologists have a number of precedents for distinguishing between assertible and unassertible knowledge" (1988, p. 445). This is crucial to Sorensen's case. The tenability of his case for junk knowledge – like Hawthorne's, who endorses the Sorensenian view *in toto* as the key element in a defense of knowledge-closure for classically valid reasoning (2014, pp. 71–3) – depends on our agreeing that (a) there is unassertible knowledge, and that (b) the apparent fact that JC is threatened by the repugnant conclusions in our anti-JC sample cases (Napoleon, JFK, Reagan, and the Mayor) can be explained away by appeal to the notion of unassertible knowledge.

Point (a) is clearly true. In accordance with Sorensen's claims, normative unassertibility (i.e. "low assertibility") is naturally exemplified by cases in which violating Gricean maxims (and kindred principles) generates misleading evidence. For instance, as I leave the conference room, I see the janitor, broom in hand, looking bored. She is waiting for the talk to end so that she can clean the room. With hope in her voice, she asks if there is anybody left in the room. I answer that four people are in there. What I said is true, since I know that there are forty people in there. I have then been "uncooperative," though. My knowledge that there are forty people in the room entitles me to infer that there are four. But, in asserting that there are four people there, I represent myself as cooperative and invite her to infer that there are *exactly four* people in the room. I have unassertible knowledge that there are four people. Unassertible knowledge typically generates misleading evidence (or perplexity of some kind by relevance failure, for instance) in a social context. It also often seems to be worthless mental clutter to the believer's own perspective.

But (b) is false: the discomfort in our anti-JC cases has nothing *exclusively* to do with normative assertibility in a social context; it has to do with perceived irrationality from an *egocentric* perspective. Sorensen's "pragmatic" approach is inadequate to account for our problem. Take the Mayor case. Our problem is not simply that the inferred disjunction is *worthless* to the believer for any practical purpose, or that it would create misleading evidence in a social setting. Our problem is the apparent irrationality of believing the disjunction when your belief system entitles you to *disbelieve* one of the disjuncts. Sometimes, as our cases seem to show, pragmatically reprehensible assertion is explained by *epistemically reprehensible belief.* So, we still need to explain what makes the relevant beliefs egocentrically reprehensible from an epistemological point of view. I can't see how we might be able to squeeze the desired explanation out of any notion of junk knowledge, rooted as it is in normative unassertibility.

From a psychological point of view, the facts seem clear. You wouldn't normally infer that someone is in the room from your belief that Roy is in the room. The awkwardness is unquestionable. It's hard to imagine a situation to which the inference might be perceived as the adequate response in an *egocentric* setting. The data are more interesting in a social context. If you believe that Roy is in the room and your interlocutor asks you if someone is in the room, "yes" is a perfect response. *Ceteris paribus*, it doesn't make you uncooperative. Asserting the weaker proposition doesn't always make you uncooperative.[20] But sometimes it does. If you believe that Jones owns a Ford and have no information on where Brown might be, and your interlocutor, who happens to have good evidence of both Jones' Ford-owning behavior and Brown's Barcelona-bound plans but no other relevant beliefs regarding those

---

[20] The point is urged by Burgess (2009, pp. 102–3) in the context of a defense of Addition. My points regarding Addition are compatible with what he writes. But his apparent defense of Addition does not protect it against counterexemplification.

co-workers, were to assert (only) that either Jones owns a Ford or Brown is in Barcelona, it would be downright misleading for you to respond simply with "yes," or "you're right." But that's because it would be *epistemically irrational* for you to believe the disjunction. By hypothesis, you have no reason to regard Brown's presence in Barcelona as a live possibility. (Maybe you have evidence that he's not in Barcelona, where he has knowingly made some deadly enemies.) The normal response on your part would include something like this: "Do you have any reason to think that Brown is in Barcelona?"[21] In the Mayor case, it looks even worse to those who haven't been contaminated by closure-dogmatism: your agreeing that the mayor is either a model citizen or Soprano's secret accomplice, based solely on your nonoverridden evidence that she is a model citizen, would normally be seen as downright pathological – as confirming that there is *a basis for suspicion* regarding the mayor's possible Soprano connection.[22] Asserting the disjunction would be perceived by those who share in your admiration for the mayor as libelous – or as insane.[23]

---

[21] When talking about Gettier's Brown-in-Barcelona case, embarrassed teachers feel compelled to say what Zagzebski (2009, 115) says about it: "Don't ask what would possess Smith to draw such an inference [and form the disjunctive belief while being ignorant of Brown's whereabouts]."

[22] In correspondence, Risto Hilpinen notes that some deontic logicians have also argued in a way that suggests opposition to combining Addition with JC. Here's how he puts it:
"Let 'E(P)' mean that P is evident to you. In this example we have:
(1) E(M) (M = The Mayor is a model citizen)
Therefore, according to the consequence principle for E [i.e., JC], we should also have:
(2) E(M ∨ C),
where C = The Mayor is a criminal. However, we also have
(3) E(Not-C).
Thus it would be odd or misleading to assert that (2). This is exactly (or very much) like Ross's paradox in deontic logic, according to which the consequence principle justifies the inference from the directive
(4) Mail this letter! (or: You must mail this letter.)
to a disjunctive directive
(5) Mail this letter or burn it!
even though you must not burn the letter. You say that, intuitively, a disjunction should present 'live possibilities,' possibilities not excluded by your evidence. In the same way, it has been suggested in deontic logic that a disjunctive directive should offer a normative subject a choice between the disjuncts." See Aloni (2016) for context.

[23] Claiming that not every truth-preserving move in reasoning deserves to be called an "inference rule" might seem to point in the right direction. Logic teachers are familiar with the need to explain that the rule of Reiteration is not a license to perform an inference of the form "p ⊢ p," since reasoning of this form instantiates a well-known fallacy, although the move seems harmless (to classicists) in the context of more complex reasoning. It is heroic – or just downright misleading – to suggest that Reiteration *transmits* justification, although it is truth-preserving. Why not treat Addition likewise? Maybe because this just delays explaining the distinction between a truth-preserving move that instantiates a justification-transmitting, bona fide inference rule and one that doesn't. Relevance logic can be seen as the project of making such a distinction.

Here again, as in relevantist onslaught, we find passionate defense of classical logic breeding closure-dogmatism.

2.5 Concluding Remarks: Cosmopolitanism on the Cheap?

I've noted that a number of epistemologists have contributed to what Kvanvig calls "the closure mess." Nowhere is the mess any messier than in work giving us the obscure SIK principle – the principle that was supposed to explain why *valid (deductive) inference* from premises that are cases of knowledge should be expected to give you more *knowledge*. To escape the mess, we must, I submit, turn to work that acknowledges a principle of transmission of epistemic *entitlement*, something like our JC. We do find some clarity in pro-JC literature. However, not all is well there either. Authors such as Klein, one of the leaders among those for whom JC is essential within any discussion of inferential knowledge, have taken a carefree approach to the default notion of entailment/validity in most epistemological theorizing, namely, classical entailment/validity. The carefree approach breeds a form of parochialism. While speaking about a Cartesian skeptical argument framed as a *modus tollens*, Klein quickly dismisses the option of refuting the skeptic on the grounds that *modus tollens* is invalid (2015, sec. 4):

> If one were to deny that *modus tollens* is a valid form of inference, one would also have to deny the validity of (i) disjunctive syllogism and (ii) *modus ponens* or contraposition, since it is easy to transform *modus tollens* arguments into ones employing the other forms of inference. Hence, if this alternative [response to skepticism] were chosen, reasoning would apparently come to a complete standstill. That, presumably, is why no one has ever seriously considered this alternative.

Klein is clearly mistaken if the neglected alternative is that of regarding *modus tollens* as invalid, as witnessed not only by the literature that specifically targets *modus tollens*, but by much of the literature according to which the material conditional is an aberration, or, in any case, something to be distinguished from the indicative "if."[24]

But, if Klein has made *that* mistake, why should we simply disregard the option of seeing a skeptical *modus tollens* as a case of non sequitur? Wasn't it Dretske's idea to disregard a skeptical conclusion reached by *modus tollens* as

---

[24] For specific discussion of seemingly paradoxical instances of *modus tollens*, see Adams (1988) and Sinnott-Armstrong, Moor, and Fogelin (1990).

irrelevant (or based on an irrelevant skeptical hypothesis, or, as Sorensen would put it, based on epistemic junk)? And isn't it the relevantist charge against classical validity that it allows for irrelevance in reasoning? Do we have any pretheoretical distinction between these two charges of irrelevance in reasoning? I submit that we do not. Dretske's anti-JC theoretical move was a form of epistemological parochialism, since it simply ignored the option of targeting classical validity/consequence instead. The relevance logician – backed by local objections to classical rules from a number of philosophical logicians who do not identify themselves as card-carrying relevantists – points in a different direction: s/he targets classical entailment/validity *and tacitly protects JC*. Relevantists, however, do not connect their efforts with the JC camp in epistemology, which turns them into purveyors of parochialism in philosophical logic.

At the opposite end of the spectrum, we find those for whom relevantist onslaught ignores, or misunderstands, conversational needs and the conceptual resources derived from Gricean/Jacksonian respect for those needs.[25] Sorensen and Hawthorne together represent the conversationalist proclosure beachhead in epistemology, as we have seen. But, as we also have seen, their notion of junk knowledge doesn't seem to gain any traction by appealing to the notion of (normatively) unassertible knowledge. Looking at cases where assertion frustrates conversational needs gives us no insight into why some conclusions seem unjustified from an egocentric perspective. And if junk knowledge is not a species of unassertible knowledge (ordinary knowledge that simply happens to be conversationally inappropriate), "junk knowledge" must be a label for some new kind of classicist dogma.

But neither of those popular warring factions, relevantists and classicists, will deny me the right to complain that JC-denial is a legitimate contender in their fight, or, more properly speaking, in a fight that they parochially thought was exclusively their own. Their objection to my proposal will be of a different nature. They might complain as Borges (2015, p. 3682) did. According to Borges, closure-deniers like me "owe" them a theory of where and how closure fails. But the complaint is unfair. A closure-denier carrying counterexamples owes nobody anything. A refutation stands on its own merits, and we obviously need all the good refutations that we can find. What is true in this general vicinity is that we do need a theory, a fully worked-out anti-JC

---

[25] Read (1995, pp. 73–4) claims to have a single-paragraph refutation of conversationalist moves of a Gricean/Jacksonian extraction.

theory as an attractive option. The modest message in this chapter is a plea for "cosmopolitanism," if you will, in our approach to the issue. Classicists, in particular, should see JC-denial as something to which they can warm up, since it tends to pull the philosophical rug from under the relevantist's feet.

Lastly, a warning: do not mistake my plea for a kind of epistemological "cosmopolitanism" for a proposal that brings grist to the mill of another brand of "cosmopolitanism," the form of relativism that goes by the epithet "logical pluralism." Logical pluralism is represented in the writings of Beall and Restall (2006) and Shapiro (2014). Their form of relativism (disagreements between them notwithstanding) is very wide in scope, encompassing a number of disputes among contemporary logicians. My point regarding their work is that they, too, see parochialism in the classicism/relevantism debate, but their criticism of that debate is anathema to the charge of parochialism offered here. I have seen a pro-JC move in the relevantist claim that classical validity sanctions non sequiturs. My claim assumes that there is a "yes/no" answer to the question "Does classical logic sanction non sequiturs?" These logical pluralists, instead of answering the question, would denounce it as the yield of large-scale *confusion*.

To appreciate the difference, consider the following excerpts. Here's how Beall and Restall introduce the relevantist challenge (2006, p. 49):

> [The] (classical) precisification of "follows from" is familiar and useful, however, it is not the only sense of "follows from" apparent in English . . . Another strongly apparent sense of "follows from" takes "from" seriously . . . [T]hat [relevantist] sense of "follows from" is more restrictive than the classical one.

In a similar vein, but offering an even more radical view, Shapiro writes (2014, pp. 207–8):

> do those expressions [namely, "valid" and "logical consequence"] have the same *meaning* (or the same content) in all contexts? . . . This matter is, I suggest, terminological, as is the general issue of monism [as contrasted with pluralism] . . . [W]ords like "valid," when used in works in logic, are terms of art. One just stipulates how it is to be used.

From that relativist perspective, there is no closure debate as I see it, simply because there can be no reasonable relevantism/classicism debate. But it's powerfully counterintuitive to think that the relevantist is *not* providing a *philosophically respectable*, if ultimately wrongheaded, "no" answer to the question of whether classical rules are infallibly truth-preserving.[26]

Regarding the relevantism-versus-classicism debate, my own perspective on the pluralist proposal is in line with Burgess' (2005, p. 728) claim that

> there would be no room for contention between classicism and relevantism if "entailment" were simply being introduced as a term previously without meaning (outside probate law) . . . There is room for disagreement only if both sides claim to be analyzing a notion of entailment that already exists, though perhaps not under that label.

So, I'd like to disagree with the pluralist, and to be perceived by her as one who *radically and legitimately* disagrees with her.[27] But I'm now pondering this question: Can a pluralist who practices the kind of "tolerance" s/he preaches at every level of discourse accept me as one with whom s/he *radically and legitimately* disagrees? Or must we remain forever incorrigible to each other?

---

[26] Again, I have not sought to establish that relevantism is a mistake.
[27] Assume, if you must, that we don't see ourselves as disagreeing with an epistemic peer, so that we can reasonably regard the opponent as mistaken.

3   Gettier Cases and Evidence

Clayton Littlejohn

3.1 Introduction

Gettier's (1963) two examples are now widely believed to be counterexamples to this account of knowledge:

JTB. A believes that *p* is true, and the thinker knows that *p* iff *p* is true, the thinker is justified in her belief.

Gettier claimed that his cases work equally well against Chisholm's (1957) account of knowledge:

ETB. A thinker knows that *p* iff *p* is true, the thinker believes that *p* is true, and the thinker has adequate evidence for *p*.

It's probably fair to say that most epistemologists agree with Gettier on these points. There seems to be a general consensus that his protagonists lack knowledge and that they meet the conditions that these theories propose would be sufficient for knowledge.

Gettier's cases, and subsequent Gettier-type cases, have played a tremendous role in shaping our understanding of propositional knowledge. As readers are certain to know, there is a vast literature in which people propose alternative accounts of knowledge that are designed to overcome the difficulties that arise for the JTB or ETB accounts, and then discover to their chagrin that further counterexamples emerge that show their proposals to be inadequate. In this paper, our primary concern will be with evidence. What can we learn about evidence and its theoretical role by studying Gettier-type cases?

In Section 3.2, we briefly discuss two Gettier-type cases and the problems that these cases cause for the ETB account. In Section 3.3, we look at some of the ways that Gettier-type cases have functioned as a tool for testing proposals about the nature of evidence. In Section 3.4 we look at some of the ways that these cases have functioned as a tool for testing proposals about the relationship between evidence and warrant (i.e. that which distinguishes mere true belief from knowledge). In Sections 3.5 and 3.6, we look at challenges to some standard operating assumptions about evidence and knowledge in the post-Gettier literature.

3.2 Gettier-Type Cases

Gettier doesn't spend much time discussing the difference between JTB and ETB. Few epistemologists have criticized him for failing to do so. Perhaps it is thought that this thesis about evidence and justification is true enough for Gettier's purposes:

Evidentialism. A thinker is justified in believing *p* iff the thinker's evidence provides adequate support for believing *p*.

Even if there are important differences between being justified and having adequate evidential support, the differences wouldn't matter for Gettier's purposes if we all agreed that his cases were ones in which a thinker didn't know *p* in spite of correctly believing *p* on the basis of adequate evidence.

Let us have a look at Gettier's first case (which we may call *Coins*). Smith is the protagonist. He has strong evidence for believing this conjunction:

(1) Jones is the man who will get the job, and Jones has ten coins in his pocket.

Smith realizes that (1) entails (2):

(2) The man who will get the job has ten coins in his pocket.

Because Smith has strong evidence for (1), he should have strong evidence for (2). As it happens, though, Smith's evidence for (1) is misleading and it is Smith, not Jones, who will get the job. While Smith's belief in (1) is mistaken, Smith's belief in (2) is not: Smith also happens to have ten coins in his pocket.

Smith believes (2), and (2) is true. The success of Gettier's case turns on whether Smith knows (2) and whether Smith is justified in believing it. If Smith knows (2), the case isn't a counterexample. If Smith is not justified in believing (2) or doesn't have adequate evidence to believe (2), the case isn't a counterexample. Perhaps most readers would agree with Gettier that Smith doesn't know (2); but what about the third condition in JTB or ETB? Does Smith have adequate evidence for believing (2)? Is Smith justified in believing (2)?

Gettier seems to assume that Smith has adequate evidence for (2) and that this means that he is justified in believing it. (Perhaps this is some weak evidence that Gettier assumes that something along the lines of Evidentialism is correct.) Some readers might want to know more about Smith's evidence before issuing a verdict on whether the evidence or justification conditions are met, but I think we should abstract away from the details and focus on two assumptions that Gettier makes explicit. He assumes that it should be possible to meet the evidence and justification conditions even if the thinker's evidence supported a false proposition:

Fallibilism. It is possible for a thinker to have adequate evidence for believing a proposition even if it is possible for a thinker to have just this evidence and be mistaken in her belief.[1]

Most epistemologists would probably agree that this fallibilist thesis is correct. We often learn from induction. If it is possible to come to know p via inference where the evidence that supports p is fallible in the relevant sense, it should be possible for the thinker to be justified in this belief. It is plausible that a thinker is justified in believing whatever she knows.

If this shows that there is no principled objection to the idea that Smith is justified in believing (1) in spite of its falsity, it seems that we can appeal to one further assumption to get Gettier's desired conclusion:

Closure. If a thinker is justified in believing p and she knows that q is a logical consequence of p, she is justified in believing q.

Provided that Smith is justified in believing (1) and knows that (2) is a logical consequence, we are home free. Smith is justified in believing (2) and he has adequate evidence for (2). Readers know that Closure is controversial. To the best of my knowledge, however, those who deny closure do not think that *Coins* is a plausible counterexample to the claim.

It should be noted that some philosophers have questioned whether Gettier's cases were genuine counterexamples, because they were concerned about the role that false propositions played in the evidential pathway that leads Smith to conclude (2). George Pappas and Marshall Swain, for example, suggested, "If an *essential* part of the reasoning from the evidence to the accepted proposition, h,

---

[1] Fallibilism, as understood here, is a thesis about the adequacy of evidence. On its own, it tells us nothing about justification. How should adequacy be understood? If we combine Fallibilism with Evidentialism, adequate evidence is sufficient for justification. If we consider Fallibilism on its own, the idea is that evidence is adequate iff a belief would not fail to have justification because it lacks the right kind of evidential support.

proceeds through a false step, then acceptance of *h* is not justified" (1978, p. 15). They might have thought that genuine evidence consists of true propositions, and that support by genuine evidence is necessary for justification.

While I have some sympathy for this suggestion about evidence, I don't think that these concerns could do much to save ETB. First, some readers will have sympathy for the idea that the operative notion of justification is connected to things like responsibility and blame, in which case it is hard to see how the truth or falsity of the operative considerations that led Smith to conclude that (2) is true could have much to do with meeting the justification condition (Lowy 1978, p. 106):

> To get at Gettier's notion of justification, we might then ask, when is a person justified in believing something in such a way that Gettier's points about justification apply? A person is justified in believing a proposition when no more can reasonably be expected of him with respect to finding out whether that proposition is true. Clearly, Gettier's points about justification hold here: there can be cases where no more can reasonably be expected of a person as a truth-seeker with respect to some proposition, and yet the proposition be false.

If this is right, then someone who wanted to press Pappas and Swain's worries would have to challenge Closure. The intuitions into which Lowy taps in motivating Fallibilism seem to support the further claim that Gettier's case isn't a counterexample to Closure. If it were, we'd have to think that if we ran two versions of Gettier's case (one in which Smith's beliefs were all true, plus the case as Gettier described it) we would have adequate evidence and justification for (2) in only one version of the case. In turn, we would have to say that Smith didn't have justification because he did not do everything that could be reasonably expected. This seems wrong, however. If Smith is internally the same in the two versions of the case, he should be equally responsible in the two cases.

Second, it seems that Gettier's point about ETB can be made without using his cases. We can sidestep Pappas and Swain's worry if we formulate Gettier-type cases in which the protagonist doesn't reason through a false step. Environmental luck cases are a good case to consider in this regard (Dutant 2015, p. 149):

Fakes. I look at a display of 50 identical-looking pens. They all have blue caps, but only one of them is a blue-ink pen. I happen to look at the blue-inked pen and believe that it is a blue-ink pen. If I had looked at any other pen I would have believed the same and been mistaken.[2]

If we wouldn't have knowledge under the conditions described, it seems that fussiness about the presence of falsehoods in the chain of supporting reasons is a distraction.

Many think that Gettier's protagonist had beliefs that met the conditions imposed by JTB and ETB, but lacked knowledge because there was too much luck involved in the connection between the subject's belief and the truth. Environmental luck cases of the kind just described seem to show that a kind of lucky connection between belief and truth can preclude knowledge even if the relevant belief is not supported by mistaken premises. It wouldn't seem that, in the environmental luck cases, there is knowledge-precluding luck even though the relevant belief is not based on any mistaken beliefs or premises or any sort of false evidence.[3]

We don't need to use cases to try to show that Gettier's point can be generalized. Linda Zagzebski (1994) argues that Gettier-type cases can be constructed for any view that incorporates Fallibilism:

Inescapability. A Gettier-type case can be generated for any view of knowledge according to which warrant does not entail truth.

Let us say that "warrant" is a technical term that stands for whatever it is that is added to true belief to give us knowledge.[4] If we introduce the term in this way, it is trivial that any warranted true belief will be knowledge, but it is not trivial that any warranted belief will be true. Given how the term is introduced, it could be that warrant is something that is common between, say, a true belief that constitutes knowledge and a false belief that does not. If a thinker has a warranted false belief – say, because the belief's falsity is due to bad luck – there is nothing that would prevent the thinker from deducing something from this belief that is true owing to some stroke of good luck. This true belief, like the false one, might be true only as a matter of luck, in which case the warranted true belief would not be knowledge. Since this is impossible, the lesson to draw from this seems to be that all warranted beliefs are true.

---

[2] Obviously, this is a variant on Alvin Goldman's (1976) example, inspired by Carl Ginet. I find that this telling of the case does a better job of eliciting the relevant intuition.

[3] It should be noted, however, that some have argued that environmental luck is not incompatible with knowledge. See Hetherington (1998) for discussion, and Madison (2011) for a response.

[4] Here I am following Plantinga (1993a).

The upshot seems to be this. If Fallibilism is correct, the truth condition is not invariably met when a belief is supported by adequate evidence. Since warrant, whatever it is, ensures that a belief is true, it should follow that a belief can be supported by adequate evidence and lack warrant. Thus, it would seem that philosophers interested in understanding warrant would want to focus their attention on the further conditions that do not supervene upon a thinker's evidence.

3.3 Gettier-Type Cases and Theories of Evidence

A Gettier-type case typically functions as a device for testing a theory of knowledge. They have recently been pressed into service for testing theories of evidence. Some appeal to intuitions about Gettier-type cases to justify claims about what a thinker's evidence supervenes upon. Some appeal to the possibility of Gettier-type cases to argue against certain proposals about the nature of evidence.

For a variety of reasons, some epistemologists now believe that a thinker's evidence is just her knowledge:

$E = K$. A thinker's evidence includes all and only the thinker's knowledge.[5]

Why should we think that a thinker's evidence is just her knowledge? First, it seems that our evidence can be propositionally specified.[6] Second, it seems that knowledge should be sufficient for the possession of evidence.[7] Third, linguistic evidence suggests that all ascriptions of propositionally specified evidence entail corresponding knowledge claims.[8] Due to space limitations, I will not attempt to defend these claims here. All I can do is to note that they have been defended elsewhere, and observe that anyone who wishes to reject $E = K$ would have to reject at least one of those claims.

Some writers have suggested that our intuitions about Gettier-type cases reveal that $E = K$ is mistaken. If we think that adequate evidential support is not sufficient for warrant, and we think that the reason why this is so is that certain kinds of harmful epistemic luck prevent a true belief that is supported by adequate evidence from being knowledge, then one thing we seem to learn is that the luck that precludes knowledge does not appear to prevent a body of evidence from providing adequate support for a belief. It seems that we might have pairs of thinkers in two possible worlds who have all and only the same

---

[5] For defenses, see Hyman (1999) and Williamson (2000).   [6] See Neta (2008).
[7] See Bird (2004) and Littlejohn (2012).   [8] See Unger (1975).

nonfactive mental states, all and only the same evidence, have beliefs that are equally accurate, but still have beliefs that differ in that one thinker has warranted beliefs and the other does not. This would seem to tell us something interesting about the supervenience bases for knowledge and evidence. Whatever it is that constitutes the supervenience base for the facts about evidence and evidential support, it doesn't include the conditions that rule out the malignant epistemic luck that threatens knowledge.

Hughes (2014) and Locke (2015) appeal to environmental luck cases (e.g. *Fakes*) to try to illustrate this point. As they see it, the conditions in environmental luck cases that defeat knowledge do not have much bearing on whether the fact, say, that a pen is blue causes the belief that it is or explains why the thinker believes the pen to be blue. Thus, they think that, while the thinker wouldn't know that the pen was blue, the fact that it was blue seems like the kind of thing that could be the thinker's reason for believing various things about the pen. Mitova (2015) and Hofman (2014) use veritic luck cases (e.g. *Coins*) to make a similar point. If we think of reasons or evidence as facts, perhaps having a reason or having some evidence is just a matter of having an attitude that is correct or accurate. As long as the thinker has a true belief (and there is nothing internally amiss), the accidental connection between belief and fact that blocks knowledge in Gettier's original cases needn't prevent the truth from belonging to the thinker's evidence. The guiding intuition seems to be that some of the conditions that make a Gettier-type case a Gettier-type case do not have any role to play in determining what the thinker's evidence is, only what the thinker is in a position to know on the basis of it.

Comesaña and Kantin (2010) argued for something slightly different, which is that E = K implies that Gettier's case wouldn't have been a genuine counterexample to JTB or ETB. They think that E = K implies the following claim:

E = K1. The proposition that *p* justifies S in believing *q* only if S knows *p*.

Comesaña and Kantin suggest that E = K1 is a consequence of E = K because an important functional role that evidence is supposed to play is that of justifying belief. If a proposition justifies some belief, shouldn't we think of it as evidence? If some such proposition can justify belief without that proposition being known, shouldn't we have our counterexample to E = K? If we think that the answers to these questions is "Yes," it looks like E = K is in trouble.

Smith comes to believe (2) by reasoning from (1). If we assume that *Coins* is a counterexample to JTB, we have to assume that Smith was justified in believing (2). Isn't this some reason to think that, if E = K1 is correct, (1) is part of Smith's evidence? Since, by hypothesis, (1) is false, E = K would be mistaken if (1) is part of Smith's evidence. If, however, (1) is *not* part of Smith's evidence, how could Smith be justified in believing (2)? If (1) isn't evidence, it doesn't seem that Smith's belief would be well-founded and thus wouldn't be something that Smith would be justified in believing. Thus, *Coins* wouldn't be a potential counterexample to JTB.

Someone who defends E = K might pursue a number of responses to this line of criticism. First, they might observe that Smith's belief in (1) is supported by further beliefs. If these further beliefs are knowledge, they might constitute Smith's evidence and provide adequate support for both (1) and (2). Thus, little might turn on whether (1) is part of Smith's evidence. Second, those defenders of E = K might argue that not all justification or knowledge comes from evidence. It is one thing to say that all evidence is such that it must be capable of offering support for a thinker's beliefs, and another to say that the support that a thinker has for her beliefs must always come from the thinker's evidence. Couldn't those who accept E = K admit that it's possible for something that isn't evidence to be psychologically operative and to generate a belief that has the properties that make it a good candidate for knowledge or for justification? Someone who accepts E = K might say that the mistaken belief in (1) is a cog in a process that generates a belief in (2) in such a way that the belief in (2) turns out to be justified even though (1) isn't part of Smith's evidence. Someone sympathetic to E = K might argue, for example, that the correct explanation as to why Smith is justified in believing (2) is not one that assumes that Smith's belief in (2) is supported by a piece of evidence corresponding to (1). While there are certainly some views of justification that imply that it's not possible for a thinker to be justified in believing something without supporting evidence for that belief, a proponent of E = K might reject that proposal. They might instead say, following Bird (2007), that a person is justified in believing something iff the thinker's belief is knowledge or it fails to be knowledge for reasons that are external to the thinker's perspective. This account of justification seems to leave open the possibility that a thinker might justifiably believe something just because they are sufficiently similar to a thinker in a case of knowledge, not because the thinker also has good evidence that supports her belief.

As with the previous objection to E = K, this line of attack runs into the problem that linguistic evidence suggests that the case cannot show what it is intended to show. The notion of a proposition that justifies a thinker in believing something is a slippery one, but if the case does what it must if it is to cause trouble for E = K then we have to assume the following:

(3) Smith's reason for believing that the man who got the job had ten coins in his pocket was that Jones had the coins and got the job.

Plausibly, (3) entails (4):

(4) Smith knew that Jones had ten coins in his pocket and that Jones got the job.

Notice that it sounds quite odd to combine (4) and (3), to assert (3) and ask whether (4), or to assert (3) and add "Not only that, but (4)." All of these are evidence of an entailment from (3) to (4). We know that (4) is false, however. It's essential to the case that Jones didn't get the job. Thus, we might wonder whether this is a case in which a problematic proposition – namely, (2) – justifies Smith in his thinking by virtue of the fact that it's a piece of evidence or a good reason, or is a case in which (3) wouldn't figure as part of the explanation of the fact that Smith is justified in believing (2).

We have seen some of the ways that intuitions about Gettier-type cases have been used to test proposals about the theory of evidence. It is unclear whether these objections to E = K succeed, and so it is unclear how helpful these intuitions might be for testing theories of evidence.

3.4 Evidence and Warrant

Let us suppose that Gettier's cases did what they were intended to do. If they did, they show us that facts about what a thinker knows at a given time do not supervene upon facts about the thinker's beliefs, the accuracy of these beliefs, and the evidence that the thinker has that supports them. The cases leave intact the idea that a thinker's evidence determines whether she is justified in believing what she does, and suggest that any further inquiry into the conditions that matter for knowledge should focus on factors beyond those that matter to evidence and/or justification. Thus, the evidence or justification condition must be supplemented or replaced.

We see this in many of the main proposed accounts of propositional knowledge in the post-Gettier literature:

- *Defeasibility theory.* Knowledge requires the absence of defeaters – truths that, if the thinker were aware of them, would defeat the thinker's justification (Lehrer and Paxson 1969).
- *Causal theory.* Knowledge requires an appropriate causal relation between the thinker's belief and that which makes it true (Goldman 1967).
- *Sensitivity theory.* Knowledge requires a belief formed in such a way that, if it had been false, the thinker would not have held it (Dretske 1971; Nozick 1981; Roush 2006).
- *Safety theory.* Knowledge requires a belief to be formed in such a way that the belief could not easily have been formed that way and been false (Luper-Foy 1984; Sosa 1999a; Williamson 2000).

Most of these authors were happy to say that the crucial conditions we would need for addressing the Gettier problem had little, if anything, to do with the makeup of the thinker's evidence or with the kinds of support it provided for her beliefs. They seem to grant that, even if a thinker had evidence that we would all agree would provide adequate support for her beliefs, some further conditions could prevent a true belief from being knowledge without having any bearing on whether the thinker was justified in her belief.

Consider, for example, the causal theory of knowledge. On this theory, the presence or absence of the right kind of causal connection between a thinker's belief and that which makes the thinker's belief true does not supervene upon this thinker's evidence (Goldman 1967, p. 341). A proponent of this view might, for example, take the thinker's evidence to be something that supervenes upon the thinker's nonfactive mental states. The facts about the relevant causal relations would not supervene upon these mental states, not when the thinker's beliefs were about states of the external world. Consider also Adler's (2002) and Dretske's (1971) suggestions that knowledge requires conclusive reasons. On their view, a thinker has conclusive reasons or evidence for her belief only if that belief is true, but their view is clear that the possession of such reasons or evidence is not necessary for justification and that it is typically a contingent fact about conclusive reasons that these are conclusive. On this view, the reasons that a thinker has in a case of ordinary knowledge would be conclusive, but it is possible for her to have the very same reasons without having conclusive support for their beliefs. As a vivid illustration of this, think about the fake-barn examples or cases of environmental luck, more generally.

While many epistemologists are happy with a hybrid view in which the factors that matter to justification are, at most, a proper subset of those that matter for knowledge, this view has recently received criticism. We shall look at John McDowell's critical discussion of the hybrid view in the next section, before discussing Timothy Williamson's knowledge-first account of evidence.

3.5 McDowell and the Hybrid View

We will be looking at two challenges to the view that there is no constitutive connection between a subject's evidence and her knowledge. The first comes from McDowell. He thinks that knowledge is a standing in the space of reasons (1998, p. 395). It looks like he means this in two ways. First, he thinks that knowledge is supported by reasons. We acquire knowledge by respond-ing appropriately to the reasons in our possession. As we shall see, McDowell defends a robust reading of this claim. Second, he thinks that knowledge is a standing or a normative status, one that we must attain if our beliefs are to be justified. If a thinker believes *p* but fails to know *p*, their belief about *p* is not justified and they have failed to meet the normative requirement that a thinker believe only on the basis of adequate reason. The adequacy of evidence, on McDowell's view, turns on whether the evidence ensures that the thinker is in a position to know *p*.

Let us consider these two points in turn. Many philosophers would agree that we come to know things by responding correctly to the reasons we have for our beliefs. It happens, most would say, when we have good reasons for our beliefs and when further factors obtain that ensure that our beliefs are correct and that we aren't in a Gettier-type case. McDowell defends a much more interesting claim than this. He thinks that a state could not be a state of knowledge unless the reasons that supported it provided us with everything required for knowledge. He explicitly rejects the prevailing view that allows that it is possible to have the kind of evidence necessary for knowledge without also having a belief that is true (1998, p. 403):

> In the hybrid conception [of knowledge], a satisfactory standing in the space of reasons is only part of what knowledge is; truth is an extra requirement. So two subjects can be alike in respect of their satisfactoriness of their standing in the space of reasons, because only in her case is what she takes to be actually so. But if its being so is external to her operations in the space of reasons, how can it not be outside the reach of her rational powers? And if it is outside the reach of her rational powers, how can its being so be the crucial element in the intelligible conception of her knowing that it is so?

What is wrong with the prevailing view, which says that the evidence that we have in cases of knowledge could provide the same support for false beliefs or for beliefs that fail to constitute knowledge for some other reason? Perhaps this passage captures McDowell's worries about the intelligibility of the hybrid view (1998, p. 390): "one's epistemic standing ... cannot intelligibly be constituted, even in part, by matters blankly external to how it is with one subjectively. For how could such matters be other than beyond one's ken? And how could matters beyond one's ken many any difference to one's epistemic standing?" On the hybrid view, matters "blankly external" to how things are from the subject's point of view turn out to be the crucial difference-making factors that explain why pairs of subjects who have the very same perspectives, the very same reasons, the very same evidence differ in terms of what they know. This seems to conflict with the idea that, when we credit someone with knowledge, we say that the relevant fact that they know is not beyond their ken, is something that is within the reach of their rational powers, or is something of which they are aware. On the hybrid view, a complete and accurate description of the subject's perspective on the world and the exercise of their rational powers would just be neutral on whether the subject was in touch with things as they actually were. How can we say both that a subject is in touch with the relevant realities and that their rational capacities put them in touch only with appearances?[9]

Relatedly, think about McDowell's suggestion that knowledge is itself a normative standing. Suppose that you should not believe what you do not know. Suppose further that, whenever you believe with justification, it is false that you should not believe what you do. If we combine these two normative claims with the assumption that you have justification to believe what you have adequate evidence to believe, we have our argument against the hybrid view of knowledge. It would be impossible for a thinker to have adequate evidence to believe p and yet to be mistaken in believing p.

If McDowell is right to reject the hybrid view, these three claims about knowledge should be correct:

Non-Doxastic Possession. A thinker knows p only if she independently possesses adequate evidence for this belief.

---

[9] For an incredibly useful guide to McDowell's conception of knowledge, see van Cleve (2004).

Normative Adequacy. A thinker knows *p* only if her evidence ensures that she conforms to the epistemic norms that govern belief.

The Knowledge Norm. A thinker should not believe *p* unless she knows that *p*.

While many epistemologists might accept the first two theses, few would accept all three. In combination, they imply that a thinker cannot know or justifiably believe *p* unless she possesses reasons independently that ensure that she is in a position to know *p*. Since we cannot be in a position to know what isn't so, and aren't in a position to know in Gettier-type cases, McDowell's view implies that knowledge and justification require the presence of supporting reasons that entail both the correctness of our beliefs and the absence of knowledge-undermining luck.

Let us briefly consider three potential problems for McDowell's position. First, there are problems associated with his handling of cases of noninferential perceptual knowledge. If we want to understand how perceptual knowledge is possible on this picture, it looks like we will have to embrace a controversial account of perceptual experience, on which experience involves both relational and representational elements. The experience would need to be understood *relationally*, because McDowell thinks that the justification of perceptual belief turns on whether the thinker is in a position to know that this belief is correct, and thinks that this epistemic property has to supervene upon the thinker's experience. (If it did not, we would be left with a version of the hybrid view.) If the thinker's experience were not a relation between her and aspects of the external world of which she would be aware in having the experience, the relevant epistemic property would not supervene upon the thinker's experience. The view also requires a *representational* view of experience because it requires that there is some logical relation between that which perception provides us and the beliefs we form in response to it.[10] If experience had no representational content, no such logical relations could hold between the perception and the beliefs we form by taking experience at face value; McDowell fears that this would mean that perception provides causes for our beliefs without providing reasons.[11]

Some of McDowell's critics have argued that this picture of experience is untenable. First, McDowell's view commits him to a disjunctive conception of

---

[10] For an important defense of the idea that experience has representational content, see Siegel (2011).

[11] For helpful discussions about whether perceptual beliefs are based on reasons, see Ginsborg (2006) and McGinn (2012) for defenses of two very different approaches.

experience because a view that identifies a subject's experience with the highest common factor between perception and hallucination cannot identify the subject's experience with a perceptual relation between the subject and things in an external reality. Some have objected on empirical grounds to McDowell's metaphysical disjunctivism.[12] Second, there are those who object that McDowell's particular brand of disjunctivism is problematic precisely because of how it tries to incorporate representationalist and relationalist elements. On the one hand, if the objects of visual awareness were particulars (e.g. substances and events), it is hard to see how awareness of them alone (that is, without the aid of something representational) could provide us with reasons that would guarantee that our perceptual beliefs formed under ideal circumstances would be knowledge. On the other hand, it is hard to see how perceptual awareness could be anything but awareness of particulars found in our surroundings. To explain how such awareness could be the source of knowledge, McDowell faces the nontrivial problems of having to show that experience has a representational aspect *and* that this further representational aspect of experience could ensure that we had facts in our possession that would provide an adequate basis for perceptual belief. He sees the need to reject the idea that the understanding operates on that which the senses independently bring into view, but it is unclear how the understanding could play any role other than this in the processes that precede perceptual judgment.

The second problem is that of squaring McDowell's view with an optimistic assessment of the scope of our inferential knowledge. While deductive reasoning from things that are certain might pose no problem for his view, the case of inductive inference poses an obvious challenge. On McDowell's view, it wouldn't be possible for a thinker to be in a position to know p via inference, unless they possessed reasons for believing p that would ensure that any thinker who had just these reasons would likewise be in a position to know p. Thus, it would seem that inference from observed to unobserved cases should not be expected to yield knowledge, since a natural description of this inference is from a set of premises to a conclusion where the conclusion's falsity is compatible with the truth of all the premises.[13]

Third, there is a local problem posed by certain Gettier-type cases involving environmental luck. McDowell thinks that when we have perceptual knowledge, the reasons that supported this belief were reasons that we had by virtue of the perceptual relations in which we stand. Consider an ordinary case of perceptual knowledge and then a similar case (e.g. *Fakes*) in which environmental luck seems to preclude our having this perceptual knowledge. Do we really think that, by virtue of the fact that these two thinkers are in a position to know different things, these thinkers stand in different perceptual relations to things in their surroundings? I think it is implausible to say that the subject in *Fakes* stands in different perceptual relations than he would have done if all the fakes had been replaced by the real article.[14] It is hard to believe that the facts about the perceptual relations in which we stand supervene upon, say, the presence or absence of fakes, particularly unobserved ones that would seem to rob us of knowledge.

If these problems are as serious as I take them to be, there is no nonskeptical view on which knowledge is a standing in the space of reasons in the two ways described above. We could embrace Evidentialism, or we could take knowledge to be the norm of belief, but we could not combine both ideas in some single nonskeptical account of knowledge.

3.6 Williamson's Hypothesis

The difficulties for McDowell arise because he combines Evidentialism with Normative Adequacy and the Knowledge Norm. If the arguments for E = K have the force I take them to have, we can use these arguments to attack Evidentialism. Once we abandon that picture of the relationship between knowledge and evidence, the problems discussed in the previous section are dissolved.

To see why E = K is in tension with Evidentialism, think about the case of noninferential knowledge. If a thinker comes to know *p*, say, as a result of seeing how things stand in her surroundings, Evidentialism tells us that the thinker could justifiably add her belief in *p* to her set of beliefs only if she independently possessed evidence that provided adequate support for that belief. On the assumption that the thinker's evidence just *is* her knowledge, we should expect this condition to be routinely violated in cases of noninferential knowledge. Of course, those who like Evidentialism will say that the fact that we need knowledge to possess evidence points to a serious problem with E = K: it implies that, in cases of noninferential knowledge, our beliefs would routinely be formed without being based on evidence!

---

[14] See Schellenberg (2017) for a helpful discussion of these issues.

One way to test which approach has the upper hand here is to recall two of the considerations offered in support of E = K. Anyone who accepts rejects E = K on the ground that it implies that many of our noninferential beliefs were not supported by evidence at the point of their formation has to decide whether they think that evidence is propositional and whether they agree that ascriptions of propositionally specified evidence entail knowledge ascriptions. If such ascriptions of evidence do indeed entail knowledge ascriptions, this is some evidence that the Non-Doxastic Possession Thesis is false. In turn, it suggests that the process that yields noninferential knowledge is not one that takes propositionally specified evidence as input and that yields belief as output. If all evidence is indeed propositionally specified, it means that cases of noninferential knowledge are cases that show Evidentialism to be mistaken.

One virtue of E = K is that it shows that there is a false choice between Fallibilism and McDowell's brand of infallibilism, on which it is only possible for a thinker to be in a position to know *p* if she has entailing evidence for that belief. A trivial consequence of E = K is that, in *every* case of knowledge, a thinker has entailing evidence for her belief as a consequence of coming to have that knowledge. Thus, the view vindicates McDowell's idea that there had better be something accessible to the subject "in the know" that distinguishes her situation from the situation of a subjectively similar subject in a bad case. There is. It is the fact that the thinker knows. It is accessible to the thinker who knows (as a consequence of knowing) but not to the thinker in a bad case. If we reject Evidentialism, we reject the idea that, by virtue of accepting this kind of infallibilism, we need independently possessed entailing evidence for knowledge. Thus, we avoid some of the awkward things that McDowell has to say in discussing inductive inference.

Of course, not everyone is happy with the consequence that this approach implies, namely that it is only possible for a thinker to have knowledge of *p* if the probability of *p* on the thinker's total evidence is 1. Jessica Brown (2013), for example, thinks that this implication of Williamson's view is problematic because his view avoids skeptical problems only because it implies that the things we know will be evidence for themselves. However, it is unclear how serious this problem is for E = K, as this is a feature of many views that accept a probability-raising conception of evidence. (If we abandon that picture of evidential support, it isn't clear whether there is any remaining problem for E = K.)

Once we embrace the idea that acquiring knowledge is how we acquire evidence and abandon the idea that the acquisition of evidence is an independent process and one that must first be completed successfully in order to put a thinker in a position to know, we might then wonder again about the possibility of Gettier-type cases. Many epistemologists think that there are Gettier-type cases only if it's possible for there to be a belief that is both justified and true that fails to constitute knowledge. How could Williamson accommodate this?

He might not be able to do so. Suppose that, at noon, Tim comes to know that p inferentially. Suppose that, by dinnertime, he has forgotten all the supporting considerations that backed this belief but retains his knowledge of p. It would seem that he would still be able to come to know the obvious consequences of p by means of competent deduction, and that such beliefs would be based on good evidence or good reasons. It doesn't seem that Tim's reason for believing q (one of p's obvious consequences) could have been the reasons that convinced him initially that p was true. His reasons would have to be the considerations in light of which he came to believe q, and would not include the things that he had forgotten long before he considered whether q. It seems that the only good candidate to play the role of Tim's reason for believing q would be that p. This is some reason to think that possessed knowledge should be sufficient for evidence even if that knowledge was acquired via inference.

Now, consider two claims about justification and evidence. First, if a thinker's belief is justified, it can be justifiably included in theoretical reasoning. This seems plausible if you think that the right to believe comes with further rights, such as the right to treat what's believed as a premise in reasoning. (Think about the contrapositive: would it make sense to say that someone lacked sufficient epistemic standing to treat p as a reason but shouldn't abandon their belief in p?) Second, a thinker's belief can only be justifiably included in theoretical reasoning if it provides the thinker with evidence or a reason that could serve as the basis for some concluding belief. If we add these two claims to the mixture, we get the result that no belief could be justified unless its content was known by the thinker to be true.[15] We lose the distinction between justified belief and propositional knowledge. If the possibility of Gettier-type cases

[15] This argument draws on some ideas from Bird (2004) and is developed in detail in Littlejohn (2012), where I argue that a factive account of doxastic justification is a consequence of the idea that reasons themselves are always facts. For a defense of that approach to the ontology of reasons, see Alvarez (2010).

requires a possible distinction between justified belief and propositional knowledge, we have an argument from E = K, and some plausible ancillary considerations, to the surprising conclusion that knowledge just is justified belief.[16]

There might still be room for some Gettier-type cases. Recall Lowy's (1978) point that it is important to distinguish the justification of *belief* from the justification of some *believer*. It might be that these points about justification and evidence are plausible only if they pertain to doxastic justification rather than to personal justification.

If readers aren't happy with that distinction, and agree that a natural consequence of E = K (combined with the ancillary assumptions mentioned above) is that there cannot be justified beliefs that are not knowledge, then we might ask what this means for the ETB or JTB accounts. Did they survive Gettier's attack? Perhaps not. There is nothing in this that should be taken to support the idea that a state of belief is knowledge *because* it is supported by adequate evidence or *because* the belief is justified and true. We might say that the belief is justified because it is knowledge, or that it does not lack adequate evidential support because it is knowledge. Gettier can still be credited with helping us to see that these are bad accounts of what makes something knowledge.

---

[16] Sutton (2007) defends this view, albeit on very different grounds. Although Williamson (2000) initially suggested that he thought that there could be false beliefs that were justified, he has come around to the idea that a fully justified belief must itself be knowledge. McDowell (1998) likewise holds that all justified beliefs are knowledge, but he differs from these authors in insisting that all such beliefs are turned into knowledge because of the incredible support that the thinker's reasons provide for such beliefs.

4   The Gettier Problem and Externalism

Rodrigo Borges

4.1 Introduction

The problem that Edmund Gettier (1963) posed in his classic paper challenges anyone who is trying to understand knowledge. Things are not different for externalists and their theories of justification and knowledge. In what follows, I look at the Gettier problem, and at three externalist solutions to this problem that have been proposed by reliabilists, by truth-tracking theorists, and by virtue epistemologists. Along the way, I identify apparent limitations in those proposed solutions.

4.2 The Gettier Problem

"The Gettier problem" traditionally refers to the problem in conceptual analysis posed by Edmund Gettier in his 1963 classic "Is justified true belief knowledge?"[1] Gettier allegedly produced two counterexamples to the claim that, necessarily, someone, S, falls under the concept KNOWLEDGE if and only if S has a justified true belief.[2] According to Gettier, Plato (Meno 98), Chisholm (1957, p. 16), and Ayer (1956, p. 34) all accepted this view.[3] Although the cases that Gettier presented did not challenge the claim that justification, truth, and belief are *necessary conditions* on KNOWLEDGE, those cases did challenge the claim that justification, truth, and belief form a *sufficient* set of conditions for KNOWLEDGE. So far, there is no consensus in the literature as to whether anyone has succeeded in solving the Gettier problem.

---

[1] It is not clear that Gettier was the first to raise that *type* of problem for accounts of knowledge. There is good evidence that medieval and ancient Indian philosophers, for example, had considered the same type of problem. See Hilpinen (2017) for discussion of the Gettier problem before Gettier.
[2] I will use capital letters when referring to concepts.
[3] It is not entirely clear whether all of them accepted this analysis of KNOWLEDGE. See Klein (2017) for some doubts concerning Gettier's exegesis here.

In his paper, Gettier argued that a subject can be shown to be ignorant of a true proposition, *p*, that she justifiably believes, if we accept two general principles about epistemic justification:

Fallibility. It is possible for a person to be justified in believing a proposition that is in fact false.

Justification Closure. For any *p*, if S is justified in believing *p*, and *p* entails *q*, and S deduces *q* from *p* and accepts *q* as a result of this deduction, then S is justified in believing *q*.

Even though Gettier did not tell us why he thought that Fallibility and Justification Closure are true, we may think that those principles are acceptable on the following grounds. Consider Fallibility: why think that it is possible for one to believe a falsehood with justification? Supposedly, because of something like the experience that all of us have undergone at some point in our lives, of being misled into believing something false on the basis of what (at the time) seemed like good evidence (optical illusions and conniving liars do just that). As for Justification Closure, the principle seems to enshrine the centuries-old idea that deduction is the safest method that we can deploy to expand our body of justified beliefs, since the information in the deduced proposition "is already contained" in the premise of our reasoning.

Once we accept Fallibility and Justification Closure, Gettier's original cases seem to show quite conclusively that Smith, the protagonist of those cases, has a justified true belief but no knowledge. In each of Case I and Case II, Smith has "strong evidence" for his belief in the false proposition in 1, and he accepts 2 as a result of a deduction from 1:

Case I	Case II
1. Jones is the man who will get the job, and Jones has ten coins in his pocket.	1. Jones owns a Ford.
2. The man who will get the job has ten coins in his pocket.	2. Either Jones owns a Ford, or Brown is in Barcelona.

Given the details that Gettier provides for Case I and for Case II, it seems clear that Smith satisfies Fallibility and Justification Closure in both cases. It seems equally clear that he also fails to know in each case. In Case I, 2 is true in virtue of the number of coins in Smith's own pocket (a fact of which Smith knows nothing), while Smith's belief in 2 is based on his counting the coins in

Jones's pocket, whom Smith mistakenly believe to be the man who will get the job. In Case II, Smith's belief in 1 is false but justified because Jones goes around pretending a rented Ford is his car, and Smith's belief in 2 is true only because Brown, whose whereabouts are unknown to Smith, is in fact in Barcelona. The prevalent intuitive judgment about Cases I and II is that Smith has a justified true belief in 2, but fails to know it. Call this *the Gettier intuition.* Epistemologists usually take the Gettier intuition to support strongly the belief that one does not necessarily fall under the concept KNOWLEDGE if one has a justified true belief.[4]

As a problem in conceptual analysis, one can solve the Gettier problem by either (a) adding more conditions to the existing set of necessary conditions (that is, justification, truth, and belief) until one gets a set of conditions that are jointly sufficient for the analysis of KNOWLEDGE, or (b) by challenging Gettier's characterizations of one or more of the existing necessary conditions. As we will see in the next section, *internalists* have, for the most part, favored the first strategy, while *externalists* have, for the most part, favored the second strategy.

Before we look at externalist solutions to the Gettier problem, it might be a good idea for us to address a particular worry. Recently, some have voiced skepticism concerning the Gettier problem. Timothy Williamson (2000, p. 31), for example, has argued that the pursuit of conceptual analyses in general (and the pursuit of an analysis of KNOWLEDGE in particular) is a "degenerating research programme" and should be abandoned. He goes on to say that KNOWLEDGE is in fact unanalyzable. If Williamson is right, the Gettier problem as Gettier presented it is a waste of time. I will not try to decide here whether Williamson is in fact right about this.[5] Instead, I would like to suggest that, even if he is right and KNOWLEDGE is unanalyzable, the Gettier problem is not a waste of time. Although the Gettier problem is traditionally a problem in conceptual analysis, this is not the only possible interpretation of the epistemological significance of the Gettier intuition. Regardless of whether we can give a noncircular analysis of KNOWLEDGE, we might still be interested in *explaining why Smith fails to know in Case I and in Case II.* Call this latter problem the *Explanatory Gettier Problem.* This problem contrasts with the related, but, strictly speaking, independent

---

[4] Of course, for all that Gettier has said, one sometimes falls under KNOWLEDGE even though one has nothing more than a justified true belief. After all, he showed at most that not *all* justified true beliefs are in the extension of KNOWLEDGE; he did not show that *no* justified true belief is.

[5] But, for discussion of this and other aspects of Williamson's views on knowledge, see Greenough and Pritchard (2009).

problem in conceptual analysis that we have been discussing, which may now be labeled the *Conceptual Gettier Problem*. Even if Williamson is right about the Conceptual Gettier Problem being a waste of time, the Explanatory Gettier Problem might still be interesting. This is so in part because Smith's situation poses a threat to the proposed analysis of KNOWLEDGE only if his justification is, other things being equal, *good enough for knowledge*. If the justification that his belief enjoys is not good enough for knowledge, then Smith does not satisfy one of the conditions on KNOWLEDGE, and Case I and Case II provide no counterexample to the analysis. If the justification that Smith's belief enjoys is, on the other hand, good enough for knowledge, then the Explanatory Gettier Problem (that is, the question of why Smith fails to know) becomes particularly salient. After all, Smith's belief in 2 has much going for it, epistemically speaking (it is true and it enjoys knowledge-grade justification). How could someone in such an otherwise strong epistemological position fail to know? This latter question should interest us regardless of whether or not KNOWLEDGE is analyzable. Or so I think.

4.3 Externalist Solutions to the Gettier Problem

Externalist views are often described as the rejection of one or more forms of internalism. The dispute between those two camps is over whether the factors that determine epistemic justification are purely internal to one's mind. Externalists say that factors *external* to one's mind may help determine whether (and to what extent) one is justified in believing a particular proposition. Internalists argue that only factors internal to one's mind can determine whether (and to what extent) one is justified in believing a particular proposition. I will expand below on the distinction between internalism and externalism views, but the bulk of this section will be devoted to three influential externalist views – reliabilism, truth-tracking views, and virtue theories – and to what they have to say about the Gettier problem.[6]

The two main versions of epistemological internalism are *mentalism* and *accessibilism*. According to mentalism, all justifying factors are internal to one's mind in the sense that the degree to which one is justified in believing that p at some particular time supervenes on the totality of one's mental state at that time. According to accessibilism, all justifying factors are internal to

---

[6] There is a vast literature on the internalism/externalism debate in epistemology, and I will not rehash it here. My focus is on how likely it is that an externalist view would solve the Gettier problem. For a good overview of the debate, see, among many others, Alston (2005).

one's mind in the sense that the degree to which one is justified in believing that p at some particular time supervenes on one's past, present, or at least potential awareness of one's reasons for believing that p. The idea animating each form of internalism seems to be that one ought to follow one's evidence where it leads, and that one can follow only that which presents itself to conscious awareness. Perhaps the best-known implementation of this idea is in the epistemology of Rene Descartes (2008), which takes all justifying factors to be objects of immediate reflective awareness (*ideas*).

It should be noted that mentalism and accessibilism are, in principle, independent of one another. That is, there is no contradiction involved in accepting only one of those views.

Accessibilism does not necessitate mentalism. For one thing, if the class of mental states on which justification supervenes includes only *pure mental states* (that is, states whose obtaining does not depend on any extramental condition being satisfied), and one's version of accessibilism allows for justification to come from one's access to mental states that are *not* purely mental (such as knowledge),[7] *then* one has a form of accessibilism that does not entail mentalism. Perhaps more controversially, if, as some (such as Kripke [1980] and Turri [2010]) have suggested, there is such a thing as *a priori* knowledge of propositions about the world outside of one's own mind, then it would in principle be possible for one to be an accessibilist without also being a mentalist. For example, Saul Kripke (1980) argued that one can know *a priori* that a certain stick, s, is exactly one meter long, if one baptizes s as the "meter stick." If he is right, then the person baptizing s as the "meter stick" has direct *a priori* access to what justifies her in believing (and knowing) that s is exactly one meter long (namely, the fact that she baptized s as the "meter stick"); but, since this justifier is not a mental state of the subject but is instead a state of the world, the view would be a form of accessibilism that does not necessitate mentalism.[8]

Mentalism does not necessitate accessibilism. Richard Feldman and Earl Conee, the main proponents of mentalism, conceive of their version of mentalism as being independent of accessibilism. They argue (Conee and Feldman 2004, p. 73) that, in some cases, a mental state plays a justificatory

[7] That is, *if* knowledge is a mental state, then it is not a pure mental state, for its obtaining depends on the extramental condition of *truth* being satisfied.

[8] I do not mean to commit myself to the view that there are cases of *a priori* knowledge of the external world. My point is just that *if* there are such cases, *then* one could be an accessibilist without also being a mentalist. As I suggested earlier, the issue of *a priori* knowledge of the external world is contentious. See Turri (2010) for detailed discussion.

role even if that state is not accessible to the subject. They imagine a case in which a huge conjunction stored in memory defeats the subject's justification for believing that p. Due to the sheer size of the conjunction, the subject is psychologically incapable of grasping it, and hence does not have reflective access to it. This shows, according to Feldman and Conee, that the conjunction plays a justificatory role even though it is not accessible to the subject.

None of this implies that accessibilism and mentalism are not compatible. One could also, in principle, accept both views. The result would be a type of internalism that takes all justifiers to be reflectively accessible mental states. Usually, however, internalists accept either one or the other version of internalism.[9]

Externalists usually reject both mentalism and accessibilism.[10] The general externalist idea is that some of the factors that help determine whether (and to what extent) S is justified are neither mental states of S nor something that S can access via reflection. For instance, it seems that evidence that one does not possess can sometimes be an external factor that determines one's degree of justification. Consider this example. I walk into the supermarket looking for bread and milk. I left my phone in the car. As I walk down the aisle looking for milk, my wife is sending text and voice messages to me, saying that we do have enough milk at home (she checked the fridge). The fact that her messages say (truthfully) that we do have enough milk seems to be a factor relevant to how justified I am in believing that we do not have enough milk. That is the case even though I currently do not have access to those messages and they are not the content of any of my mental states. There might also be a more general argument against the claim that all factors that are relevant to justification are internal to subjects in the way mentalists and accessibilists say that those factors are relevant. For any ground, g, that the internalist considers relevant

---

[9] The distinction between mentalist and accessibilist forms of internalism has its limitations. One of those limitations is brought out by Williamson's knowledge-first epistemology. According to him, knowledge is not only a mental state but is also the only thing that can justify belief. (Experience, although an evidence-provider, is not itself a justifier, on this view.) This suggests that Williamson is a mentalist, for the justification of belief supervenes exclusively on mental states (that is, on knowledge). Moreover, Williamson's arguments against the principle according to which S is in a position to know that S knows that p whenever S knows that p, seem to amount to a rejection of accessibilism. This package of views complicates the distinction between accessibilism and mentalism, because knowledge is not usually seen as a mental state in its own right, but only as a special form of the mental state of belief.

[10] One possible exception is Williamson's knowledge-first view, which rejects accessibilism but accepts a form of mentalism. See note 9 for discussion. Another possible exception is the synthesis between reliabilism (an externalist view) and mentalism proposed by Alvin Goldman (2011).

to how justified S is in believing that *p*, there is a further fact (call it a "supporting fact") having to do with whether g is a good or a bad reason for S to believe that *p*. Clearly, the obtaining of a supporting fact is relevant to whether S is justified in believing that *p*. The problem for the internalist is that supporting facts are relevant to one's justification even if they are not reflectively accessible to one or if none of one's mental states are about that fact (cf. Comesaña 2005b).

I will now discuss three externalist views and their proposed solution to the Gettier problem.

4.3.1 Reliabilism

David Armstrong (1973), Alvin Goldman (1979), Fred Dretske (1971), and others articulated the view according to which one's awareness of the reasons why one believes what one does is not a requirement on one's belief justifiedness. All that is required for epistemic justification, they contended, is the *reliability* of the cognitive process that causes the belief in question. For example, according to reliabilism, beliefs caused by vision are justified not because the subject who is holding those beliefs is (or could be) reflectively aware of something, but rather in virtue of vision being a reliable cognitive process, one that tends to produce true beliefs more often than false ones when used in favorable enough circumstances (such as good lighting conditions). The reliability of vision, of other cognitive processes that normally we deem reliable (such as the other sensory modalities), and the justification of the beliefs that they cause contrasts sharply, says the reliabilist, with the unreliability and the consequent lack of justication of beliefs caused by processes such as guesswork, wishful thinking, and motivated reasoning. The point that the reliabilist is making here applies not only to innate cognitive processes such as our sensory modalities, but also to learned methods such as calculus, Newtonian mechanics, and the prediction of future events based on the "reading" of chicken entrails. Supposedly, only the first two methods are, once mastered, reliable in the desired sense.

We need to make one final distinction before we are ready to look at what the reliabilist has to say about the Gettier problem. This is the distinction between *conditional* and *unconditional* reliability. According to the reliabilist, the reliability of processes (e.g. reasoning) whose inputs involve beliefs should be assessed differently from the reliability of processes (e.g. vision) whose inputs do not involve beliefs. That is because the former type of process tends to output true beliefs *conditional on the input-beliefs also being true*. Since beliefs are not part of the input to the latter type of cognitive process, their propensity to output true beliefs is independent of the truth of other beliefs.

With this in mind, let us look at what the reliabilist has to say about the Gettier problem. Given the influential version of reliabilism proposed by Goldman (1979), for example, Smith fails to know in Case I and in Case II, because he is using a conditionally *unreliable* method. Deduction is a conditionally reliable method. As such, it can only produce justified beliefs if its input-beliefs (that is, the premises in one's deductive inference) are true. The problem is that Smith's deductive inferences have false input-beliefs, thereby yielding an unjustified belief in the conclusion.

Although this solution to the Gettier problem is a direct consequence of the reliabilist account of inferential justification, the latter might be problematic. For one thing, it is not so clear that it yields the right result in cases where the input-belief to one's deductive inference is justified and true but one's belief in the conclusion does not seem to amount to knowledge. Consider, for instance, the following deductive inference:

(1) My ticket lost.
(2) If my ticket lost, I cannot buy a Lamborghini.
(3) Hence, I cannot buy a Lamborghini.

Suppose that I know 2 because I know that I have no way to afford a Lamborghini unless I win the lottery. Suppose further that, although it is true that my ticket lost, I had not checked the lottery result before I performed this deduction. Instead, I based my belief in 1 solely on my statistical knowledge of the odds of any single ticket winning this large and fair lottery. Most philosophers think that I do not know 3 in these circumstances. And they think this in spite of the fact that they also think that I know 2 and that I have (at least) a justified true belief in 1. This is a potential problem for the reliabilist account of inferential justification because my belief in 3 is not a case of knowledge, even though I am not in a Gettier situation, and even though my belief in 3 is true and the output of a conditionally reliable method (hence it is also justified). Given the reliabilist account of conditional reliability and justification, and its treatment of the Gettier problem, cases such as the lottery case should not exist. The view should exclude the possibility of a reliably acquired true belief that is not a case of knowledge. The view seems unable to do that, however. This case raises doubts about the reliabilist treatment of deduction and the way in which this method transmits justification and knowledge. Since the reliabilist solution to the Gettier problem depends on this view of the reliability of deduction, it is also subject to doubt.

4.3.2 Truth-Tracking

The truth-tracking theory of knowledge proposed by Robert Nozick (1981), Fred Adams and Murray Clarke (2005), among others, radicalizes the externalist position. Even though the reliabilist rejected mentalism and accessibilism, she still saw herself as offering an account of *epistemic justification*. Nozick, on the other hand, dispensed in his analysis of KNOWLEDGE with the notion of justification. Truth-tracking accounts pursue the idea that a belief is an item of knowledge just in case this belief is *sensitive* to changes in the truth-value of the target proposition in circumstances that are similar enough to the actual circumstances in which the belief is formed. If the subject's belief displays this sensitivity, the truth-tracking theorist says that the belief *tracks the truth* and that the subject thereby *knows* the target proposition. According to this view, one knows that p via a certain method, M, if and only if one not only believes truly that p, via M, in one's actual circumstances, but also tracks the truth of p in close enough circumstances where one continues using M. Whether one tracks the truth of p in close enough circumstances is, in turn, a matter of satisfying the following two subjunctive conditionals:

- If p were false and S were to use M to believe that p, then S would not believe, via M, that p.
- If p were true and S were to use M to believe that p, then S would believe, via M, that p.

To the extent that satisfying these conditions is what turns true belief into knowledge, the conditions play a role that is similar to the one played by the justification condition in the analysis of KNOWLEDGE that Gettier criticized. In that sense, we may speak of Nozick's externalist account of justification, since whether S satisfies either of those subjunctive conditionals in a particular circumstance is a fact that is usually neither accessible to, nor the content of, a mental state of S.

As an illustration of the view, consider my knowledge of the fact that there is a computer screen in front of me right now. According to the truth-tracking account, I know this to be the case because I believe truly that there is a computer screen in front of me right now via normal vision, and if there was no computer screen in front me right now I would not believe (while still using normal vision) that there was one, and if there was a computer screen in front of me right now, I would believe (if still using normal vision) that there was one.

What does the truth-tracking theory say about the Gettier problem? According to this view, Smith fails to know because he fails to track the truth of the conclusion of his inferences. The view says that one knows something via inference only if one would not believe the premises in one's inference if the conclusion were false, and if one would still believe the conclusion if the premises were true.[11] Smith fails the first condition, for he would believe that Jones is the man who will get the job and that Jones has ten coins in his pocket, even if it were not the case that the man who will get the job has ten coins in his pocket. Smith would also believe that Jones owns a Ford even if it were not the case that either Jones owns a Ford or Brown is in Barcelona.

In order for this solution to the Gettier problem to work, the account of inferential knowledge on which it rests should not exclude cases of inferential knowledge. However, there is some reason to worry whether the truth-tracking theory can in fact do that. To see that, consider the following case.[12] After counting fifty-three people in the audience for my talk, I conclude, on that basis, that the 100 handouts that I printed will be enough. However, unbeknownst to me, there are in fact fifty-two people in the audience: I double-counted an audience member who changed seats during my counting of heads. Most people seem to agree that I know that the 100 handouts that I printed will be enough, even though this knowledge is based on a false premise.[13] The problem is that the truth-tracking theory does not seem able to deliver this result, for my belief that 100 handouts will be enough seems to fail the condition according to which I would still believe that there are fifty-three people in the audience in close-enough circumstances in which my hundred handouts are enough. Arguably, I fail to satisfy this subjunctive conditional in close-enough circumstances where I still believe that my 100 handouts are enough but where I count only fifty-two people in the audience because – in some close-enough scenario – the one person whom I double-counted in the actual scenario does not move. The upshot is that the account of inferential knowledge to which the

---

[11] Cf. Nozick (1981, pp. 233–4).   [12] This case is adapted from Warfield (2005).
[13] But see Montminy (2014), Schnee (2015), and Borges (2017) for some push-back on this claim.

truth-tracking theory appeals in its proposed solution to the Gettier problem needs to be mended.

4.3.3 Epistemic Virtues

Finally, according to virtue theorists such as Linda Zagzebski (2000) and Ernest Sosa (2007a), a belief is justified in an externalist sense only if this belief is the output of a virtuous cognitive process. This view is a form of externalism because the fact that one's belief is true in virtue of its being the output of a virtuous cognitive process is neither something to which one usually has reflective access, nor is among one's mental states. According to Sosa, for instance, one knows that p if and only if one's belief that p is not only true, but is true *in virtue of* being the output of a virtuous cognitive process. Now, the idea of a belief being true in virtue of being the output of a virtuous cognitive process might sound peculiar at first: one might think that the view confuses what makes the believed proposition true with what causes one to believe the proposition. This is not what the virtue theorist has in mind, however. Rather, he is trying to explain why the subject has a belief that is true. An example might make this distinction clearer. The fact that I cooked dinner might explain why there is dinner, without explaining why dinner is delicious. In fact, given how bad a cook I am, dinner is delicious *in spite* of the fact that I cooked it! Similarly, the fact that my cognitive process, c, caused my belief that p might explain why I have the belief that p, without explaining why my belief that p is true. The thought is that the fact that a certain belief was caused by a *virtuous* cognitive process helps to explain not only why one has the belief, but also why one has a belief that is true: that's what virtuous cognitive processes do – they cause true beliefs a lot more often than they cause false ones. According to Sosa (2007a, pp. 95–6), this distinction explains why Smith fails to know in Case I and in Case II: Smith's belief is true, but it is not true in virtue of being deduced from his premise belief, for this premise is false. However, this proposed solution to the Gettier problem is threatened by cases such as the handout case above, for in those cases the subject seems to have knowledge even though her deduction depends on a false premise.

4.4 Conclusion

Reliabilism, truth-tracking accounts, and virtue theories are externalist views with plenty to say about the Gettier problem. However, it is not a settled matter whether those views succeed in explaining why Smith fails to know in Case I and in Case II. In particular, the view of inferential knowledge on which those views rely might not be as sound as their solution to the Gettier problem would suggest and require.

5   The Gettier Problem and Context

Delia Belleri and Annalisa Coliva

5.1 Introduction

Epistemic contextualism is known as the view that the truth-value of knowledge ascriptions depends on the epistemic standards operative in the attributor's context (Cohen 1998, 1999; DeRose 1992; 1995; 1999; Lewis 1996; Heller 1999). The higher the standards, the easier it is for a knowledge ascription "S knows that P" to be false. Typically, when standards are high, the subject's evidence is unable to rule out some *relevant alternatives* where the proposition *p* under discussion is false (Goldman 1976; Dretske 1981).

Contextualism has been proposed primarily as a way of dealing with skeptical problems, such as evil demon or brain-in-a-vat scenarios (DeRose 1995; Cohen 1999; Neta 2003). It also purports to explain the apparent contextual variability of "know"-statements in everyday contexts, where practical stakes seem to affect our epistemic position: Cohen's (1999) "airport case" and DeRose's (1992) "bank case" provide apt illustrations of the close relationship between practical stakes and the truth-value of knowledge ascriptions.

Contextualism seems nicely to explain how and why contextual factors, such as high epistemic standards, can "destroy" knowledge. Skeptical and certain high-stakes practical worries are certainly good examples of this phenomenon, but they are not the only ones. Three further examples in which knowledge is somehow "destroyed" will be the focus of the present chapter: "fake-barn" cases, "lottery" cases, and Gettier cases. Let us briefly review them one by one.

(1) *Fake-barn cases.* Suppose that Henry is driving through a country that is replete with barn façades, and only contains a few real barns. Henry is not

Thanks to Giorgio Volpe, Chris Kelp, and Duncan Pritchard for their helpful comments on earlier drafts of this paper. Delia Belleri gratefully acknowledges support from the Humboldt Foundation.

privy to this situation. He looks at what appears to him as a barn, and comes to believe that he is seeing a barn. Indeed, the barn at which he is looking is a real one, but, given how few real barns there are in the country, he could easily have been looking at a fake one. In such a scenario, it would seem false to say that Henry knows that he is seeing a real barn (Goldman 1976).

(2) *Lottery Cases.* John has just bought a ticket in a fair lottery. There is a 99.99 percent chance that his ticket will lose; and suppose his ticket is indeed not the lucky one. John declares, "I know that I will lose the lottery." Despite there being an extremely high chance for this to happen, John's self-ascription of knowledge seems nevertheless wrong, because, for all that he knows, his ticket could be the lucky one.[1]

(3) *Gettier Cases.* Smith's wrist-watch has stopped, even though he hasn't realized it yet. Smith looks at his watch, which tells him that it is 8:29, so he comes to believe that it is 8:29. As it happens, it is 8:29, so Smith's belief is true. Yet it does not amount to knowledge.[2]

Does contextualism offer a good account of cases like (1), (2), and (3), too? In his influential 1996 paper "Elusive Knowledge," David Lewis answers that it does. He links fake-barn cases and lottery cases to Gettier cases, *plus* he argues that his brand of contextualism can account for Gettier cases.

In this chapter, we wish to argue that Lewis's view has only a limited reach. Not only it is contentious to argue that fake-barn and lottery cases are closely linked to Gettier cases, as Lewis suggests, it is also generally objectionable to regard contextualism itself as a good framework for thinking about Gettier cases. In what follows, we first reconstruct Lewis's contextualist take on Gettier cases, fake barns, and lottery cases. Secondly, we compare Gettier cases with lottery cases. Thirdly, we compare Gettier cases with fake-barn cases. Lastly, we point at the limitations of contextualism as an account of Gettier cases.

5.2 Lewis's Contextualism About Epistemic Predicates

Lewis (1996) introduces contextualism as a way of escaping the skepticism that threatens an infallibilist account of knowledge. In order to avoid the pitfalls of skepticism, Lewis opts for a qualified form of infallibilism, whereby

[1] For discussion of such cases, see Hawthorne (2004).
[2] Gettier (1963) is obviously credited with the first Gettier cases that ever appeared. The stopped-watch case is owed to Russell (1948).

a subject knows that *p* if and only if *p* obtains in a specific set of possibilities – namely, all the possibilities left uneliminated by her evidence. Equivalently stated, S knows that *p* if and only if S's evidence *eliminates all non-p possibilities*.

The set of *uneliminated possibilities* is a set of possible worlds where the subject has the same experience and memories as those she actually has. Knowledge is infallible only relative to this restricted set of possibilities, insofar as in every scenario where the subject has that particular experience and memory, the proposition *p* that she believes is true. Yet what if, among the uneliminated possibilities, there were still scenarios where *p* is false? Lewis manages to deal with these threatening possibilities by allowing that they may be *ignored* in the context of the knowledge attributor – for instance, on the grounds that they are not salient. This delivers Lewis's final formulation of his brand of contextualism, as follows (1996, p. 54):

> S knows that P iff S's evidence eliminates every possibility in which not-P – Psst! – except for those possibilities that we [attributor and hearer] are properly ignoring.

Which criteria determine whether a possibility is, or is not, properly ignored? Lewis gives a list of rules to serve this purpose. We only need to mention two of them. First, according to the *Rule of Actuality*, the possibility that happens to be actual is never properly ignored. Next, the *Rule of Resemblance* has it that if one possibility resembles another, and one of the two is not properly ignored, then neither is the other.

Let us now go back to cases (1)–(3), listed earlier. Following Lewis, we may say that knowledge is "destroyed" because, from the perspective of the attributor, the subject violates one of the rules listed above, thus *improperly ignoring* certain possibilities. The rest of this section reconstructs in closer detail Lewis's account of (1)–(3).

He purports to diagnose and resolve Gettier cases by invoking his *Rule of Resemblance*, according to which if one possibility saliently resembles another, and one of the two is not properly ignored, then neither is the other.

Suppose that Sue believes that either Nogot or Havit owns a Ford. She believes that Nogot owns a Ford on the basis of her having seen him driving a Ford, while she has no evidence suggesting that Havit is the owner of a Ford. Suppose, however, that Nogot owns no car at all: the vehicle he was driving when he was spotted by Sue was rented. Havit does own a Ford, although he almost never drives it and Sue never saw him doing so. Then

Sue's belief *that either Nogot or Havit owns a Ford* is true (because Havit owns a Ford) and justified (on the basis of Sue's spotting Nogot on a Ford), yet it is not knowledge. Why does Sue fail to achieve knowledge in this case? According to Lewis, it is because – from the point of view of a knowledge attributor – she *improperly ignores* a possibility that is still compatible with her evidence: namely, that Nogot drives a Ford he does not own, while Havit neither drives nor owns a car. Why is this possibility improperly ignored? Because, first, actuality is never properly ignored; and, second, because this possibility *saliently resembles actuality* as far as Sue's evidence is concerned, and, since actuality is not properly ignored, neither is this resembling possibility.

Notably, Lewis believes that the same explanation holds for fake-barn cases and lottery cases. These respond to the same resemblance considerations that, in Lewis's view, seem *central* to explain Gettierization. To the extent that they contain these central ingredients, too, it seems safe to say that he considers them as very close to Gettier cases.

Imagine that Ida is traveling in a country full of fake barns and finds herself in the fake-barn situation described in (1). On the Lewisian account, Ida lacks knowledge, in that she is improperly ignoring a possibility that her evidence leaves uneliminated: namely, that she is looking at one of the many barn façades in the country. This possibility is not properly ignored, because it resembles actuality (relative to the evidence at her disposal) too closely to be set aside, given the amount of bogus barns in Ida's surroundings.

Further support for the idea that fake-barn cases are closely linked to Gettier cases in Lewis's sense seems to come from contrastivism (Schaffer 2004; 2005). Contrastivism has it that knowledge attributions generally have the form "S knows that *p* rather than *q*." As Schaffer notes (2005, p. 243), contrastivism fits particularly well the way in which perception works – namely, through *discrimination*. Sensory discrimination seems to enable us to reject some possibilities based on the inputs that we receive. For instance, outside fake-barns country, if Ida had the visual experience as of the façade of a building, this input, together with the reasonable assumption that she is in the real world and that façades are usually parts of whole buildings, would enable her to rule out the possibility that she is merely seeing a façade. It would then be true to state "Ida knows that she is seeing a real building *rather than a mere façade*." In a fake-barns case, however, the environmental conditions are such that Ida's visual experience is not sufficiently discriminating to license such a knowledge ascription. Why so?

Lewis would say that Ida is improperly ignoring certain possibilities; Schaffer would say that the salient contrast for the knowledge attribution is the one between fake and real barns. This implies that, on Schaffer's account as well as on Lewis's, it is true to say, regarding the fake-barns scenario, "Ida does *not* know that she is seeing a real barn rather than a mere façade," because a salient, knowledge-threatening element has not been ruled out.

Finally, let us move to lottery cases. Imagine that Jane, who has just purchased a lottery ticket, finds herself in the situation portrayed in (2). Her intuitive lack of knowledge is explained, in Lewis's contextualism, by her improperly ignoring a possibility that is compatible with her evidence: namely, that the ticket will win. As Lewis explains (1996, p. 557), either every one of these possibilities may be properly ignored, or none may be. But one of them may not properly be ignored: namely, the one that actually obtains. So, given that actuality may not be properly ignored, neither can the possibilities that saliently resemble it.

Is Lewis's suggestion on the right track, to the effect that fake-barn cases and lottery cases are so closely linked with Gettier cases? In order to establish this, a careful comparison between Gettier cases and lottery cases and fake-barn cases needs to be conducted. This is what we set out to do in Sections 5.3 and 5.4. Is Lewis's contextualist diagnosis of Gettier cases viable? This question is tackled in Sections 5.5, 5.6, and 5.7, where we point out some limitations of contextualism (including Lewis's version) in capturing the ultimate source of Gettier problems.

5.3 Gettier and Lotteries

In this section, we compare lottery cases with Gettier cases, arguing that the parallel put forward by Lewis only works up to a certain point. As will emerge, the key difference lies in the *luck* component.

First, recall that, in Lewis's view, when the subject states "I know my ticket will not win," her self-attribution is false because she is improperly ignoring the possibility that the ticket will win. Cohen (1988, p. 106) provides a similar explanation when he says that the statistical information concerning lotteries makes salient the possibility of error. DeRose (1996, p. 569), too, voices a similar view when he says that we judge that the subject doesn't know, because we realize that she would have the same belief even if her ticket were in fact to win, thus being insensitive to the obtaining of certain possibilities.

An alternative way of spelling out the problem is offered by Hawthorne (2004), who in turn draws on Vogel (1990). Key to this explanation is the so-called "Parity Reasoning Principle," which begins with the question of what special reasons the subject has to believe that her ticket will lose. Apparently, she has none. Therefore, if she knows her ticket will lose, she has to know that any other ticket will lose, on pain of being arbitrary. Yet it is unacceptable that the subject knows that every ticket will lose. Therefore, it should be inferred that the subject does not know her ticket will lose either.

Now, Parity Reasonings are quite sophisticated: they take some time and some effort to be spelled out. Philosophers may be able to create conversational contexts where the epistemic standards are so high as to demand that the Parity Reasoning be considered and dispelled; however, in less philosophical circumstances, it may be legitimate for us to deem as true sentences such as "S knows that her ticket will lose." This, observes Hawthorne (2004, p. 18), is especially likely to happen when certain practical aims are at stake. Suppose that Sarah suggested to Ida, who is planning to buy a new car, that she purchase a lottery ticket to get the cash that she needs. This would seem like insane advice. Ida would be well within her right to claim "I know I am not going to win," at least relative to these practical purposes. Indeed, Hawthorne suggests that, if one's plan or practical deliberation were to depend on a lottery win, then the huge probability that one's ticket will lose would suffice for one to *know* that one's ticket will indeed lose.

These considerations provide support for the view that contextualism can account for the problem underlying lottery cases. The contextualist is in a position to say that (a) to the extent that the standards in the attribution context are suitably high, it is true to claim that the subject does not know she will lose – because (following Lewis, Cohen, and DeRose) she cannot rule out certain salient possibilities, or, alternatively (following Hawthorne and Vogel), she cannot avoid the Parity Reasoning; (b) conversely, when the standards in the attribution context are suitably low, it is true to state that the subject knows that she will lose the lottery.

The full details of the contextualist account in play are not essential here. What is important is that the lottery problem can be accounted for with the resources typical of a contextualist theory – namely, the idea of the attributor-sensitivity of the truth-value of knowledge ascriptions and the "shiftiness" of epistemic standards.

Can contextualism equally well articulate the Gettier problem? In Lewis's view, it seems like it can. Lewis contends that the subject lacks knowledge of the Gettierized proposition because, from the attributor's standpoint, she is improperly ignoring a possibility that saliently resembles other possibilities that are not properly ignored. So far, Lewis's reconstruction of the problem behind Gettier examples exactly parallels his reconstruction of the problem behind lottery cases. There is nothing wrong with this parallel. It seems that the subjects involved in Gettier cases *are* indeed guilty of the error that Lewis imputes to them. Lewis's explanation is therefore so far accurate and we will not question it. The issue to be discussed is that of whether his explanation is *exhaustive*. Gettier cases do not seem to present only a problem of improperly ignored possibilities. They do more than that. A commonly acknowledged source of the problem is that the subject knows by pure "luck."

The notion of luck in epistemology has received increasing attention in the last decade, allowing philosophers to better understand this phenomenon and its relation to knowledge.[3] As Duncan Pritchard (2005) notes, some forms of luck are epistemically benign, while others are malignant. For instance, it does not threaten knowledge that the subject's capacity to acquire knowledge is the product of luck – as when a subject fortuitously survives dangerous circumstances, and as a result becomes capable of knowing certain facts (2005, pp. 135–6). Neither does it threaten knowledge that the evidence is merely accidentally presented to the subject – as when somebody accidentally acquires evidence by overhearing a conversation (2005, pp. 136–7). By contrast, it *does* threaten knowledge that a subject who acquires a belief based on a certain body of evidence, gets it right only as a matter of luck – in the sense that, although she is right, she could have easily been wrong. This is what Pritchard calls *veritic epistemic luck*, which he describes in modal terms as follows (2005, p. 146; see also 2015a, p. 98):

> the agent's belief is true in the actual world, but . . . in a wide class of nearby possible worlds in which the relevant initial conditions are the same as in the actual world – and this will mean, in the basic case, that the agent at the very least forms the same belief in the same way as in the actual world . . . the belief is false.

---

[3] For an overview, see Rabinowitz (2011), Broncano-Berrocal (2016), and Broncano-Berrocal and Carter (2017).

We wish to argue that lottery cases and Gettier cases importantly differ with respect to the role of veritic epistemic luck. Consider again the stopped-watch case. The subject believes that it is 8:29; her belief is justified on the basis of her consultation of the watch, a procedure that in normal circumstances is reliable; however, to put it in Pritchard's terms, it seems like in (almost) all close possible worlds where she acquires her belief as she actually does – namely, through a glance at the watch – she wrongly believes that it is 8:29. This implies that her belief that it is 8:29 is actually true by sheer chance, simply because the actual world "plays in her favor" by instantiating a possibility that is not instantiated in the nearby worlds.

Think now of the lottery case. The subject believes that her ticket will lose; she is justified on the basis of statistical information about the workings of lotteries; yet the fact that she believes truly is not lucky at all: it is the most expected result! We may say, again in Pritchard's terminology, that in almost all the nearby possible worlds where she believes she will lose on the same grounds, she gets it right. Of course, the fact that her true belief is not lucky does not yet mean that she *knows* that her ticket will lose. It is compatible with what we have said so far that the subject has a nonlucky true belief that does not amount to knowledge, perhaps because a further requirement about strength of evidence is in place.

Interestingly, Pritchard contends that the belief of the lottery subject is in fact lucky, at least in one sense of the word. He first distinguishes between the probability of an event and its modal closeness – that is, how much of the actual situation needs to change in order for a certain possibility to obtain. Then he argues that, although losing the lottery is a very probable event, the truth of one's belief to the effect that one will lose is still the result of luck, because *very little would have had to change* in order for the winning possibility to be instantiated – after all, it was only a matter of which configuration of balls would have been drawn (Pritchard 2005, p. 163; 2015a, p. 97; 2016b). Although this is an intriguing analysis, it seems to us that it can be trumped by the following consideration: there are very few nearby possible worlds where the subject wins. So, even though the winning obtains in virtue of a very tiny variation from one nearby world to the next, it is still true that the nearby modal space is almost entirely occupied by losing worlds. At the very least, the idea that only a tiny change would have sufficed to turn a losing ticket into a winning one and the idea that there are many more worlds where the ticket loses than worlds where the ticket wins are in tension with one another, which renders luck intuitions extremely unstable. The burden of proof seems to lie on Pritchard to explain why considerations of modal nearness should

override considerations that have to do with a prevalence of losing alternatives in the surrounding modal space. As formulated, then, the proposal is
doubtful, for it is not yet clear that the subject who believes truly that she lost
the lottery is in any way lucky.

The conclusion of this section is that luck is a central component of Gettier
cases – which, however, seems (*pace* Pritchard) absent from lottery cases.
In order to achieve a fulfilling explanation of Gettier examples, the contextualist should therefore strive to provide an account of this phenomenon by
accommodating it in its theory. Can the phenomenon of epistemic veritic luck
be satisfactorily captured in the contextualist framework? We postpone an
answer to this question until Sections 5.5, 5.6, and 5.7. In the next section, we
compare Gettier cases with fake-barn scenarios.

5.4 Gettier and Fake Barns

The aim of this section is to compare Gettier cases and fake-barn cases.
As will emerge, the two scenarios share the luck component, with only
minor and marginal differences. Given these similarities, it will be urged
that if it is possible to give a rendering of fake-barn cases in contextualist
terms (as some have proposed), then it should be possible to do the same
with Gettier cases.

It is easy to realize that both fake-barn cases and Gettier cases involve
epistemic veritic luck, or believing the truth by accident. Applying
Pritchard's formulation, we may see that, in both cases, in (almost) all
nearby possible worlds where the subject acquires the belief as she actually
does – by seeing a barn façade or by glancing at the watch – she ends up with
a false belief. To be sure, the two examples differ in a number of respects: in
the fake-barn case, the subject is supposedly exercising her visual capacities
from a distance, whereby this increases the chances of error; in the stopped-
watch case, the subject glances at the watch from a much less problematic
distance. Moreover, the subject in the fake-barn scenario seems overall to
be in a more epistemically hostile environment, given the extent and
unpredictability of the deception to which he is exposed; the stopped-
watch case seems, in comparison, a rather mundane epistemic mishap.
Still, it is conceivable that these differences be erased or significantly
lessened, which would reveal the strong structural similarity between the
two cases.

In light of these similarities, it seems that, if fake-barn cases can receive
a contextualist treatment, the same should happen for Gettier cases. John

Greco illustrates how the verdict to the effect that the fake-barn subject does not know that there is a barn ahead of him may depend on assumptions about what is at stake (2010, p. 80):

> suppose that we are government employees, charged with counting barns in the area for the purposes of determining property taxes. Suppose also that barn facades are not taxed in the same way that working barns are. However, Henry is a new employee who does not realize that the area is populated with fake barns, and who has not yet received the special training needed to distinguish barns from barn facades. In this context, Henry sees a barn from a hundred yards and pulls out his log to record this ... [I]f Henry were in this context to say, "I know there is a barn over there," we would not view his claim as true. But now consider a different practical reasoning context. Still in Fake-Barn Country, we are working on a farm where we know that there are no barn facades. In fact, we know that there is only one structure on the property – a working barn. We and Henry are charged with getting a cow back to the barn. In this context, Henry sees a barn from a hundred yards and starts walking the cow in that direction. Now ... if Henry were in this context to say, "I know there is a barn over there," we most likely would view his claim as true.

A discussion of the merits of this contextualist treatment would lead us too far astray, so we will not pursue it. What matters to us for our present purposes is that, given the strong resemblances so far detected between fake-barn cases and Gettier cases, the contextualist should be able to provide a similar story with, for instance, the stopped-watch case or the Nogot–Havit case. Specifically, the contextualist should be able to offer an account whereby knowledge-denials in Gettier cases (as well as knowledge-ascriptions, if any) can depend on features of the attributor's context – for instance, stakes, epistemic standards, properly ignored possibilities. As we saw in Section 5.2, Lewis's contextualism is certainly an option here. It is now time to assess this option.

5.5 Gettier and Contextualism: From Attributor-Sensitivity to Subject-Sensitivity

As a point of departure, let us first discuss an objection to contextualist accounts of Gettier-style cases that has been offered by Cohen (1998, p. 297). The contextualist theory says that the possibilities salient in the attributor's context determine whether the knowledge attribution is true.

Thus, if in context C_1 the attributor is attending to the possibility that the watch tells 8:29 while it is really, say, 8:40, she will "call the shots" on the evaluation of the knowledge ascription. In C_1, she would be right to say "The subject does not know that it is 8:29." However, suppose that in context C_2 the attributor was (appropriately) not attending to this very possibility. In the contextualist framework, it would follow that in C_2 it would be true to state "The subject knows that it is 8:29," despite the obtaining of the Gettier conditions. This, Cohen maintains, "is strongly counterintuitive" (1998, p. 297), for it seems implausible that a subject might *know* – in any sense of the notion – that it is 8:29 when the conditions described above obtain, even if the attributor is not paying attention to some knowledge-threatening possibility.

It could be replied that the trouble for contextualism is really just its exclusive focus on the ascriber, whose standards "call the shots" in the knowledge ascription. This is what primarily creates the problem in C_2: on the one hand, by virtue of her being (appropriately) unaware of the Gettier possibility, the attributor truly ascribes knowledge to the subject; on the other hand, the subject's Gettierized circumstances seem independently to suffice for denying knowledge. Contextualism should admit that, in this context, the subject's (improper) ignorings *trump* the attributor's (proper) ignorings. Thus, one could argue that if contextualism allowed bracketing the possibilities salient to the attributor, and allowed the possibilities salient to the subject to affect the truth-value of the knowledge attribution, it would deliver the desired result in C_2 – namely, that the subject of the Gettier case does not know that it is 8:29. Cohen identifies the trouble of Lewis's contextualism with Gettier cases as follows (1998, p. 304):

> it is problematic to use an attributor-sensitive rule of relevance to solve the Gettier problem. There is no reason not to view the subject's failure to know in these Gettier cases as fixed across contexts of ascription – as holding regardless of who the attributor is. So any rule that solves the Gettier problem must be attributor-insensitive.

Cohen's suggestion is that Lewis's contextualism may better capture Gettier problems by becoming more subject-sensitive. One way for contextualism to achieve this aim is, according to Heller (1999, p. 125), to assume as part of the attributor's very own interests a concern for the *subject's capability* to distinguish between, say, a situation where it is 8:29 and one where it is 8:40; or to distinguish between a situation where Nogot owns a Ford and one where he owns no Ford. Once this concern for the subject is integrated into the attributor's own interests, it will be part of the attributor's job to carefully look into the possibilities that the subject is or is not ignoring, regardless of whether or not they are salient in the attributor's context.

Regardless of whether or not Heller's suggestion helps, our persuasion is that making contextualism more subject-sensitive would be insufficient in order fully to capture the problematicity of Gettier cases, for reasons we explore in the next section.

5.6 Gettier and Contextualism: Failure to Capture the Luck Component

Can a more "subject-sensitive" version of contextualism capture the real problem with Gettier cases? In order to be able to answer this question, we need to establish what the "real problem" underlying these cases is. Recall our comparison between lottery and Gettier scenarios. There, we took the first steps toward making explicit at least one of the main problems of the Gettier examples – namely, *epistemic veritic luck*. We also noticed that epistemic veritic luck is shared by fake-barn cases. There is therefore some pressure for contextualism to account for this element in its own framework.

Suppose that we recruited the "subject-sensitive" version of contextualism suggested by Cohen and Heller in order to account for epistemic veritic luck. Would it provide a fulfilling account? Our persuasion is that it would not: to explain Gettier cases exclusively in terms of improperly ignored possibilities would seem to offer an incomplete and unfair reconstruction of the case.

Our argument for this claim is quite simple. Think of the elements that compose the stopped-watch case. (1) The subject forms the belief that it is 8:29. (2) This belief is justified. (3) It is also true by accident. (4) The subject is ignoring the possibility that the watch says 8:29 while it is really 8:40. Now, suppose that somebody asked "Why does the subject fail to know that it is 8:29?" We might answer, "Because she is ignoring a possibility she should be considering (and ruling out)." By giving this explanation, we would have taken care of the intuition of the lack of knowledge, but we would have failed to capture what is peculiar in the Gettier situation. In effect, our explanation would seem to locate the stopped-watch case on the same level as, say, a bank case, where the attributor denies knowledge to the subject in virtue of the fact that the subject fails to consider, and therefore cannot rule out, the possibility that the bank will be closed on

Friday despite evidence indicating that it will be open. But, clearly, there is more to a Gettier case than the ignoring of certain possibilities (listed as element (4) above). There is also what we have listed as element (3) – namely, the accidental truth of the belief. This is exactly what sets a Gettier case apart from a bank case, and thus should be the target of an explanation aiming to account for the subject's lack of knowledge. Therefore, explaining the Gettier subject's lack of knowledge in terms of the ignoring of certain possibilities will have the cost of neglecting the most distinctive detail of the story, thus offering an incomplete and unfair representation of it.

The contextualist might retort that there is a systematic connection between element (3) and element (4), to be characterized as follows: the subject's belief to the effect that it is 8:29 is accidentally true. This affects the epistemic standards in the subject's scenario in such a way that she would have to consider and rule out certain possibilities which he would not have had to rule out if not for the luck component. (The natural candidates here are those possibilities where the subject embraces a false belief despite using the same method of belief acquisition – for instance, the possibility whereby it is 8:40 but she still comes to believe that it is 8:29 based on her consultation of the watch.) Since these possibilities remain improperly ignored, the subject fails to know. In this scenario, luck acts as an element capable of modifying the epistemic standards operative in the subject's situation, and consequently capable of affecting which possibilities are properly ignored and which are not. Yet even if luck could play this role, this would render the changing of the standards a quite explanatorily idle step. For the fact that the subject believes the truth by luck seems already independently sufficient to deny knowledge, with no need to further process this element in the contextualist machinery of "shifty standards" and "improperly ignored possibilities." That is to say, the fact that the subject's belief is true by chance seems already effectively to explain why she fails to know that it is 8:29, with no need to mention a change in epistemic standards and the consequent improper ignoring of certain possibilities.

The conclusion of this section is that either a contextualist explanation of Gettier cases is incomplete and fails to do justice to the distinctive feature of these examples (namely, veritic epistemic luck); or, if it attempts to incorporate the luck element into the explanation, it turns the typically contextualist account in terms of shifty standards (and improper ignoring of possibilities) into an idle wheel. This implies that contextualism offers an unsatisfactory account of all the cases reviewed so far where luck bears on the knowledge attribution: stopped-watch cases, Nogot–Havit cases, and fake-barn cases.

Having achieved this result, our discussion could potentially stop here. Yet there is a further aspect to Gettier cases that has not emerged so far, and that reveals a further way in which contextualism has difficulty in accounting for Gettier cases.

5.7 Gettier and Contextualism: Failure to Capture Lack of Causal Connection

So far, we have argued that contextualism inadequately accounts for the luck component of Gettier cases. Based on our discussion so far, Gettier cases comprise stopped-watch examples, Nogot–Havit cases, and fake-barn scenarios. This is not completely accurate, though. There is an important, further difference that has not emerged so far between fake-barn cases and the rest of the "standard" Gettier examples. We contend that contextualism fails to account for this differentiating feature. This provides additional reasons to think that contextualism's relation with Gettier cases is highly problematic.

The further difference that we wish to emphasize lies in the *connection* between the subject's evidence and her true belief. Arguably, while this connection nonproblematically obtains in the fake-barn case, it fails to obtain in Gettier examples.

Consider again the subject in the fake-barn country: he looks from a distance and happens to see the only real barn in the surroundings. Now, if we ignore possible defeaters and set aside epistemic veritic luck, we notice that all goes well when it comes to the *link* between the subject's evidence and the truth of his belief. The subject acquired some evidence as to the presence of a barn when there is indeed a barn ahead of him, so the evidence in this case is *truth-conducive*. Thus, we can say that the subject acquires the true belief that there is a barn ahead of him "thanks to" the fact that he had that particular evidence. Both the evidence and the process of its acquisition were connected to the true belief in an acceptable way. The fake-barn subject is therefore *creditable* to his true belief. Note that this is likely to generate a clash of verdicts about fake-barn examples: on the one hand, the subject being lucky would seem to push in the direction of a knowledge denial; on the other hand, the subject's creditability would seem to push in the direction of a knowledge ascription. If this is so, then we are happy to leave it open whether fake-barn cases are cases of knowledge;

our consideration from now on will be restricted to more "traditional" Gettier cases, like the stopped-watch or the Nogot–Havit case.

The link between evidence and true belief that we detected in fake-barn cases is absent in the other Gettier cases we have been scrutinizing. John Greco brings this point out in his own terminology (2010, p. 74):

> in Gettier cases, S believes the truth, and S believes from an ability, but S does not believe the truth because S believes from an ability. ... the "because" is here intended to mark a causal explanation.

Thus, in Gettier cases, the subject believes the truth on the basis of evidence acquired through an epistemically acceptable method, but she does not come to believe the truth *because of*, or *thanks to*, the evidence acquired through that method. In the stopped-watch case, the subject comes to believe that it is 8:29, based on her looking at the watch. Her belief is true, her method of belief acquisition is generally reliable, and her evidence is sufficient; however, that very evidence and the process through which she acquired it "deserve no credit for" causing her to believe something true. For if it hadn't been for a lucky coincidence (it actually being 8:29), the subject's evidence would have led her to a false belief. Similarly, in the Nogot and Havit case, the subject forms the belief that either Nogot or Havit owns a Ford, based on evidence she has for the first disjunct of the proposition, consisting of visual experience and memories of Nogot driving a Ford. Although this evidence decently supports the first disjunct, the disjunction is true because the second disjunct is true. Here, too, the evidence that the subject has "deserves no credit" for leading her to believe the truth, because it provides epistemic support for the false disjunct, and the fact that the other disjunct (and thus the whole disjunction) was true was an altogether fortuitous result.

Now, it seems to us that this defective liaison between evidence acquisition and true belief acquisition is simply not articulable in the contextualist framework. It is one thing for the subject to have or to lack the quality and amount of evidence demanded by the standards relevant in a certain context (whether the subject's or the attributor's); it is another thing to have evidence that defectively connects with the true belief she acquires on its basis. The master consideration supporting the latter claim is the following: It is perfectly possible to imagine that in a Gettier case the subject has exactly the quality and amount of evidence demanded by the relevant contextual standards (which may range from ordinary to extremely low), but the evidence is defectively linked to the true belief, thus endangering knowledge for independent reasons. These seem precisely the conditions in which the problematicity of the Gettier case best emerges. In the stopped-watch case it indeed seems that, at least relative to *ordinary* epistemic standards in the context of the ascription, the subject has the adequate quality and amount of evidence required for her to know that it is 8:29; and the same goes for the Nogot and Havit case. The subject's evidence is unassailable, given ordinary standards; what engenders the intuition of a lack of knowledge is something *other* than the failure to meet epistemic standards – plausibly, the defective nexus between evidence and (lucky) true belief.

The contextualist might reply that, when a subject's evidence fails to be the appropriate cause for the subject's true belief, the evidence fails certain contextual standards required for belief to count as knowledge. Thus, this defective connection between evidence and true belief has a correlate in terms of epistemic standards within the contextualist framework. Yet it is difficult to see the epistemic standards in any Gettier scenario as being significantly higher than they are in ordinary circumstances. This already casts suspicion on the idea that, with Gettier cases, the theorist is managing to raise the contextual standards in a way comparable with, say, bank examples. Moreover, it is extremely difficult to imagine a context where these standards are loosened: there would hardly seem to be any situation in which the epistemic standards could be *so relaxed* as to allow that, even if evidence and true belief bore such a defective relation, the subject would still have knowledge. That evidence and true belief are related in a specific, non-Gettier-like way does not seem to be a requirement that may legitimately hold in some contexts and not in others, as one would expect to happen in a contextualist theory. Rather, this requirement would seem to hold in *all* contexts of ascription, no matter how low their standards, thus violating the "shiftiness" that is typical of context-sensitive aspects of knowledge.[4]

---

[4] Contextual variation need not have to do with epistemic standards; importantly, it could concern causal relations. Greco (2004, pp. 391–2) defends a contextualism about "because" whereby, depending on the context, the subject might or might not have knowledge based on whether her evidence acquisition appropriately caused her true belief – typically, through the exercise of intellectual virtue. Yet even this contextualism would not help with Gettier cases; for, in order to do some explanatory work, it would have to be compatible with a context in which "because" is applied in such a way that evidence acquisition for the Gettier subject is appropriately causally connected to the true belief. Yet there seems to be no context where the conditions of application of "because" are so relaxed as to admit that evidence acquisition in a Gettier case appropriately causally connects with true belief, for this would imply excessively disregarding the subject's intellectual abilities and virtues. If there is no such context, then it seems that the same explanation available to a contextualist is also available to someone who is not a contextualist about "because."

We therefore conclude that if what sets Gettier cases apart from fake-barn cases is the defective connection between evidence and true belief, then the fact that this defective connection cannot satisfactorily be captured by a contextualist account gives us a further reason to believe that contextualism is not well positioned to offer a complete explanation of the problem under-lying "traditional" Gettier cases – like stopped-watch cases and Nogot–Havit cases.

Perhaps, though, we have not considered one last possible type of contextualism, which could stem from a *rejection* of the distinctive Gettier intuition to the effect that the subject lacks knowledge. Stephen Hetherington (1999; 2006) has argued that, in Gettier scenarios, although it is false to say that S knows that p in the standard sense of knowing, it is true to say that S knows that p in a *nonstandard* sense of knowing. Such a nonstandard sense of knowing would be one explicitly admitting "lucky knowledge" – that is, knowledge that could have easily failed to be so.

The crucial point for the present discussion is that of whether this position can be developed into a form of contextualism. One way to do so would be to argue that "know" is *ambiguous*, and that, depending on the context, either the standard sense of "know" may be used, which demands an absence of luck, or a less strict sense of "know" may be employed, which does not demand an absence of luck. In the spirit of contextualism, this thesis would require further backing by means of evidence stemming from a close examination of our linguistic practices. It would also require a significant departure from the overall monistic attitude concerning knowledge that contextualists have had so far. For they have usually main-tained that "knowledge" has a univocal sense and that it picks out just one kind of epistemic property, which can then be either attributed or denied depending on contextual shifts of standards.

Another possibility would then be to argue that "know" has only *one* sense and picks out just one property. Still, its sense is, upon reflection, more permissive than one might have thought. This would imply that subjects in Gettier scenarios know that p in the same sense of "know" in which subjects in non-Gettier scenarios know that p, in virtue of the fact that the only sense of "know" available is, upon philosophical reflection, sufficiently broad as to encompass cases in which knowledge obtains by luck. Hetherington's own proposal might be read exactly in this fashion, when he remarks "There is a real possibility of our having been thinking about knowledge in a way that is more conceptually restricted than we have realised" (2006, p. 219; see also p. 223; see also 1999, p. 586). Since Plato's rejection of Theaetetus' second definition of knowledge, philosophers have been quite skeptical of such a possibility. Hence, its proper defense would require substantial elaboration.

An examination of the latter two proposals falls outside the scope of the present chapter, whose goal was to examine what extant contextualist theories have to offer in the way of a diagnosis of Gettier cases.

5.8 Conclusion

We have explored the question of whether contextualism can provide a satisfactory account of the Gettier problem. Our point of departure was Lewis's contention that Gettier cases crucially involve the improper ignoring of certain uneliminated possibilities, where this feature also makes lottery and fake-barn scenarios very close to Gettier cases. By comparing Gettier cases with lottery cases and with fake-barn cases, we have isolated some features that are distinctive of a Gettierized scenario, and that should be accommodated by a contextualist account. These features are (i) epistemic veritic luck and (ii) a defective relation between evidence and true belief. We have found no convincing way in which contextualism could accommodate these features within its framework. We have therefore concluded that a contextualist account of Gettier cases would at best be partial or incomplete.

6   The Gettier Problem and Epistemic Luck

Duncan Pritchard

6.1 Two Gettier Problems

Philosophers often mean different things when they talk about the Gettier problem. I am interested in two core disambiguations of what this problem might be. On the first reading, the Gettier problem is the problem of offering a plausible, informative – and possibly reductive – theory of knowledge (where this means, of course, a theory that can deal with Gettier-style cases). Call this the *analytic Gettier problem*.

On the second reading, the Gettier problem is concerned with determining what the anti-luck condition on knowledge is. One of the core intuitions about knowledge is that it cannot be lucky, in the specific sense of *veritic luck*: given how you formed your belief, it shouldn't be a matter of luck that the belief is true.[1] Prior to the emergence of Gettier-style cases, we thought that having a justification was enough to ensure that one's true belief wasn't subject to veritic luck. Learning that there can be Gettier-style cases of justified true belief that are not knowledge, because the subject's belief is veritically lucky, leads us to wonder what kind of condition would exclude veritic luck.[2] Call this the *luck Gettier problem*.

Note that these two renderings of the Gettier problem, while closely related to each other, are also distinct. In particular, it needn't follow that, in resolving the luck Gettier problem, and thereby formulating the anti-luck condition on

---

Thanks to Stephen Hetherington.

[1] Elsewhere, I have refereed to this as the *anti-luck platitude*. See, for example, Pritchard (2005, *passim*). Almost all epistemologists accept this platitude, at least in some form. For a dissenting voice, see Hetherington (2013), which is in turn a response to Pritchard (2013). See also Hetherington (2016a).

[2] Note that this way of putting things tends to presuppose the commonly held view that the tripartite account of knowledge was the default position in epistemology prior to Gettier's article. However, there are reasons to doubt this fact, though this is not an issue that we can usefully engage with here. For further discussion, see Dutant (2015).

knowledge, one is able to offer as a result a complete theory of knowledge. Solving the luck Gettier problem *might* potentially be a way of resolving the analytical Gettier problem, but then again it might not. In contrast, if one is able to solve the analytical Gettier problem, then that will presumably mean that one has found an answer to the luck Gettier problem.

With this point in mind, we will begin by focusing on the luck Gettier problem, which is in any case the formulation of the Gettier problem that is closest to the topic that concerns us. But later on we will briefly consider afresh how an answer to the luck Gettier problem might inform an answer to the analytical Gettier problem.[3]

6.2 The Luck Gettier Problem and Anti-Luck Epistemology

The initial discussion of the Gettier problem (construed along either of the disambiguations noted above) focused on what kind of condition we should add to justified true belief to ensure that it was not subject to Gettier-style cases, and hence that it amounted to knowledge. Note that this is a rather ad hoc way of approaching the problem, since it is effectively the search for the anti-Gettier condition on knowledge. Not surprisingly, it wasn't very successful, in that it turned out to be very hard to reverse-engineer such a condition on knowledge.[4]

In the wake of this record of failure, however, epistemologists began to think more deeply about the nature of the problem that they faced. What we are after is not a gerrymandered anti-Gettier condition, but rather to determine just what it is about the tripartite account that ensures that it is unable to eliminate the kind of veritic epistemic luck at issue in Gettier-style cases. In turn, this means understanding the nature of our anti-luck intuition about knowledge. Note that this project is much broader than formulating an anti-Gettier condition, since Gettier-style cases are not the only ones to trade on the anti-luck intuition. In responding to the anti-luck Gettier problem in this way, we are thus significantly broadening our focus. What we have here, therefore, is the embryonic beginnings of a methodology that I have described as *anti-luck epistemology* (about which I will say more in a moment).[5]

---

[3] I distinguish between these two formulations of the Gettier problem in Pritchard (2015a; 2017), where each paper is concerned with one of these formulations.

[4] For a comprehensive survey of this first wave of responses to the Gettier problem, see Shope (1983).

[5] For more on anti-luck epistemology, see Pritchard (2005; 2007; 2012). For a critique of this sort of proposal, see Hetherington (2013; 2016a). As we will see in a moment, there is a broad and a narrow way of understanding the methodology of anti-luck epistemology. (In addition, as I also expand on later – see notes 12 and 20 – there may be good reasons to focus on the notion of *epistemic risk* rather than of epistemic luck.)

What other kinds of case trade on the anti-luck intuition? One key case that we need to describe is the *lottery problem*. Imagine that you've bought a ticket for a free and fair lottery, with astronomical odds (a million-to-one, say). The draw has happened, but the result hasn't been announced yet. Now suppose that you reflect on the astronomical odds against your ticket winning and so form the belief that your ticket is a losing ticket. Perhaps, as a result, you tear up your ticket without seeking out the results. What's odd about this is that, even with the odds so massively in favor of your belief being true, it doesn't seem right to say that you *know* that your ticket is a loser prior to hearing the results. (If you're not sure about this, imagine that it's someone else who reflects on your odds of losing and forms the belief that your ticket is a loser. Now imagine that they tear up your ticket, without checking the results first. Wouldn't you say that they shouldn't have done that because they didn't *know* that you'd lost?)

So, one can fail to know even when one has evidential support for one's belief that – from a probabilistic point of view, anyway – is massively in one's favor. This is especially puzzling because often we come to have knowledge while having evidential support for our beliefs that, again from a probabilistic point of view, is not nearly as strong. Imagine someone who also bought a ticket for this lottery, but who knows nothing about the astronomical odds involved. Instead, she bases her belief that she has lost entirely on what she reads about the results in a reliable national newspaper. Here's the thing, though: the odds of her belief being true when formed on this basis, while very high, don't seem to be *astronomically* high, as they are in the case of our subject who merely reflects on the odds involved (newspapers sometimes make mistakes, after all).

One upshot of the lottery problem is that knowledge is not straightforwardly a function of the probabilistic strength of one's evidence. Antecedently, one might have expected that whether one has knowledge tracks how strong the probabilistic strength of one's evidence is, so that the stronger it is, the more likely it is that you know. But it seems that this simply isn't the case, as one person can lack knowledge even while having overwhelming evidence of this kind, while a counterpart with weaker evidence of this kind does know.

The reason why this case is relevant for our purposes is that the natural explanation for why the subject knows in the second case but not the first is the anti-luck intuition. If you form your true belief that you've lost the lottery merely by reflecting on the odds involved, then, although the odds are massively in your favor, it still seems a matter of luck that your belief is true. After all, you could have very easily formed a false belief on this basis – all that it would have taken is for a few colored balls to fall in a slightly different configuration and your belief would have been false. In contrast, the subject who forms her true belief by reading the result in a reliable national newspaper doesn't seem to have a belief that is true merely as a matter of luck, even though the odds of her being right on this basis are much lower. National newspapers go to great lengths to ensure that they get lottery results right – for obvious reasons, as the consequences of failure on this score would be very serious – and so they have lots of checks built in to ensure that they get it right. But this means that, although the odds of error are still higher than in the other case (where the belief is merely based on the odds involved), it doesn't seem to be an easy possibility that one is wrong if one forms one's belief on this basis.

What is going on here? I noted earlier that there is a broad, or embryonic, rendering of anti-luck epistemology methodology at work when we shift our attentions from the specific project of seeking an anti-Gettier condition to the broader project of seeing a general anti-luck condition on knowledge. How might we flesh out this embryonic methodology? I've argued elsewhere that a fully fledged anti-luck epistemology would proceed in the following three stages in order to properly unpack what is at issue in the anti-luck condition on knowledge. First, we need to develop an account of luck. Second, we need to develop an account of the specific sense in which knowledge is incompatible with luck. Third, and finally, we put the first two parts together to determine the anti-luck condition on knowledge.[6]

This more refined methodology is important for our purposes in that it offers us a way to make sense of what is going in the lottery problem. This is because luck seems to be a *modal* notion. Very roughly, on the modal account of luck, for an event to be lucky means that it is an event that (keeping relevant initial conditions fixed) could very easily have not occurred. This explains why lottery wins are lucky, in that there are plenty of very close possible worlds where one doesn't win. It also explains why it isn't lucky that the sun rose this morning (although this is also an event over which, like a lottery win, we lack control), in that there is no close possible world where the sun doesn't rise.[7]

---

[6] See Pritchard (2005; 2007; 2012) for further discussion of anti-luck epistemology in this sense.
[7] I defend the modal account of luck in a number of places. See especially Pritchard (2014). See also Pritchard (2005; 2007; 2012). For a collection of articles on the philosophy of luck, including some pieces that are critical of the modal account of luck, see Pritchard and Whittington (2015).

Suppose now that we combine this modal account of luck with our notion of veritic luck – *viz.* luck that one forms a true belief, given how one forms one's belief. The idea, recall, was that it was in this specific sense that knowledge excludes luck. (Some bona fide knowledge is lucky, after all. There can be lucky discoveries where one is lucky to have the evidence that one does, but where one makes good use of this evidence to gain knowledge. But such luck is not veritic. Given how one formed one's belief, it is not a matter of luck that one forms a true belief. *Evidential luck* is not veritic luck.)[8] The result is that we get an account of the anti-luck condition such that, given how one formed one's belief, one's belief should not be false in close possible worlds.

The reason why this is relevant to the lottery problem is that an interesting feature of possible worlds, on the standard similarity ordering of possible worlds anyway, is that low-probability events can occur in close possible worlds.[9] Indeed, that's just what a lottery win is: a modally close but low-probability event. Although the odds are against its happening, not much needs to change about the actual world to make it happen (just a few colored balls need to fall in a different configuration), and so the possible world where you win the lottery is close to the actual world. Indeed, this is why people play lotteries but don't generally place bets on events with similar astronomical odds (which will typically concern modally far-fetched events, such as someone as unfit as yours truly swimming the Atlantic).[10]

Anti-luck epistemology can thus explain what is going on in the lottery problem. Knowledge is not a straightforward function of our probabilistic evidence because one needs a true belief that is not subject to veritic luck. This is now unpacked in terms of a modal theory of luck, such that one's basis for belief should not result in false belief in close possible worlds.

---

[8] For a detailed discussion of different kinds of epistemic luck, some of them malignant (like veritic luck) and some of them benign (like evidential luck), see Pritchard (2005).

[9] For more on the similarity ordering of possible worlds, see Stalnaker (1968) and Lewis (1973).

[10] For a long time the advertising slogan for the British National Lottery was "It Could Be You!," accompanied by a video advertising campaign which depicted a God-like finger selecting a lottery winner. The UK has notoriously strict advertising laws, and one certainly can't have a slogan that is false or misleading, and yet this advertising campaign was not objected to. This is interesting, since if one construes the slogan in a probabilistic sense then it seems the slogan should be problematic, as realistically it *couldn't* be you, as the odds are astronomically against you winning (they are, or were at the time, around 14 million to 1). But clearly that's not the reading of the slogan that the advertisers have in mind, as the advertising video that went with the slogan makes clear. The intended reading is *modal* rather than probabilistic. And, of course, in this sense it really could be you.

But of course that's just what goes wrong in the lottery case. Forming one's belief that one has lost the lottery just by reflecting on the odds involved, despite the odds being overwhelmingly in one's favor, is a veritically lucky way of forming one's belief, since it could so very easily have led to a false belief (one could have won, after all, and one would still have believed on this basis that one had lost). In contrast, although the odds are not so massively in one's favor, forming one's true belief that one has lost by reading the result in a national newspaper is not veritically lucky, in that one couldn't easily have ended up with a false belief via this process. This much is secured by the checking processes that national newspapers employ to ensure that they don't get this result wrong.[11]

So, anti-luck epistemology has delivered us an account of the anti-luck condition. Moreover, it also gets us a particular rendering of this condition. On the modal account of luck, we can order the degree of luckiness of the target event in terms of how modally close the nonobtaining of this event is. For example, in the actual world I am not shot by the sniper's bullet, which whizzes past nearby. But I am luckier to be alive in the world where it whizzes past a few inches from my head than in the world where it flies by a few meters away. Luck thus admits of degrees, and so our anti-luck condition should admit of degrees. We are intolerant of high levels of luck when it comes to knowledge, and tolerant of low levels of luck. In between, there is a sliding scale of tolerance. For example, we are opposed to knowledge in the lottery case (forming beliefs by reflecting on the odds involved) because we recognize that we could very easily have formed a false belief, unlike in the corresponding case (by reading the result in a reliable national newspaper) where we couldn't have easily formed a false belief. In between, there is a sliding scale, leading to penumbral cases where the level of luck involved is such that we aren't confident either way.[12]

---

[11] As it happens, I have personal experience of this point, from my brief time doing work experience (as a 16-year-old) on the Wolverhampton *Express and Star* newspaper. I remember being intrigued by the lengths they went to in order to check the lottery results, which far exceeded the usual copyediting rules in play at this paper. And remember that this is just a (respected) local newspaper, not a (respected) national newspaper.

[12] Note that these days I put the point in terms of the closely related notion of *epistemic risk* rather than epistemic luck (and hence I argue for an *anti-risk epistemology*). For an explanation of why this change is philosophically important, see Pritchard (2016b; forthcoming). For more on the modal account of risk that underlies this shift, and how this account diverges from the modal account of luck, see Pritchard (2015b).

6.3 Anti-Luck Epistemology and the Safety/Sensitivity Debate

An interesting feature of anti-luck epistemology is that it offers us an independent basis for settling a dispute in epistemology regarding which modal condition is entailed by knowledge. In the one corner are the proponents of *sensitivity*. According to this view, when one knows that *p*, one has a belief that *p* that is sensitive to the truth in just this sense: had *p* been false, then one wouldn't have believed that *p* on the same basis. Sensitivity can account for both Gettier-style cases and the lottery problem.[13]

In the former case, this is because these beliefs are clearly insensitive. Consider the Gettier-style case of (appropriately) forming your belief that there is a sheep in the field by looking at a big hairy dog that looks just like a sheep, but forming a true belief regardless because there is a sheep in the field, hidden by the big hairy dog.[14] You thus have a justified true belief that doesn't amount to knowledge because it's just a matter of luck that it's true. But the belief is also clearly insensitive. Had what you believed been false and there was no sheep in the field hidden from view, but everything else stayed the same, then clearly you would have continued to believe that there is a sheep in the field regardless (because you are still looking at the big hairy dog). So, proponents of sensitivity can explain why Gettier-style cases are not cases of knowledge, on the basis that they involve insensitive belief.

Proponents of sensitivity can explain why knowledge is lacking in the lottery case in the same way. The point is that forming one's belief that one has lost simply by reflecting on the odds involved isn't knowledge since in the closest possible world where you do win, and your basis for belief is the same, you will continue to believe that you have lost regardless. Knowledge is thus lacking because your belief is insensitive. In contrast, forming one's belief that one has lost by reading the results in a reliable newspaper is a route to knowledge because in the closest possible world where your basis for belief is the same but you've won, you will read the winning numbers in the newspaper and so believe that you have won. Your belief is thus sensitive.

These kinds of considerations might seem to offer decisive support for the sensitivity condition on knowledge, but the problem is that its chief competitor, *safety*, can also handle these two kinds of case. According to

---

[13] For some key defenses of the sensitivity condition, see Dretske (1970), Nozick (1981), and Becker (2007). See also the papers collected in Becker and Black (2012).

[14] This Gettier-style case was originally offered by Chisholm (1977, p. 105).

safety, when one knows, one's true belief must be such that it couldn't have easily been false (when formed on the same basis).[15] Gettier-style cases essentially involve unsafe beliefs. Given how one was forming one's belief about the sheep in the field, one could very easily on this basis have formed a false belief (i.e. if the sheep that was hidden from view had wandered out of the field). The same goes for forming one's belief that one has lost the lottery simply by reflecting on the odds involved. After all, there is a very close possible world where this basis for belief leads to a false belief (i.e. the world where a few colored balls fall in a slightly different configuration). In contrast, forming one's belief that one has lost by reading the results in a reliable newspaper will result in a safe belief. Given all the checks that reliable newspapers have in place to ensure the accuracy of these reports, it is not an easy possibility that this basis for belief will result in a false belief.

So how do we adjudicate between sensitivity and safety? The standard line is to argue case-by-case, and thereby determine which one fares better overall. One consideration in this regard is that sensitivity struggles with cases of inductive knowledge.[16] Suppose I accidentally knock a pot plant off the balcony of my apartment. Even if I don't see the fate of the pot plant directly, I will naturally infer, correctly as it happens, that the plant pot is now in pieces on the pavement below (given that there is nothing below the balcony that would break its fall, or otherwise alter the trajectory of the fall). Moreover, one would be entirely right to so infer, as this seems to be a fairly clear-cut case of inductive knowledge.

But now consider the closest possible world where the pot plant isn't on the pavement. This won't be a particularly close possible world, since we will have to suppose that something quite incredible has happened, such as that a passing gull has somehow caught the plant pot as it fell and carried it off somewhere. Since I haven't seen the fate of the pot plant, however, in this possible world I would continue to believe on the same inductive basis that the pot plant is on the pavement. My belief is thus insensitive, and hence on the sensitivity view it cannot amount to knowledge.

Safety, however, predicts the right result. Since there isn't a close possible world where the plant pot fails to hit the pavement, one couldn't on this inductive basis have easily formed a false belief. The belief is thus safe, and hence can be bona fide inductive knowledge. Note, too, why safety gets the

---

[15] For some key defenses of safety, see Sainsbury (1997), Sosa (1999b), and Williamson (2000). See also Pritchard (2002; 2005, *passim*; 2007; 2012).

[16] This was originally pointed out by Sosa (1999b).

right result here but sensitivity does not. The problem seems to be that sensitivity asks us to consider the closest possible world where what one believes is false, no matter how far out that possible world is. That's why we have to consider the far-fetched possible world where, say, the gull catches the plant pot and spirits it away. But intuitively such possible worlds simply aren't relevant to whether we have knowledge, precisely because they are so far-fetched. Safety avoids this problem since by its nature it only considers what is going on in close possible worlds – one's *modal neighborhood*, if you will.

Anti-luck epistemology offers us another, independent route to motivating the adoption of the safety condition over sensitivity. This is because our anti-luck epistemology methodology has led us to an account of the anti-luck condition such that knowledge demands true belief that could not have easily been false, and this, of course, is essentially safety. Note as well that anti-luck epistemology generates a specific rendering of this principle. For we might ask how far this modal neighborhood extends, and whether our basis for belief needs to be generating true beliefs in all of them or just in most of them. Anti-luck epistemology gives us an answer to this question. What we need is a continuum account of safety, in line with our continuum account of luck. We are highly intolerant of the possibility of error (on the same basis) in the very close possible worlds, with our tolerance increasing as we move further outwards, to the point where the possibility of error (on the same basis) becomes completely irrelevant to our assessment of knowledge.[17]

6.4 *Contra* Robust Anti-Luck Epistemology

So, we seem to have determined what the anti-luck condition on knowledge is, and have thereby solved the luck Gettier problem. Can we use this result to solve the analytical Gettier problem, too? Well, it certainly can't be the case that we can understand knowledge as merely true belief that satisfies the anti-luck condition, a position I have elsewhere termed *robust anti-luck epistemology* (as opposed to the *modest anti-luck epistemology* that merely contends that the anti-luck condition is a necessary condition on knowledge).[18]

---

[17] For further discussion of safety, sensitivity, and anti-luck epistemology, see Pritchard (2008).

[18] See Pritchard (2009, chs. 3, 4). See also Pritchard (2012) and Pritchard, Millar, and Haddock (2010, chs. 2–4) (although note that in some places I use the alternative nomenclature of *strong versus weak* anti-luck epistemology).

The reason for this is that besides the anti-luck intuition there is also another fundamental intuition about knowledge, which I call the *ability intuition*. This is the idea that when one knows, it must be down to one's cognitive agency in some significant way that one's belief is true. It is, after all, *you* who acquired the knowledge, so it must be the case that you did something cognitively significant in forming the target belief. The ability intuition can easily seem like just the other side of the coin to the anti-luck intuition. If your true belief isn't due to your cognitive agency then, presumably, it must be down to luck, right? And if your belief is due to luck, then surely that must be because it's down to your cognitive agency?

In fact, the relationship between these two intuitions is more complex, in that they come apart in both directions (i.e. one can satisfy the anti-luck intuition without thereby satisfying the ability intuition, and vice versa). What is of particular interest to us is the claim that there can be nonlucky cognitive successes that are not significantly attributable to your cognitive agency. The crux of the matter is that the anti-luck condition only ensures that there is a certain match between your belief and the truth across the relevant close possible worlds, but one's belief can have this modal profile and yet this have nothing at all to do with one's exercise of cognitive agency.

Imagine a subject who is forming beliefs about a certain domain in an entirely unreliable fashion. Perhaps, for example, they form their belief about the current temperature by picking three numbers between 1 and 10 at random and adding them together. (It need not concern us why they are doing this. Perhaps they have been tricked into thinking that this is the way to work out the temperature.) Now suppose that there is a helpful demon who is intent on ensuring that this subject has true beliefs in this domain. (Again, we needn't worry too much about why. Perhaps they have been set this as a task by the overarching demon, who will destroy them if they fail.) In order to achieve this aim, the helpful demon simply makes sure that every time our agent forms a belief about the temperature, the actual temperature changes to match with what they believe. Accordingly, our subject not only forms true beliefs via this strange method, but in fact is effectively *guaranteed* to form true beliefs in this way.

This subject's beliefs clearly satisfy the anti-luck condition, since there is nothing at all lucky about the fact that they are true. In particular, she doesn't just get to the truth in the actual world, but also in all close possible worlds too, since whenever she forms a belief about the temperature the demon will ensure that this belief is true. Crucially, however, her true belief – much less the fact that her true belief is safe – has nothing significantly to do with our agent's cognitive agency, but rather has everything to do with the demon helper. Our subject's belief thus satisfies the anti-luck intuition without thereby satisfying the ability intuition.

An immediate upshot of this point is that robust anti-luck epistemology is simply not tenable as a response to the analytical Gettier problem, in that one can satisfy the anti-luck condition in such a way that doesn't satisfy the ability intuition. Note, too, that merely adding justification into the mix here wouldn't make any difference. The subject's belief in this case may well be justified – perhaps she has been given good reason for thinking that her method is the right way to determine the temperature. It follows that adding the anti-luck condition to the justified-true-belief condition, while it will deal with Gettier-style cases, will not thereby present us with a complete theory of knowledge. So how, then, should we respond to the analytical Gettier problem?

6.5 Resolving the Analytical Gettier Problem

Although robust anti-luck epistemology fails, what we have learned so far points toward where the right answer lies. Naturally, the question of what a complete theory of knowledge demands is beyond the scope of this chapter, but we can at least offer some suggestive remarks.[19] What we need, I claim, is a theory of knowledge that demands that one's nonlucky cognitive success is significantly attributable to one's cognitive agency. This is, after all, what is missing in the case considered in the previous section. While the agent in this scenario is forming safe beliefs about the temperature, her cognitive agency is playing no, or next to no, explanatory role in accounting for why her beliefs are safe (the explanatory burden instead falling overwhelmingly on the interventions of the demon helper).

Elsewhere, I have described such a view as *anti-luck virtue epistemology*, where the "virtue" in question is meant to be capturing the contribution of

---

[19] And it should be noted that some prominent epistemologists maintain that the very idea of offering a theory of knowledge is problematic. See especially Williamson (2000) and his defense of knowledge-first epistemology. (Though one should also bear in mind that Williamson's stance primarily concerns the idea of a *reductive* theory of knowledge. This is relevant because it's not clear to me that the analytical project in epistemology ought to be committed to offering reductive accounts of knowledge anyway.)

the subject's cognitive agency.[20] Note that this position is not merely the conjunction of an anti-luck condition with an ability condition on knowledge. A proposal of this kind would be easily Gettierized, in that one would simply need to formulate a scenario where both the first and the second condition are met, but for completely independent reasons. Perhaps, for example, one manifests a high degree of relevant cognitive agency, and one's belief is also true in a nonlucky fashion, but the reason for the latter has nothing to do with the former, it rather reflects some purely environmental factor.

What we are looking for is instead a conception of knowledge such that one's nonlucky cognitive success is significantly attributable to one's manifestation of cognitive agency. What I mean by this is that there is an important explanatory connection between one's nonlucky cognitive success and one's manifestation of cognitive agency, such that the former cannot be merely incidentally correlated with the latter. It would take us too far afield to defend this proposal here, but hopefully I have said enough for the reader to see how it might respond to the analytic Gettier problem, and to recognize that it does so by drawing on how one should respond to the luck Gettier problem.[21]

---

[20] For the main defense of this position, see Pritchard (2012). See also Pritchard, Millar, and Haddock (2010, chs. 2–4). Note, too, that these days I express this position in terms of an anti-risk virtue epistemology: for more details, see Pritchard (2016b; forthcoming).

[21] In particular, one thing that I haven't done is explain why anti-luck virtue epistemology offers a superior response to the analytical Gettier problem to that which is offered by the highly influential kind of robust virtue epistemology found in Sosa (1991; 2007a; 2009; 2015), Zagzebski (1996; 1999), and Greco (2010). What makes this form of virtue epistemology robust is that it doesn't involve any appeal to an anti-luck condition, but rather eliminates such luck by appealing only to a virtue condition on knowledge. Such a proposal thus offers a very different way of responding to the analytical Gettier problem. For a critical assessment of robust virtue epistemology in light of anti-luck virtue epistemology, see Pritchard (2012).

7   The Sensitivity Response to the Gettier Problem

Kelly Becker

7.1 Introduction

Gettier cases have spawned, directly or indirectly, a host of new ideas about the nature of knowledge. A common reaction to a Gettier case is to think that its agent, Smith, lacks knowledge because the connection between his belief and the fact that makes it true is somehow deficient. In turn, one way to understand that deficiency is to think that, while Smith has a justified true belief, his way of believing does not *track* the truth. In both original Gettier cases, given his reasons, Smith would have believed what he in fact believes even if it had been false. This is the central insight for sensitivity theorists.

While not the first attempt to account for Gettier cases in a revamped characterization of knowledge, a version of sensitivity theory was on the scene already by 1971 in Fred Dretske's "Conclusive Reasons," with a sneak preview of sorts in his 1970 "Epistemic Operators." The best-known and best-developed version of sensitivity comes from Robert Nozick's *Philosophical Explanations* (1981), which will be the focus of much of my discussion. Nozickean sensitivity met with serious objections soon after the publication of his book, but it is certainly worth mentioning that, despite the serious criticisms leveled at sensitivity, the most central of which will be explained herein, it handles most Gettier cases quite nicely.

This chapter will first briefly review the history of sensitivity in the works of Dretske, Alvin Goldman, and Nozick. We then turn to a more detailed discussion of Nozick's version, pausing along the way both to see how it accounts for Gettier cases and to note a problem inherent in Nozick's articulation of his "tracking" theory. That will position us to look at three of the most persistent and severe objections to sensitivity. I think it is fairly clear that some of the problems will not go away, and so the remaining question for anyone who takes sensitivity to be an otherwise plausible condition on knowledge[1] is that of whether the problems are too damaging to pursue the theory further.

7.2 Historical Background

With no other organizing principle readily to hand, a brief history of epistemic sensitivity might as well begin with its roots in post-Gettier epistemology. Goldman recognized early on that, in Gettier cases, there is a crucial disconnection between the agent's belief and the fact that makes the belief true. Goldman's (1967) first attempt to forge the requisite belief–truth link focuses on the point that, in Gettier cases, there is no *causal* connection between the fact making true Smith's belief *that the person who will get the job has ten coins in his pocket* and Smith's believing that proposition. Smith comes to believe it because he has evidence that Jones will get the job and that Jones has ten coins in his pocket, but what makes Smith's belief true is that he (Smith) will get the job and also has ten coins in his pocket. Goldman concludes that S knows that *p* if and only if S's belief that *p* stands in some appropriate causal relation to the fact making *p* true.

Goldman's causal theory of knowledge is not, of course, a version of sensitivity, but it is a precursor to his subsequent view about perceptual knowledge, which is in the sensitivity family. Interesting, too, is that one of his motivations for abandoning the causal theory is a kind of counterexample that is recognizably a relative of Gettier cases. Goldman reports the famous example of fake barns, one that he attributes (1976, pp. 772–3) to Carl Ginet. Henry is driving along a country road when his son, pointing to what is in fact a barn, asks "What is that?" Henry replies truthfully that it is a barn. However, almost all of the other barn-looking structures along this stretch of road are excellent papier-mâché facsimiles of barns. Henry has a true belief, and the espied object is directly causally connected, via perception, to Henry's belief about it. Still, it seems that Henry does not know that it is a barn, for, as is the case in the original Gettier examples, Henry seems to have obtained a true belief only luckily. If his son had pointed to any one of the facsimiles, Henry would have said that it is a barn, too.[2]

---

[1] In very original work, Guido Melchior (ms.) argues that sensitivity is not necessary for knowing, but it is necessary for checking whether or not *p*. He develops the notion of checking and uses it to diagnose puzzles surrounding conflicting intuitions about aspects and cases of knowledge.

[2] While most philosophers agree that Henry does not know that the object he sees is a barn, there are dissenters. See, for example, Hetherington (1999) and Lycan (2006).

Goldman proceeds to say, roughly, that S knows that p through perception only if there is no alternative state of affairs that is perceptually equivalent to what one actually perceives but where p is false. Two notions stand out in Goldman's revised account. The first is that of a relevant alternative state of affairs. Generally, relevant alternatives theorists claim that S knows that p only if S is somehow able to rule out *relevant* alternatives to p. Suggested by this formulation is that not all alternatives are relevant, so one need not rule out all logically possible alternatives to p in order to know that p. This generates some anti-skeptical traction, provided that skeptical hypotheses are not relevant alternatives. So, what constitutes relevance? There are several different theories of relevance, but common to sensitivity theorists is the idea that an alternative is relevant if it is what would have or might have been the case if p were false. For Goldman, to threaten a lack of knowledge these alternatives must also be perceptual equivalents of what one actually perceives. In the fake-barn example, if it were false that what Henry sees is a barn, it would have been a similar-looking facsimile. Since Henry cannot distinguish the facsimiles from the real barn, he cannot rule out the possibility that he's seeing a fake. So Henry does not know. The second important notion here is that knowledge requires the ability to discriminate states of affairs where p is true from what would be the case if p were false. S must be able to distinguish between states of affairs. This is a central insight for sensitivity theorists.

Goldman's discrimination theory of perceptual knowledge counts, for our purposes, as a version of sensitivity because (a) it takes the aforementioned capacity to distinguish between states of affairs as being necessary for knowledge, and (b) it glosses "relevant alternatives" as those that would or might be the case if p were false. Goldman famously moved on from his discrimination account to develop and articulate process reliabilism (1979; 1986), but it is probably fair to say that the discrimination account was an important step on the path.

After Goldman's causal account, but before his discrimination theory, Dretske articulated a similar idea, also recognizably in the sensitivity vein. Dretske couched his view in terms of the reasons on the basis of which one forms belief: S knows that p on the basis of (conclusive) reason R only if "R would not be the case unless p were the case" (1971, p. 1). Applying this to Gettier cases shows why their agents do not know. Smith's reason R for believing that p (*the person who gets the job has ten coins in his pocket*) is his evidence that Jones is getting the job and has ten coins in his pocket. Here, R would be the case – Smith would still have that reason – even if p were false. Also, Henry would still have his reason to believe that the object he sees is a barn even if it were just a facsimile of a barn.

The "sneak preview" of Dretske's version of sensitivity that I mentioned above appears in his "Epistemic Operators" (1970), where he argues that knowledge is not closed under known entailment. His discussion of relevant alternatives in that paper suggests that he is already working with a notion like sensitivity. The vexed issue of knowledge "closure" is one with which we will have to contend, but let us shelve it until we have a fuller view of sensitivity and its implications.

We come finally to Nozick's version of sensitivity. It is clear from his presentation that getting Gettier cases right is a major desideratum, as he gives his theory a grueling test-run through just about all of the tough examples of which he can think. Nozick is concerned, however, not just to get those cases right, but to give a fully general theory of knowledge, one that handles even knowledge of necessary truths. This is one of the reasons why his version of sensitivity has two distinct conditions:

Variation. S knows that p only if, were p false, S would not believe that p.

Adherence. S knows that p only if, were p true, S would believe that p.

Nozick dubbed these twin conditions "sensitivity," and claimed that properly tracking the truth requires meeting both conditions. For most of this chapter, we will construe sensitivity as only the variation condition. Still, it is instructive to see how adherence is meant to help with accounting for knowledge of necessary truths.

If p is necessarily true, it is not possibly false; hence, the variation condition is vacuously satisfied for any true belief about a necessarily true proposition. That is, the antecedent of "if p were false, S would not believe that p" cannot be satisfied when p is necessarily true; hence, the variation condition is always satisfied. Even so, surely S can believe that p for very bad reasons, intuitively not knowing that p. But if S's reasons are bad, then there are close worlds where p is true but S doesn't believe that p. For example, if S believes *that 51 is not a prime number* because he thinks that his least favorite ballplayer, who wears #51, is not a prime player, so that his jersey number cannot be prime, then it could easily have been the case that (or there are close worlds where) he believes 51 is prime – say, if that player were his favorite. (Never mind just how confused S is about prime numbers!)[3]

You might have noticed that I've appealed to close possible worlds to explicate sensitivity. Nozick himself preferred to construe subjunctive conditionals intuitively, without reference to possible worlds, though he includes a long footnote (1981, pp. 680–81n8) explaining how he could interpret sensitivity in a possible worlds framework. On that interpretation, variation is satisfied, roughly, if, in the closest worlds where p is false, S does not believe that p. Adherence is satisfied, roughly, if, in the closest worlds where p, S believes that p. You might then also have noticed that Nozick's interpretation of his subjunctive conditionals is somewhat nonstandard, when compared to Lewis (1973). For Lewis, the subjunctive "if p were true, S would believe that p" is satisfied when S has a true belief, because the world closest to the actual world is the actual world itself, and in that world both antecedent and consequent are true. Thus, Nozick is required to interpret adherence somewhat nonstandardly – by reference not just to the closest possible world (actuality), but also by reference to close *worlds* – to make sense of S's sometimes not knowing that p when p is necessarily true and S believes that p. On the one hand, though some might deem Nozick's interpretation faulty because it contradicts Lewis's, it is surely coherent. On the other hand, as we will see in the next section, Nozick is not consistent in his application of the adherence condition to various cases, some of which involve ordinary empirically known contingent truths. Seeing the problems that emerge from Nozick's appeal to the adherence condition will be our cue to leave adherence behind and to focus on variation, more commonly called "sensitivity."

7.3 Exploration of Nozickean Sensitivity

It is the variation condition that "solves" the Gettier problem for Nozick. If it were false that the person who gets the job has ten coins in his pocket, Smith would believe it anyway, because he wouldn't have ten coins in his pocket, but Jones would, and he believes Jones is getting the job. If it were false that either Jones owns a Ford or Brown is in Barcelona, Smith would believe it anyway,

---

[3] One wonders whether Nozick would have been open to an alternative semantics of "counterpossibles" – nonvacuously true counterfactuals with necessarily false antecedents. See, for example, Nolan (1997). As we shall see, the adherence condition creates problems for Nozick beyond the stock objections to variation and arguably does little work except to account for knowledge of necessary truths.

because Brown would not be in Barcelona but Smith would still believe that Jones owns a Ford. If it were false that the object Henry sees is a barn, he would believe it anyway, because he would be looking at a facsimile, an object he cannot distinguish from a real barn.

Here are some more cases. Lehrer and Paxson (1969, p. 229) offer the following Gettier example. I have good evidence that Nogot, a student in my class, owns a Ford, and on that basis alone I infer that someone in my class owns a Ford. It turns out that Nogot does not own a Ford, but, unbeknownst to me, another student – Havit – has a Ford. I have a justified true belief that someone in the class owns a Ford, but I don't know it. My belief violates the variation condition, since, if it were false that someone (Havit) owns a Ford, I would believe it anyway.

Harman (1973) presents the case of the dictator. The dictator is assassinated, and S, an early riser, hears the news on an early morning radio report. However, to keep the peace, soon thereafter government officials spread false information to all of the media outlets, stating that the dictator is relaxing on vacation. S does not read or hear any of these reports. Harman's suggestion is that S doesn't know that the dictator was assassinated. Of the cases discussed so far, this intuition is among the least stable, since one could surely think that S does know – she received the information from a reliable source and her belief satisfies the variation condition. Nozick, however, takes the bait on this case and argues that S does not know because there are close worlds where it is true but S does not believe it – worlds where S listens to a later radio broadcast or reads in a newspaper that the dictator is on vacation – thus violating the adherence condition.

Assuming that one shares the intuition that S does not know that the dictator was assassinated, Nozick's appeal to a violation of his adherence condition seems a plausible diagnosis. For the remainder of this section, we will explore his problematic treatment of adherence. To see the concern, we turn to the next topic in Nozick's book, which is the source of trouble for adherence. There, he discusses the issue of methods of belief formation, an issue whose importance he brings out in another example (1981, p. 179). A grandmother is sick in the hospital. Her family comes to visit, and she sees her grandson, who looks to be quite well. But if the grandson were ill, the other family members would lie and tell her that he is at home, doing just fine. The grandmother clearly knows that her grandson is well, but if it were false, she would believe that he is well anyway. Nozick claims that cases like this motivate indexing the sensitivity conditionals to the method of belief formation that S actually used in forming belief. Put differently, in determining whether Nozick's subjunctive conditionals are satisfied, we must hold constant S's actual belief-forming method. The revised conditions, then, are these (1981, p. 179):

Variation. S knows that p only if, if p were false and S were to use her actual method M, S would not believe, via M, that p.

Adherence. S knows that p only if, if p were true and S were to use her actual method M, S would believe, via M, that p.

If the grandson were ill, his grandmother would not believe that he is well, using her actual method, which involves looking directly at the grandson, seeing his rosy cheeks and healthy glow.

There are a number of questions about how best to construe belief-forming methods. Ought they to be narrowly construed, including, for example, S's very specific perceptual experiences? Or more broadly, for example, in the grandmother case, as *vision-based*?[4] Should they be individuated internally, by reference to how things appear to the agent? Or externally, by reference to external causes? It would detain us considerably to explore these questions to any depth, and because my aim here is to bring out an internal tension in Nozick's applications of his conditions to diagnose cases, we will focus on his preferred construal (see Becker 2012 for discussion).

Nozick favored a metaphysically internalist, narrow (specific) construal (1981, pp. 184–5):

A person can use a method (in my sense) without proceeding methodically, and without knowledge or awareness of what method he is using. Usually, a method will have a final upshot in experience on which the belief is based, such as visual experience, and then (a) no method without this upshot is the same method, and (b) any method experientially the same, the same "from the inside," will count as the same method.

This approach appears to handle the grandmother case well. If the grandson were ill, the grandmother would not believe, by seeing his rosy cheeks, that he is healthy! The questions are those of whether Nozick's preferred individuation of methods, by "upshot in experience," is consistent with his appeals to adherence to diagnose agents' knowledge statuses in a variety of cases, and of whether, if it is not, there is a plausible alternative individuation of methods.

---

[4] Is there an independently motivated criterion of individuation along this dimension, or is sensitivity theory vulnerable to an analog of the generality problem for process reliabilism?

Nozick claims that S does not know that the dictator was assassinated, because there are close worlds where S reads or hears a different report than the one she actually heard and upon which she based her belief. But in that case the upshot in her experience would not have been the same as it actually was. Adherence is violated, but only if we do *not* hold the upshot in experience constant when evaluating it.

Nozick's treatment of the dictator case also appears to be inconsistent with his handling of other crucial cases. For example, S sees a bank robber running from the bank. The robber's mask slips, and S sees that it's Jesse James. There are lots of close worlds where the mask does not slip, hence where S does not believe that it's Jesse James. And yet it is clear that S does know it's James. Nozick says (1981, p. 193), "His method is looking and concluding that it is Jesse James on the basis of seeing certain things. By that method . . . he would know in other cases also. To be sure, some other situations might not allow that method to be used . . . but that causes no difficulty for [adherence], properly understood." In the Jesse James case, Nozick says that S knows because, even though some other upshot in experience might have led to another belief or none at all, what matters is that S's actual method varies with and adheres to the truth: she knows Jesse James when she sees his face. Here, Nozick holds to his claim that the upshot in experience must be held constant, whereas in the dictator case he says that S does not know because some other upshot in experience might have led S not to believe that the dictator was assassinated.[5]

Perhaps by individuating methods more generally, we could reconcile Nozick's inconsistency. In the dictator case, the method might be that of *basing belief on whatever is said in a particular [normally reliable] radio broadcast*; in the Jesse James case, *basing belief on whatever I see when I look at that man with a clear view of his face*. This approach highlights the significance of the specific upshot in experience, but does not require holding it constant. This approach also appears to generate the desired verdicts. S does not know that the dictator was shot, because there are close worlds where it is true but something contradictory is reported on that normally reliable news broadcast. S does know that the bank robber is Jesse James, because if it were false she would not believe it, and if it were true she would believe it, based on what she sees when she looks at the man with a clear view of his face.

---

[5] Nozick also fails to hold "upshot in experience" constant in his explanation of why the brain-in-a-vat (BIV), who is "informed" by the vat scientist that she is a BIV, does not know that she is a BIV (1981, pp. 175f.).

There is, however, a serious drawback to generalizing methods in this way. Timothy Williamson presents an argument against sensitivity, based on the idea that knowledge requires a margin of error. Suppose that S sees a ship with a mark on it roughly one meter from the water line. Does S know that the mark is less than twenty meters from the water line? Intuitively, yes, but even so the belief could easily be insensitive, violating the variation condition. In the closest worlds where it's false that the mark is less than 20 meters above the waterline, it is just barely above 20 meters, and S's powers of discrimination may not suffice to prevent her from believing it's less than 20 meters (Williamson 2000, p. 160). To solve this problem, we should individuate methods by upshot in experience. Based on that upshot – where the mark simply looks far less than 20 meters from the waterline – S would only ever believe that it is less than 20 meters. Some other upshot might lead to a different belief, but, as Nozick says with the Jesse James case, that is irrelevant. If, on the other hand, we were to individuate methods more generally, we would get the wrong result. Such a method might be *basing belief on whatever I see when I look at the distance between the ship's mark and the waterline.* If the mark were 20.1 meters above the waterline, S might judge that it is less than 20 meters because her margin for error in making such judgments is greater than 0.1 meters. S's belief would violate the variation condition, but intuitively she knows. In short, the variation condition seems to call for something like Nozick's preferred individuation of methods, whereas adherence seems to demand a more coarse-grained individuation.[6]

Perhaps there would be nothing wrong with individuating methods for variation and adherence differently, but any such suggestion is bound to seem ad hoc. Without a clear means of individuating methods consistently for adherence and variation, one that gets the cases right, perhaps it is best to abandon adherence and to focus on variation. Such a course is warranted

---

[6] Luper-Foy (1987) notices that Nozick's method-indexed conditionals founder on one-sided methods – methods that are suited only to believing that *p*. For example, if the grandson were ill, the grandmother would not use her actual method (say, judging by rosy cheeks and healthy glow) to form a belief about his health, and so the antecedent of the variation condition couldn't be satisfied. It might be thought that, by taking this point into account and reconstruing how methods figure into Nozick's conditionals, we could avoid the problem I've just been rehearsing. For example, suppose that adherence should read: "If *p* were true, then S would believe that *p* via M." But this would undermine Nozick's diagnosis of the Jesse James case, for there are lots of close worlds where *p* is true but S does not believe that *p*, via M – worlds where the mask does not slip.

anyway, because adherence is not at all a widely held condition on knowledge, and because, as we have seen, the core sensitivity notion involves a discrimination requirement, which is captured only by variation. Let us then focus our attention on the variation condition (hereafter "sensitivity"). In the next section, we will investigate criticisms of sensitivity (variation) as a necessary condition on knowledge.[7]

7.4 Core Objections to Sensitivity

As you might imagine, there are numerous counterexamples to sensitivity, as there are to just about every proposed condition on knowing (other than true belief). There are, however, three particularly persistent problems worthy of discussion.

The first problem is that sensitivity appears impossible to satisfy for any belief that one has a true belief. Jonathan Vogel (2000) presents the case for the prosecution. Assume that I know that Omar has new shoes. Surely, in some such cases, not only do I know, but I also know that I have a true belief. Take the proposition *I have a true belief that Omar has new shoes*. The problem, says Vogel, is that no such higher-order belief is ever sensitive. If I believe that I have a true belief, then I believe that it is not the case that I believe falsely. Now, if that belief were false, it would be the case that I believe falsely (that Omar has new shoes). In the closest world where my higher-order belief is false, I would still have the belief that Omar has new shoes, and would of course believe that I do not have a false belief. My higher-order belief violates sensitivity.

The point is perfectly general, having nothing in particular to do with Omar's shoes. Here is a schematic presentation:

Suppose that S knows that p.
   S believes that it is not the case that she has a false belief that p:

(1) $B(not\text{-}(B(p) \& not\text{-}p))$

In the closest worlds where this higher-order belief is false,

(2) $not\text{-}not(B(p) \& not\text{-}p)$

---

[7] If we abandon adherence, how do we diagnose lack of knowledge of believed necessary truths? One way might be to construe such cases as violating variation by allowing for false counterfactuals with necessarily false antecedents. (See note 3: "If 51 were prime, Jones would believe that it is not prime.") Or one might consider replacing adherence with a process reliablilist condition (Becker 2007). It's worth mentioning that Robert Shope (1984) also noticed Nozick's inconsistent application of his conditionals to tough cases –as sometimes holding the method constant, and sometimes not.

or, more simply,

(2*) B(p) & not-p.

Thus, in the closest worlds where the higher-order belief is false, S believes that p, and because she believes that p (is true), she believes that it is not the case that her belief that p is false. More succinctly, then, in the closest worlds where the higher-order belief content in (1) is false, (2*) is true, and S holds the higher-order belief (1) anyway.

One reply to this (Becker 2006) is to ask whether Vogel has accurately formulated the relevant higher-order belief. Saying that S believes that she has a true belief is an alternative to saying that S believes that she does not have a false belief. If, for example, my belief that I have a true belief were false, and assuming I do know that Omar has new shoes, then, in the closest worlds where it's false that I have a true belief, perhaps I do not believe that Omar has new shoes, and thus do not believe that I have a true belief, which satisfies sensitivity. Here is the alternative schematic presentation:

Suppose that S knows that p.
  S believes that she has a true belief:

(1') B(B(p) & p)

In the closest worlds where this higher-order belief is false,

(2') not-(B(p) & p)

which is equivalent to

(2'*) not-B(p) ∨ not-p.

In the closest worlds where S's higher-order belief is false, either she does not believe that p – in which case, she won't believe that she has a true belief that p – or p is false (or both). In the closest worlds where p is false, again S does not believe that p (on the assumption that S knows, hence has a sensitive belief, that p). It appears that in either case S might well not believe that p, and thus not believe that she has a true belief that p: in either case, her higher-order belief might be sensitive.

Further support for characterizing higher-order belief in this alternative way is that it implies that one actually has the first-order belief – S believes that she has a true belief – whereas Vogel's characterization – S believes that it is not the case that S has a false belief – does not imply that S has the first-order belief.

While I rather like this idea, it's nonetheless open to Vogel to say that it is a problem that, according to sensitivity, one can never know that one does not have a false belief. It is left to the reader to determine how damaging this is.

The second persistent criticism of sensitivity is that it cannot account for inductive knowledge. Again, Jonathan Vogel originally registered this complaint, this time in a chapter in Luper-Foy's (1987) volume of essays devoted to Nozick's epistemology.[8] But let us begin with a similar criticism presented by Ernest Sosa, because with regard to the present objection, I think, some examples are more compelling than others, and it's instructive to compare them. Sosa imagines dropping a bag of garbage down a trash chute in a high-rise condo (1999b, p. 145): "Presumably, I know my bag will soon be in the basement." The problem is that if it were false that the trash bag will soon be in the basement, I would believe it anyway. Here, however, there may be a little wriggle-room for the sensitivity advocate. One could say that I know only that it is very likely that the bag will drop to the basement. Suppose that there are close worlds where the bag does not drop – for example, where a clog occurs or a rivet snags the bag. It's not implausible to think, then, that I do not know the bag will drop, even if it's very likely that the bag will drop. It's not implausible to say that I know only that it's likely that the bag will drop. This latter belief could easily be sensitive, for if it were not even likely that the bag will drop (for example, in the closest world where the chute often doesn't work properly) then I might well not believe that it is likely that it will drop.

Compare the trash chute case with Vogel's (2007) "Heartbreaker" example. Suppose that there are sixty golfers in a golf tournament at a course with a hole that is short but very difficult. It seems that I know that not all sixty golfers will make a hole-in-one on the Heartbreaker. But if it were false, I would still believe it. One reason why this example is different from the trash chute case is that it's very difficult to deny that one can know that not all sixty golfers will ace the Heartbreaker. And this might be because, intuitively, worlds where all sixty golfers make a hole-in-one are more distant than those where the trash bag gets snagged on a rivet – they are far enough away to seem irrelevant to whether one knows. (Do I really have to know what would be the case in a very strange circumstance, in order to know what happens in the actual world?) So,

---

[8] In my view, Luper-Foy's book (1987) remains one of the best critical investigations of Nozick's epistemology, treating just about every aspect and implication of the position.

if there is a clearly damaging objection based on sensitivity's inability to handle inductive knowledge, it will involve cases where the closest worlds where *p* is false are far from actuality.

Nozick himself anticipated worries about whether sensitivity is consistent with inductive knowledge, and he takes up an example that is more like the Heartbreaker, less like the trash chute. Suppose the question is that of whether I know that the sun will come up tomorrow. At first glance, one might think that if it were false that the sun will come up tomorrow, I would still believe it. But Nozick replies (1981, p. 222): "If the sun were not going to rise tomorrow, would we have seen that coming, would that alteration in the earth's rotation have been presaged in the facts available to us today and before?" The suggestion is that, if it were false that the sun will come up, then some large cosmic event would have had to occur, and I would presumably know about that and therefore not believe that the sun will rise.

We saw earlier how Nozick had to deviate from Lewis's theory of subjunctive conditionals on pain of rendering his adherence condition ineffective. Here we see Nozick flouting Lewis's (1979) widely accepted view that the correct reading of counterfactual conditionals (at least those used to explicate causation) does not permit "backtracking" – does not permit, that is, interpreting counterfactuals as Nozick does in the sunrise example: if *p* were false, then something else would have had to occur. Simple examples favor Lewis's view. Consider this counterfactual: if I were an NFL lineman, I would be crushed on the first play of the game. That seems true. (I weigh roughly 150 pounds.) But if one were to say, "No, Kelly, if you were an NFL lineman, you would have to have grown much larger and stronger, and in that case you'd be fine," it would typically strike us as a misunderstanding of the counterfactual conditional. Lewis allows that there will be contexts where such a backtracking argument is acceptable (perhaps where one's interlocutor asks incredulously, "How could you be a 150 pound NFL lineman?"), but goes on to argue that his favored "standard" resolution of the vagueness of counterfactuals is preferable. In general, when assessing a counterfactual, one must hold the past constant. The lineman example illustrates, I think, both possibilities – that normally one must hold the past constant, and that we can, in some contexts, accept backtracking.

Perhaps Nozick could rightly use the wedge offered by Lewis's suggestion, that in some contexts backtrackers are acceptable, to defend his response to the sunrise example; and perhaps he's right to say, in that example, that if the sun were not to rise tomorrow, we would all know about it. Even though I think Lewis is right that this is a somewhat strained interpretation of the counterfactual, I suggest that for the sake of argument we allow Nozick's response to stand.[9] The problem is that it doesn't generalize very well – given the earlier point that inductive knowledge in the actual world does not seem hostage to whether one would know what would be the case in a far-off world.

To see this, let us apply Nozick's suggestion to the Heartbreaker example in an attempt to support the implication of his view that one's belief (that not all sixty golfers will ace the Heartbreaker) is sensitive. If it were false that not all sixty golfers will ace the Heartbreaker, then something very strange would need to have occurred. Maybe in that world the hole has been enlarged to 100 feet in diameter. Maybe each golf ball was fitted with a homing mechanism that tracks precisely to the hole. Would I know these things? Suppose that I do, and that therefore my belief is sensitive: if it were false that not all sixty golfers will ace the hole, I would not believe it, because there would have been a strange occurrence of which I would have known. The obvious concern is that, in order to know that not all sixty golfers will ace the hole, I do *not* need know about whatever strange occurrence would have happened if they did all shoot holes-in-one. Knowing what I know about golf, I already know that not all players will ace the hole. My suggestion is that the Heartbreaker case is more difficult than the trash chute case for sensitivity advocates, because worlds where all of the golfers ace the hole are significantly more distant than worlds where the trash bag does not drop. I don't need to know about what would happen in such distant worlds if I am to know inductively in the actual world that not all of the golfers will make a hole-in-one.

So, we see that the strength of the objection (to sensitivity) from inductive knowledge depends partly on the example chosen to illustrate the objection. Worse still, the stronger the intuition that one has inductive knowledge, the more the appeal to backtrackers – which is used to reconcile sensitivity and inductive knowledge – seems irrelevant. Those intuitions are stronger when the falsity of the known proposition occurs only in distant possible worlds; but then whether I would know about the counterfactual events that would have led to the falsity of the inductively known proposition has no bearing on whether I actually know that proposition. This is a large and unresolved – perhaps

---

[9] Troy Cross (2010) suggests that the sensitivity theorist might help herself to backtracking counterfactuals. See, especially, note 10 therein.

unresolvable – problem for sensitivity. (Note that it does not afflict Goldman's version of sensitivity, which is meant to apply only to perceptual knowledge.)

The third and final major criticism of sensitivity that I want to address is that it implies violations of the principle that knowledge is closed under known entailment. The closure principle says that if S knows that p and S knows that p entails q, then S knows that q. The principle, as stated, is clearly false. What if S doesn't draw the relevant inference? What if S forgets or loses her knowledge that p? There have been many attempts to formulate the closure principle to make it watertight, but let us simply refer to the state-of-the-art formulation:[10]

Closure. If S knows that $p_1, \ldots, p_n$, and S competently deduces q from $p_1, \ldots, p_n$, and S thereby believes that q, then S knows that q.

Whatever one's preferred understanding of closure, the present concern is that, on the sensitivity account, one can know that p, know that p entails q, and yet be in no position whatsoever to know that q, even if one competently deduces q while retaining knowledge of the closure premises. For example, S knows that she has hands (for if it were false that she has them, then she would not believe that she does). S knows that if she has hands, then she is not just a BIV. But S is in no position to know that she is not a BIV; for if it were false, she would have experiences similar to her ordinary ones and would believe that she is not a BIV.[11]

Dretske's early "Epistemic Operators" paper (1970) argues valiantly that knowledge is not closed under known entailment, but suffice it to say that not many are persuaded. The common rebuttal is that deduction is the securest way to extend one's knowledge to new propositions, whereas closure

---

[10] See Becker (2016) for general discussion of knowledge-closure principles. Compare Williamson (2000, p. 117) and Hawthorne (2004, p. 82).

[11] Sherri Roush (2006) presents a version of sensitivity that deviates from Nozick's in at least two important ways. First, she cashes Nozick's conditionals in terms of conditional probabilities rather than subjunctives. Second, and more importantly in the present context, she adds a recursion clause in an attempt to save closure, such that, roughly, S knows that p if either S tracks p or S knows both that q and that q implies p and believes that p on that basis. The latter move is, of course, open to any sensitivity theorist. For an alternative approach, see Murphy and Black (2012). They suggest that one's ordinary belief-forming methods are different from a BIV's, and so that if it were false that I am not a BIV then I would not believe it using my actual method, making my actual belief that I'm not a BIV sensitive (2012, p. 41). It's just that most sensitivity theorists, especially Nozick, deem to be a datum our *lack* of knowledge of antiskeptical hypotheses that are entailed by known ordinary propositions.

violations imply that in some cases one cannot extend one's knowledge through competent deduction.

Nozick is rather insouciant about this. His approach is to craft a theory of knowledge that handles as many tough cases as he can dream up, and to accept the implications as fallout. He thinks (and I, for one, think he's right) that we can't know we're not BIVs, but we can know many ordinary empirical truths. So be it. I am inclined to accept closure violations as the least worst option in accommodating the Nozickean facts just stated, but closure-deniers are typically met with derision. Following Nozick's lead, one could attempt to revise and constrain closure, formulating it in such a way as to be valid for most cases but not when one merely presupposes the truth of the proposition entailed by what one knows. (See, for example, Baumann [2012].) But even the most sophisticated proposal implies violations of the original closure principle, and that is the relevant unacceptable implication for most philosophers.[12]

The three core objections to sensitivity that I've chosen to discuss are now well known. I have suggested that, on an improved gloss of the higher-order belief at issue in Vogel's criticism, one can easily show how sensitivity is compatible with higher-order knowledge, while acknowledging that, on Vogel's reading of higher-order belief, there is a problem for sensitivity. Then the remaining questions asked whether Vogel's reading is appropriate, and, even if it is not the favored gloss on higher-order belief, whether it remains a deep concern for sensitivity theorists that their view implies that one cannot know that one does not have a false belief. With regard to the issue of closure, the sensitivity theorist might just bite the bullet and accept closure violations, citing the fairly strong intuition that one cannot know the denials of some skeptical hypotheses. Of course, this is a very unpopular position. But even if sensitivity theorists are content with their responses to the higher-order belief and closure criticisms, there is little hope for them to reconcile sensitivity with very plausible cases of inductive knowledge, such as the Heartbreaker.

7.5 Concluding Remark

But why end on a down-note? The central purpose of this chapter was to explore the sensitivity response to the Gettier problem. We've seen that

---

[12] As this chapter is dedicated to sensitivity, I will mention only in this footnote that the problem of closure is partly responsible for the recently widely popular safety principle, which ostensibly upholds closure. Concerns about closure violations are also a driving force for contextualists (see, especially, DeRose 1995, in which sensitivity plays an important role, but is not construed as a necessary condition for knowledge) and subject-sensitive invariantists (Hawthorne 2004).

sensitivity does a fine job showing why one does not know in Gettier cases, including fake barns. The point of rehearsing objections to sensitivity was to explore the theory more fully after having described its successes, and it certainly succeeds with Gettier cases.

Well, why not end on a down-note? There are some Gettier-like cases for which even sensitivity cannot account, cases where the link between one's belief and the fact that makes it true is not accidental but is intuitively insufficient for knowing. Imagine a hologram of a vase that is indistinguishable from a real vase and is caused to appear when and only when there is a vase directly behind where it would be. In the closest worlds where there's no vase, there is no vase hologram, and where there is a vase, there is a hologram. Imagine that the hologram obstructs any view of the vase, so that I can see only the hologram. If it were false that there is a vase before me, I would not believe it. If it were true, I would. My belief that there is a vase satisfies sensitivity (variation *and* adherence), but I don't know that there is a vase. The general lesson, perhaps, is that a counterfactual analysis of any interesting philosophical notion – for example, *knowledge, disposition, cause* – implies counterexamples where the counterfactuals are "rigged" to be satisfied without satisfaction of the analyzed notion (or vice versa).[13] And yet one could be forgiven for thinking that "S does not know that *p* if she would believe that *p* even if it were false" rings true.

---

[13] Lars Bo Gundersen (2012) argues that the standard objections to counterfactual analyses of dispositions are the same as those to counterfactual analyses of knowledge, and he proceeds to argue that the former objections are merely apparent, hence so are the latter.

8   The Gettier Problem and Intellectual Virtue

8.1 Introduction

Virtue epistemology begins with the idea that there are intellectual virtues as well as moral and practical virtues. Likewise, virtue epistemology exploits a distinction between virtuous intellectual agency and nonvirtuous (or even vicious) intellectual agency. Virtuous intellectual agency is thinking that is appropriately competent, responsible, and otherwise excellent. Nonvirtuous intellectual agency is thinking that falls short of relevant excellence in significant ways. We need not think of intellectual virtues and agency as strictly analogous to moral or practical virtues and agency, and many virtue epistemologists do not. The more important idea is that thinking or cognizing is an activity of agents, and that it can, like other such activities, be done well or poorly. Virtue epistemology uses virtue-theoretic resources to understand such evaluations and to understand epistemic value and epistemic goods, more broadly.[1]

One important kind of epistemic good is *knowledge,* and in recent years the following virtue-theoretic account of knowledge has gained several adherents:

In cases of knowledge, S has a true belief *because* S believes from intellectual virtue.

Alternatively:

In cases of knowledge, S's believing the truth is *attributable* to S's virtuous intellectual agency.

I would like to thank Stephen Hetherington and Sahar Joakim for useful comments on an earlier draft.
[1] Virtue epistemology goes back at least to Aristotle, but the approach was introduced into the contemporary literature by Ernest Sosa, most famously in Sosa (1980). Virtue epistemology is elaborated and given more systematic defense by Sosa (1991; 2007a), Kvanvig (1992), Zagzebski (1996), Greco (2010), and Pritchard (2010).

We will see below that there are many variations on this theme, but even this very general idea has substantial theoretical power. Most importantly for present purposes, it suggests the following diagnosis of Gettier cases:

> In Gettier cases, S believes the truth, and S's belief is formed in an intellectually virtuous manner, but S does not believe the truth *because* S's belief is formed in an intellectually virtuous manner. Rather, S believes the truth because of mere coincidence, or dumb luck, or something else.

Alternatively:

> In Gettier cases, S believes the truth, and S's belief is formed in an intellectually virtuous manner, but S's believing the truth is not *attributable* or *creditable* to S's belief's being formed in an intellectually virtuous manner. Rather, it is attributable to mere coincidence, or dumb luck, or something else.[2]

The remainder of this chapter explores the history and prospects of this approach to understanding knowledge and Gettier cases. Section 8.2 further explicates the general approach, notes its main theoretical advantages, and details some variations on the general theme. This section also introduces an important distinction between two kinds of Gettier case. Sections 8.3 through 8.5 explore an important objection to the virtue-theoretic account of knowledge and its attendant diagnosis of Gettier cases – that such an account cannot explain testimonial knowledge, and cannot accommodate social-epistemic dependence, more broadly. We will see that the most important versions of the objection take the form of a dilemma: Depending on how a virtue-theoretic account understands the idea that knowledge is *attributable to S's virtuous agency*, either (a) it cannot adequately account for testimonial knowledge, or (b) it cannot adequately diagnose Gettier cases. Sections 8.6 and 8.7 explore various responses to the objection. We will see that attempts to

---

[2] As early as 1988, Sosa writes that, in cases of knowledge, one's belief must "non-accidentally reflect the truth of P through the exercise of . . . a virtue" (1988, p. 184). Likewise, consider Sosa (2003, p. 174):

> We prefer truth whose presence is the work of our intellect, truth that derives from our own virtuous performance. We do not want just truth that is given to us by happenstance, or by some alien agency, where we are given a belief that hits the mark of truth *not* through our own performance, not through any accomplishment creditable to us.

However, Sosa does not suggest in these papers that the idea can be used to address Gettier cases. The strategy for addressing Gettier cases was first suggested in Greco (1994) and then elaborated in Greco (2003). The strategy is also elaborated at length in Sosa (2007a) and Greco (2010). Zagzebski (1996) pursues a similar strategy, citing Greco (1994). See also Riggs (2002; 2007; 2009) and Pritchard (2010).

preserve or improve upon the virtue-theoretic approach to Gettier cases have in turn driven thinking about the nature and scope of intellectual virtue and intellectually virtuous agency.

8.2 Intellectual Virtue, Knowledge, and Gettier Cases: The Big Idea.

Suppose that a skilled archer shoots skillfully at a target, but that an unexpected gust of wind blows the arrow off its intended course. Suppose also that a second gust of wind blows the arrow back on course, resulting in a bulls-eye. We might say that the shot was a success, and that the shot was skillfully performed, but that the shot was not a success *because* it was skillfully performed. Rather, the shot's success was lucky, being attributable to the lucky coincidence of two gusts of wind.[3]

The structure of this case provides a model for the virtue-theoretic approach to knowledge and Gettier cases. In cases of knowledge, S's belief is true *because* it is virtuously (or skillfully, or competently) formed. Put differently, S's believing the truth is *attributable* to S's forming her belief in an intellectually virtuous way. In Gettier cases, S's belief is true and virtuously formed, but it is not true *because* it is virtuously formed; S's believing the truth is *not attributable* to S's forming her belief in an intellectually virtuous way.

Consider two standard Gettier cases, which serve to illustrate the point.

Office Worker. On the basis of excellent reasons, S believes that her co-worker Mr. Nogot owns a Ford: Nogot testifies that he owns a Ford, and this is confirmed by S's own relevant observations. From this, S infers that someone in her office owns a Ford. As it turns out, S's evidence is misleading and Nogot does not in fact own a Ford. However, another person in S's office, Mr. Havit, does own a Ford, although S has no reason for believing this.[4]

In **Office Worker**, S reasons well, and S arrives at a true belief in doing so, but S does not arrive at this true belief *because* she reasons well. Rather, it is just a coincidence that someone else in her office owns a Ford.

Sheep in the Field. A man with excellent vision looks out over a field and sees what he takes to be a sheep. Due to an unusual trick of light,

---

[3] The example is from Sosa (2007a).   [4] The example is from Lehrer (1965).

however, what he takes to be a sheep is actually a dog. Nevertheless, unsuspected by the man, there is a sheep in another part of the field.[5]

In **Sheep in the Field**, the man employs reliable perception, and he forms a true belief in doing so, but his forming a true belief is not *attributable* to his employing reliable perception. Rather, it is just good luck that there is a sheep in another part of the field, out of his view.

Another way that we can describe our cases is in terms of *achievement*, as opposed to *mere lucky success*. In general, achievements are attributable to the skillful performance of an agent, and can be contrasted with mere lucky successes. The virtue-theoretic approach that we are considering understands knowledge as a kind of achievement, and Gettier cases as a kind of mere lucky success.[6]

One significant advantage of this approach is that it explains epistemic normativity, or at least the kind of normativity involved in knowledge attributions, in familiar terms. That is, in any domain of human activity that allows for success and failure, we make a distinction between success due to competent agency and success due to luck. The present account exploits this familiar distinction to understand *epistemic normativity* as simply a species of *performance normativity*, more generally.[7]

A second major advantage of the account is that it yields an elegant explanation of the *value* of knowledge. In general, we think that successful agency is both intrinsically and finally valuable. That is, we think that *achievements* are both valuable "in themselves" and "for their own sake." Since the present account understands knowledge as a kind of achievement, it can explain the value of knowledge as an instance of this more general kind of value. In the same way, the account elegantly explains the *superior* value of knowledge over mere true belief, in terms of the superior value of achievements over mere lucky successes.[8]

We now have in view the central themes and advantages of the virtue-theoretic approach to knowledge and Gettier cases. Before considering objections to the view, it will be helpful to first consider some variations, and then a complication.

In respect of variations, a number of ideas have been put forward, regarding how to understand the attribution relation, or the idea that success is attributable (or not) to virtuous agency. Greco (2003) understands the relation in

---

[5] Adapted from Chisholm (1977, p. 105).   [6] Cf. Greco (2010, esp. ch. 5).
[7] Cf. Greco (2010, esp. ch. 1) and Sosa (2015).   [8] Cf. Greco (2003; 2010, esp. ch. 6).

causal-explanatory terms: to say that S's true belief that p is attributable to S's virtuous agency is to say that S's virtuous agency explains why S has a true belief regarding whether p, as opposed to a false belief, or no belief at all. Sosa (2007a; 2011) and Turri (2011) understand the relation in terms of dispositions and their characteristic manifestations. On their accounts, intellectual virtues are dispositions to manifest some intellectual success. Accordingly, to say that S believes the truth because S believes virtuously is to say that S's true belief manifests S's intellectual virtue. A third option for understanding the attribution relation is to take it simply as theoretically primitive in one's account.[9] The idea is that we already have a good grip on the relation across various phenomena and domains. For example, we smoothly attribute various kinds of success and failure to human agency in everyday life, and smoothly withhold such attributions as well. Likewise, we competently use the related "because"-language in nearly every domain of activity. This suggests that we have more than a good grip on the relation, and that it is available for use in theorizing, without further analysis. That thought is even more compelling, in that virtue epistemology under-stands knowledge and epistemic normativity as species of achievement and performance normativity in general, and the relevant attribution relation and "because"-language are already familiar and indispensable in that broader explanatory context.

Finally, it is necessary to add a complication to the foregoing account: namely, virtue epistemologists typically divide Gettier cases into two different categories, and give them different treatment. First, consider the structure of standard Gettier cases such as **Sheep in the Field** and **Office Worker**. These may be characterized in terms of what Duncan Pritchard (2010, p. 36) calls "intervening luck": in some plausible sense, "the kind of epistemic luck in play in standard Gettier-style cases 'intervenes' between the agent and the fact, albeit in such a way that the agent's belief is true nonetheless." Greco (2010; 2012) suggests that standard Gettier cases involve something akin to a deviant causal chain. In such cases, S exercises virtuous intellectual agency, and such agency is part of a total causal structure that ends in S's having a true belief, but the route from virtuous agency to true belief is somehow unusual or irregular, as in a deviant causal chain.

Second, consider the structure of the famous barn façade case, which is typically considered to be a Gettier case as well:

---

[9] For example, see Zagzebski (1996). Riggs (2009) might be interpreted in this way as well.

Barn Façade. Henry is driving in the countryside and sees a barn ahead in clear view. On this basis, he believes that the object ahead is a barn. Unknown to Henry, however, the area is dotted with barn façades that are indistinguishable from real barns when viewed from the road. However, Henry happens to be looking at the one real barn in the area.[10]

This kind of case can be characterized in terms of what Pritchard calls "environmental luck." In this kind of case, the agent "really does get to see the barn and forms a true belief on this basis – although the epistemically inhospitable nature of the environment ensures that his belief is nevertheless only true as a matter of luck" (Pritchard 2010, p. 36). Moreover, there is nothing deviant in the causal route from visual perception to true belief – nothing "intervenes" between believer and world.

Here is another case with a similar structure:

Room Full of Liars. S is a normally competent epistemic agent, but is situated in a room full of unusually good liars. At one point he talks to Nancy, the only sincere and reliable person around. Nancy reliably tells S that *p*, and he believes her.[11]

Following the literature, let's continue to call the first kind of case "standard Gettier cases" and the second kind of case "barn façade cases." The present point is that virtue epistemologists sometimes treat the two kinds of case in different ways. For example, Greco (2003) applies the central strategy described above to standard Gettier cases, but takes a different approach to barn façade cases.[12] Specifically, Greco understands abilities as relative to environments. Thus, one might have an ability to perceptually discriminate objects in a normal environment under normal conditions, but lack such an ability relative to a different environment, where perceptual illusions abound. Likewise, in **Barn Façade** S does not have a perceptual ability to discriminate barns from nonbarns, relative to the environment that she is in. And therefore, in such cases S's true belief is not explained by ability.[13] Sosa (2007a, p. 96n1) likewise treats barn façade cases differently from standard cases. Sosa's picture is somewhat complicated and will be considered in more detail later. But the main idea is that, in **Barn Façade**, S's belief that there is a barn does manifest S's perceptual ability, and so

[10] The example is from Goldman (1976). Goldman attributes the example to Carl Ginet.
[11] Adapted from Goldberg (2007)
[12] See also Greco (2009; 2010; 2012), Millar (2010), and Littlejohn (2014).
[13] For similar approaches, see Millar (2010) and Littlejohn (2014).

S does know in this case. Another aspect of Sosa's view explains why this result seems counterintuitive: namely, although S enjoys a kind of basic or animal knowledge in barn façade cases, she lacks a more robust and reflective kind of knowledge.

8.3 The Objection from Testimonial Knowledge

An early objection to the virtue-theoretic account of knowledge is that it does poorly with testimonial knowledge (Lackey 2007; 2009; Goldberg 2007; Pritchard 2010). More broadly, the view seems to conceive knowledge in an overly individualistic way, thereby failing to accommodate the various ways that knowledge can involve dependence on others (Goldberg 2010; 2011; Kallestrup and Pritchard 2012). Jennifer Lackey (2007, p. 352) pushes the objection with the case of Morris, which has now become standard in the literature:

> Having just arrived at the train station in Chicago, Morris wishes to obtain directions to the Sears Tower. He looks around, approaches the first adult passer-by that he sees, and asks how to get to his desired destination. The passer-by, who happens to be a Chicago resident who knows the city extraordinarily well, provides Morris with impeccable directions to the Sears Tower by telling him that it is located two blocks east of the train station. Morris unhesitatingly forms the corresponding true belief.

Lackey comments on the case as follows (2007, p. 352):

> it is nearly universally accepted that a situation such as Morris's not only can but often does result in testimonial knowledge. Yet ... what explains why Morris got things right has nearly nothing of epistemic interest to do with him and nearly everything of epistemic interest to do with the passer-by. In particular, it is the passer-by's experience with and knowledge of the city of Chicago that explains why Morris ended up with a true belief rather than a false belief.

Lackey concludes that it is therefore implausible to attribute success to Morris in the case (2007, p. 352):

> Thus, though it is plausible to say that Morris acquired knowledge from the passer-by, there seems to be no substantive sense in which Morris deserves credit for holding the true belief that he does. Still further, if a subject can have knowledge without deserving credit for holding the true belief ... then

obviously deserving credit for holding such a true belief can be neither what renders knowledge different from, nor more valuable than, a belief that is true merely by luck.

An initial reaction by virtue epistemologists was that Lackey is incorrect that "what explains why Morris got things right has nearly nothing of epistemic interest to do with him and nearly everything of epistemic interest to do with the passer-by." In particular, various social-cognitive abilities are in play on Morris's part, and these play an important role in Morris's arriving at true belief in the case (Greco 2007; Sosa 2007a; Riggs 2009; McMyler 2012). Putting the point differently, even if Morris's virtuous intellectual agency is not the most important factor in his arriving at true belief, it is nevertheless one important factor, and this is enough for attributing the intellectual success in question to Morris's agency. Even in testimonial knowledge, then, we can say that knowledge is an achievement of the knower's.

A second early response, related to the first, was that success can be achieved in cooperation with others. Moreover, cooperation with others does not undermine credit to the individual. As Greco (2007, p. 65) puts it, "credit for success, gained in cooperation with others, is not swamped by the able performance of others. It's not even swamped by the outstanding performance of others. So long as one's own efforts and abilities are appropriately involved, one deserves credit for the success in question."

The point is illustrated by considering a pass play in some sports.

Soccer. Playing in a soccer game, Ted receives a brilliant, almost impossible pass, and then scores an easy goal as a result. In the case we are imagining, it is the athletic abilities of the passer that stand out. The pass was brilliant, its reception easy.

Nevertheless, Greco argues, Ted deserves credit for the goal. That is not to say that the passer does not deserve credit for the goal, or even that he does not deserve more credit than Ted. It is to say, however, that Ted was involved in the right sort of way so as to also get credit (2007, pp. 64–5).[14]

Later, we will return to the idea that testimonial knowledge involves a virtuous cooperation between speaker and hearer, and is in that sense

---

[14] The idea that testimonial knowledge involves virtuous or competent teamwork is found in Greco (2007; 2010; 2012; 2013; forthcoming a), Sosa (2007a; 2011; 2015), Green (2012; 2014), and McMyler (2012). The idea that testimonial knowledge is a kind of team achievement is developed extensively in Green (2017) and Greco (forthcoming b).

a cooperative or shared achievement. For now, we turn to a more powerful statement of the present objection.

8.4 The Objection Sharpened: Lackey's Dilemma

So, why not say that Morris gains a true belief *both* in virtue of his own efforts (his own exercise of relevant abilities) *and* in virtue of the speaker's efforts? Lackey argues that this would ruin the earlier diagnosis of Gettier cases. For in Gettier cases, too, S gains a true belief *partly* in virtue of her own efforts. Accordingly, Lackey's objection (2007; 2009) is best understood as a dilemma: either (a) we understand the attribution of success to S's own agency strongly, in which case we cannot account for standard cases of testimonial knowledge, or (b) we understand the attribution of success to S's own agency weakly, in which case we lose our diagnosis of Gettier cases.

In Section 8.2, we saw that one way to understand the attribution of success is in causal-explanatory terms: to say that S's true belief that *p* is attributable to S's virtuous agency is to say that S's virtuous agency *explains why* S has a true belief regarding whether *p* (as opposed to a false belief, or no belief at all). In Gettier cases, we said, something else explains why S has a true belief. Here is Lackey's dilemma (2009), adapted to these terms:

(1) The present account claims that, in cases of knowledge, S's competent agency explains why S has a true belief, rather than a false belief or no belief at all. But this is ambiguous between (a) S's competent agency being *the most important part* of the explanation of why S has a true belief, and (b) S's competent agency being *one important part* of the explanation of why S has a true belief.
(2) If (a), then the account rules incorrectly on cases of testimonial knowledge, since, in at least many such cases, S's competent agency is *not* the most important part of the explanation of why S has a true belief.
(3) If (b), then the account does not give an adequate diagnosis of Gettier cases, since, in many of those cases, S's competent agency *is* an important part of the explanation for S's true belief.

Therefore,

(4) Either way, the account fails to rule correctly on some cases.

We might try to go through the horns of the dilemma here, claiming that in cases of knowledge S's contribution is "important enough" in an explanation why S's believes the truth, whereas in Gettier cases S's contribution is not "important enough." One problem with this reply is that it relies too much on intuitions regarding where and why a hearer's contribution is "important enough." Without a more principled treatment of cases, the account remains to that extent uninformative. On the other hand, virtue epistemologists might insist that we have a very good grip on the concepts and language involved in positing causal explanations, and that this conceptual-linguistic competence figures in an informative and principled adjudication of cases. A similar move can be made for other variations of the view, including ones that take the attribution relation as metaphysical or as a primitive. Be that as it may, a number of virtue epistemologists have tried to respond to the dilemma in ways that rely less on intuitions about cases. We will take a closer look at those in Sections 8.6 and 8.7.

8.5 The Objection Sharpened: Pritchard's Dilemma

We saw that a persistent objection to the virtue-theoretic account of knowledge and Gettier cases is that the account faces a dilemma. Such an account must either (a) understand the attribution of success to the knower's virtuous agency strongly, in which case it cannot account for cases of testimonial knowledge, or (b) understand the attribution of success to the knower's virtuous agency weakly, in which case it loses its account of Gettier cases. A different version of this dilemma is developed by Pritchard (2010).[15]

Whereas Lackey's dilemma focuses on standard Gettier cases, Pritchard's dilemma focuses on barn façade cases and the problem of environmental luck. Pritchard (2010, p. 25) directs his objection at "robust virtue epistemology" – that is, theories that try to analyze knowledge exclusively in virtue-theoretic terms. Robust virtue epistemology is also characterized as accepting the thesis that "knowledge is a type of achievement" – or the "KA" thesis, for short (2010, p. 29).

Pritchard's objection begins by considering the following nonepistemic case, which also involves environmental luck (Pritchard 2010, p. 35):

Force-field. Archie . . . selects a target at random, skillfully fires at this target, and successfully hits it . . . Suppose, however, that unbeknownst to Archie there is a force-field around each of the other targets such that, had he aimed at one of these, he would have missed it. It is thus a matter of luck

---

[15] See Goldberg (2010) and Vaesen (2011) for analogous worries about virtue epistemology and extended cognition. For responses, see Greco (2012), Green (2012), and Kelp (2013).

that he is successful, in the sense that he could very easily have not been successful.

Pritchard comments on **Force-field** as follows (2010, p. 35):

> It is thus a matter of luck that [Archie] is successful, in the sense that he could very easily have not been successful. Notice, however, that luck of this sort does not seem to undermine the thesis that Archie's success is a genuine achievement ... It is, after all, *because of* his skill that he is successful, even though he could very easily have not been successful in the case. That is, his success in the case is still primarily creditable to his archery abilities, even despite the luck involved in that success.

As Pritchard notes, this verdict is problematic for the virtue-theoretic approach, insofar as **Force-field** and **Barn Façade** share a similar structure (2010, pp. 35–6):

> consider the case of "Barney," which is structurally analogous to the "Archie" case. Barney forms a true belief that there is a barn in front of him by using his cognitive abilities ... Accordingly, we would naturally say that Barney's cognitive success is because of his cognitive ability, and so we would, therefore, attribute a cognitive achievement to Barney ... The twist in the tail, however, is that, unbeknownst to Barney, he is in fact in "barn façade county" where all the other apparent barns are fakes. Intuitively, he does not have knowledge in the case because it is simply a matter of luck that his belief is true.

Pritchard argues that if we attribute an achievement to Archie, then we must attribute an achievement to Barney as well, and this shows that there can be achievement without knowledge. Specifically, Pritchard argues, the cases show that achievement is consistent with environmental luck, even if knowledge is not.

Next, Pritchard argues that there can be knowledge without achievement. Here he invokes a version of Lackey's **Chicago Visitor** case. Even if testifiers in the environment are generally reliable, and even if a hearer (in Pritchard's case, "Jenny") has a general ability to discriminate good testifiers from bad, true belief in the case is not primarily attributable to Jenny's abilities. Rather, Pritchard argues (2010, p. 41), Jenny's true belief about the location of the Sear's Tower is "because of the cognitive abilities of the informant who knows this proposition on a non-testimonial basis."

Once again, Pritchard (2010, p. 43) puts the argument in terms of a dilemma:

> whatever the defender of the KA thesis says in response to the "Jenny" example, remember that she must also simultaneously deal with the other problem outlined above – concerning the apparent possibility of cognitive achievements which are not cases of knowledge. Indeed, notice that it is significant that these two problems pull robust virtue epistemologists who endorse the KA thesis in different directions. Whereas the "Jenny" case puts pressure on them to *weaken* their robust virtue epistemology and thus allow cases of knowledge which this view would ordinarily exclude, the "Barney" case, in contrast, puts pressure on them to *strengthen* their account in order to explain why merely exhibiting a cognitive achievement does not suffice for knowledge. That is why, when these two problems are expressed in tandem, they pose such a tricky difficulty for the robust virtue epistemologist.

Finally, Kallestrup and Pritchard (2012) offer what might be thought of as a "social" barn façade case – that is, a Gettier case that trades on environmental luck, but in this case on social environmental luck.[16]

First, consider a competent epistemic agent H, who is embedded in an epistemic community GOOD. In GOOD, most testifiers are reliable. Moreover, most conversations are monitored and policed so as to ensure reliable testimonial exchanges. Kallestrup and Pritchard assume that H can acquire knowledge in GOOD by accepting a reliable speaker's testimony. Now consider a second case (2012, pp. 94–5):

> [I]magine that H is unwittingly transported to epistemic community BAD which also mostly contains reliable testifiers. The difference is that while the testimonial processes in GOOD are monitored and policed in a knowledge-enabling manner, the corresponding processes in BAD are monitored and policed in a knowledge-precluding manner vis-à-vis H. That is to say, third party epistemic agents reliably ensure that H is mostly exposed to unreliable speakers. H has no inkling of the systematic way in which reliable informants are being screened-off from the testimonial processes. Most of the competent-looking speakers with which H comes into contact are in actual fact not trustworthy. Now assume that H forms a true belief on the basis of hearing reliable speaker S's testimony. The proposition in question is again an ordinary one which nearly every reliable speaker will know.

---

[16] **Room Full of Liars**, above, is also a "social barn façade case."

Kallestrup and Pritchard argue (2012, p. 96) that H lacks knowledge in BAD and that robust virtue epistemology cannot account for this. In particular, they argue, H exercises the same ability in BAD that she does in GOOD. The difference in knowledge in the two cases, then, cannot be explained in virtue-theoretic terms.

8.6 Some Virtue-Theoretic Responses to the Two Dilemmas

A number of philosophers have responded to the objections reviewed in Sections 8.3 through 5. Here we consider some of those.

Sosa (2007a) responds to Lackey's dilemma by emphasizing a distinction between (a) S's virtuous agency's explaining the *existence* of S's belief, and (b) S's virtuous agency's explaining the *truth* of S's belief. Commenting on **Office Worker**, Sosa (2007a, p. 96) writes, "The reasoning by way of Nogot does of course explain why the believer has that belief, but it does not in the slightest help explain its *correctness*. In order to do so, it would have to be a factor that, either singly or in combination with other factors, accounts for how the belief is true rather than false." On the contrary, Sosa argues (2007a, p. 97), in cases of testimonial knowledge, the exercise of the hearer's abilities does partially explain why she has a true belief rather than a false belief.

As we noted earlier, Sosa (2007a) takes a different approach with barn façade cases. In **Barn Façade**, Sosa argues, Henry's belief manifests his perceptual ability and therefore Henry does know that there is a barn. However, Sosa exploits a distinction between animal knowledge and reflective knowledge to explain why, in barn façade cases, S's belief still falls short in a way. Specifically, animal knowledge requires only that S's true belief that *p* manifests her intellectual virtue, and S's belief does so in barn façade cases. Reflective knowledge, however, requires that S have a knowledgeable perspective on her knowledge that *p*, including knowledge that conditions are normal, that her belief is reliably formed, etc. This is what S lacks in barn façade cases. Henry does not know that perceptual conditions are normal, for example, since he could easily be in deceptive conditions, looking at a mere barn façade, and he would not know the difference (2007a, pp. 22–43, 96–7, esp. n1).[17]

Turri (2011) follows the general strategy described in Section 8.2 for handling standard Gettier cases. In Turri's terms, in cases of knowledge, S's

---

[17] See also Sosa (2011, pp. 92–5; 2015, pp. 79–80).

true belief manifests S's cognitive competence. In standard Gettier cases, S exercises cognitive competence and S arrives at a true belief, but S's having a true belief does not manifest S's cognitive competence. Turri offers several different approaches to barn façade cases, including denying the intuition that S lacks knowledge in such cases. A second proposal accepts the intuition that S lacks knowledge in barn façade cases, and strengthens the conditions required for knowledge so as to accommodate this. Turri's earlier proposal was that, in cases of knowledge, the *truth* of S's belief manifests competence. An alternative proposal is that the *safety* of S's belief manifests competence (2011, p. 9):

> A third response involves a natural but more radical change to my theory of knowledge … A performance is ample just in case its *safety* manifests the agent's competence. A performance is safe just in case it (i) succeeds and (ii) would not easily have failed. We then propose that knowledge is ample belief. Henry's belief is adept but not ample, so he doesn't know.

As Turri points out, a belief's safety manifests competence only if its truth manifests competence, and so his alternative proposal handles standard Gettier cases in the same way as the earlier proposal does.

We noted that one strategy from Turri (2011) is to deny that S lacks knowledge in barn façade cases. Turri (2017b) presents empirical evidence that nonphilosophers regularly attribute knowledge in such cases. Turri (2015d; 2016d) also presents evidence that nonphilosophers regularly attribute knowledge in the absence of reliability, thereby contradicting the standard virtue-theoretic idea that knowledge requires the manifestation of reliable intellectual virtues or abilities. Turri (2015b; 2016d) puts forward an account that accommodates these results. Specifically, he proposes (2015b) that knowledge is true belief manifesting *cognitive ability*, where ability (unlike virtue) is defined in a way that does not imply reliability:

> I accept the following metaphysical thesis about powers in general:
> If a person possesses an ability/power to produce an outcome (of a certain type and in conditions of a certain sort), then when he exercises that ability/power (in those conditions), he produces the relevant outcome at a rate exceeding chance.
> The basic intuition here is that abilities and powers are understood relative to a baseline of chance … You are *enabled* or *empowered* to produce an outcome to the extent that your prospect of producing it

exceeds chance ... Empowerment is the antithesis of helplessness. To the extent that you are enabled or empowered, your helplessness diminishes.

The resulting view allows that subjects in barn façade cases have knowledge, and diagnoses standard Gettier cases as including a true belief that does *not* manifest cognitive ability.

Greco (2012) argues that we can avoid Lackey's dilemma by understanding explanatory salience in qualitative rather than quantitative terms. More specifically, we may say that a success is attributable to S's own competent agency just in case S's agency contributes to that success *in the right way*, where "in the right way" means "in a way that would regularly serve relevant purposes." This idea is already illustrated in the soccer case that we saw in Section 8.4. In the soccer case, it is the excellent performance of the passer that stands out. The pass was brilliant, its reception easy. In quantitative terms (the amount of effort, the degree of skill), Ted's contribution is minor. Nevertheless, Ted was involved *in the right way* so as to attribute success to him. We can compare this case with another: Ted is playing in a soccer game but not paying attention. Never seeing the ball, a brilliant pass bounces off his head and into the goal. Here we do not attribute success to Ted's competent agency. He was involved in a way, *but not in the right way.*

A pressing question for this approach, of course, is how are we to understand "in the right way"? Various accounts have been proposed here, some of which we will see below. Greco (2012) argues that "in the right way" may be understood *pragmatically*, as "in a way that would regularly serve relevant purposes." In the soccer cases, relevant purposes are those that are intrinsic to playing the game of soccer. In the first case, Ted's agency is involved in a way that would regularly serve soccer-relevant purposes, whereas in the second case Ted's agency is not so involved.

What counts as "relevant purposes" when we make knowledge attributions? Greco (2012) follows Edward Craig (1990) and others, who have argued that an important purpose of knowledge attributions is to govern the flow of quality information. For example, Craig has argued that the concept of knowledge functions to flag good informants, and a number of philosophers have argued that knowledge is the norm of action and/or practical reasoning. In cases of knowledge, then, S's competent intellectual agency contributes to her having a true belief "in the right way" just in case S's agency contributes in a way that would regularly serve relevant informational needs, i.e. informational needs associated with some relevant domain of action and practical reasoning (Greco 2012, esp. sec. 5).

With these resources in hand, Greco (2012) resolves Lackey's dilemma as follows. In cases of testimonial knowledge, but not in Gettier cases, S's competent agency contributes to S's believing the truth *in the right way* – i.e. in a way that would regularly serve relevant informational needs. In standard Gettier cases, that does not happen: S ends up with a true belief, and S's competent agency even contributes to that, but not in a way that can be regularly exploited, not in a way that is dependable or reliable. It is in this respect that standard Gettier cases involve something akin to a deviant causal chain – S's competent performance is part of the total causal structure leading up to S's having a true belief, but the route from performance to truth is deviant.

We saw that Greco (2003; 2009; 2010; 2012), Millar (2010), and Littlejohn (2014) all address barn façade cases by arguing that abilities are relative to environments.[18] The idea is that, in **Barn Façade**, Henry lacks the perceptual ability to discriminate barns from non-barns, and therefore he does not *manifest* such an ability. More generally, barn façade cases feature environments that are "epistemically hostile": that is, environments that are inconsistent with a knowledge-producing ability. An important point in defense of this view is that abilities *in general* are defined only relative to relevant conditions or environments, and so it is not an ad hoc maneuver to understand cognitive abilities in this way.[19]

Pritchard (2010) and Kallestrup and Pritchard (2011) agree that abilities should be understood as relative to an environment, but argue that the relevant environment here is the one that the agent is typically or normally in. On the Pritchard–Kallestrup account of abilities, then, the subject in a barn façade case retains her relevant perceptual ability (2011, p. 343; see also Pritchard 2010, pp. 37ff.):

> Abilities are relative only to the stable environment in which whoever has them is typically located. That is to say, abilities are possessed as long as they are reliably manifested in ... the normal circumstances in which abilities are acquired through learning and sustained through practice. Temporary abnormal environments cannot rob a subject of an ability that she otherwise reliably manifests in the normal run of things.

Pritchard (2010) argues that, since subjects in barn façade cases retain their relevant ability, such cases demonstrate that success from ability is not in itself

---

sufficient for knowledge. Rather, he argues, the conditions for knowledge must include an independent anti-luck condition. In particular, he argues for an independent safety condition on knowledge (2010, p. 54):

> What is essential to anti-luck virtue epistemology is thus that it incorporates two conditions on knowledge, an anti-luck condition and an ability condition, and that it accords each condition equal weight . . . Let us describe any true belief that couldn't have easily been false as *safe*. The general structure of the account of knowledge offered by an anti-luck virtue epistemology can now be described as follows: knowledge is safe belief that arises out of the reliable cognitive traits that make up one's cognitive character, such that one's cognitive success is to a significant degree [but need not be primarily] creditable to one's cognitive character.

By weakening the ability condition and adding an independent safety condition, Pritchard argues (2010, pp. 55–6), his anti-luck virtue epistemology resolves the dilemmas posed above. In particular, a range of testimony cases continue to amount to knowledge, insofar as such beliefs are both safe and, to a significant degree, creditable to hearer ability. Barn façade cases, on the other hand, are now ruled as not knowledge because not safe.

Finally, a number of virtue epistemologist have approached Gettier cases by taking a "knowledge-first" approach (Millar 2010; Miracchi 2015; Kelp forthcoming).[20] The general strategy here is to give up the project of providing a traditional analysis of knowledge, i.e. a set of necessary and sufficient conditions that explain what knowledge is, and that define its extension. Gettier cases find their home in that traditional project, insofar as they are designed to show that some set of proposed conditions are not in fact sufficient for knowledge. A knowledge-first approach, on the other hand, does not pretend to adjudicate all such cases. Neither does it, more generally, try to describe the conditions for knowledge in nonepistemic terms. Rather, the explanatory power of the account comes elsewhere.

A virtue-theoretic version of the knowledge-first approach continues to think of knowledge as a kind of achievement, and continues to understand achievement as success from ability. But now the idea is that knowledge is success from *knowledge*-producing ability. For example, perceptual knowledge can be understood as true belief grounded in a "perceptual-recognitional ability," where such abilities are understood as abilities to know perceptually

---

[20] For an extensive defense of "knowledge-first" epistemology, see Williamson (2000).

(Millar 2010). Clearly, such an approach is not as informative as would be one that successfully spells out the conditions for knowledge in nonepistemic terms. However, the approach continues to give a partial account of the nature of knowledge (knowledge is a kind of success from ability, or success grounded in virtuous agency), and it preserves much of the standard virtue-theoretic approach to explaining the value of knowledge.[21]

8.7 Testimonial Knowledge, Knowledge Transmission, and Joint Agency

Greco (2012) suggests that in cases of knowledge, but not in Gettier cases, S's intellectually virtuous agency is involved "in the right way" in producing S's true belief. Likewise, the hearer's virtuous agency is involved in the right way in cases of testimonial knowledge. A related theme is that, in cases of testimonial knowledge, the speaker and hearer are involved in a kind of competent teamwork.[22]

Sosa (2007a, pp. 93–4) develops the teamwork idea in terms of socially seated virtue. The idea is that, in cases of testimonial knowledge, the hearer's true belief is attributable to a social competence that involves both speaker and hearer, and perhaps others as well: "If the correctness of [testimonial belief] is attributable to a competence, it is not one seated in the believer individually. Any such competence would have to be socially seated instead, in some broader social unit." Testimonial knowledge, then, can be understood in terms of social achievements, more generally (Sosa 2007a, pp. 94–5):

> Something similar holds good of socially seated competence generally. A quarterback may throw a touchdown pass, for example, thus exercising a competence. But this individual competence is only one part of a broader competence, seated in the whole offensive team, that more fully explains the successful touchdown pass, the apt performance of that quarterback ... If we think of animal knowledge as apt belief, and of belief as apt when correctly attributable to a competence, then they fullest credit often belongs to a group, even a motely group. Seated in the group collectively is a competence whose complex exercise leads through testimonial links to the correctness of one's present belief.[23]

---

[21] Knowledge-first virtue epistemologists claim other explanatory advantages of their approach as well. See, for example, Williamson (2000) and Millar (2010).

[22] See Greco (2007; 2010; 2012; 2013; forthcoming), Sosa (2007a; 2011; 2014; 2015), Green (2012; 2014; 2017), and McMyler (2012).

[23] For criticism of Sosa's proposal, see Lackey (2009) and Kallestrup and Pritchard (2012).

Greco (forthcoming a; forthcoming b) develops the teamwork idea by exploiting the notion of *joint agency* from action theory. First, Greco makes a distinction between (a) the generation of knowledge, understood as competent information-acquisition, and (b) the transmission of knowledge, understood as competent information-distribution. The central idea is that competent information-distribution is best understood as a kind of joint achievement, involving the virtuous joint agency of speaker and hearer cooperating together. Importantly, not all testimonial exchanges, and not even all testimonial knowledge, involve the kind of purposeful cooperation that characterizes joint agency. The idea, rather, is that *some* testimonial exchanges can be characterized in this way, and it is these that constitute the important social phenomenon of knowledge transmission.

The account defended in Greco (forthcoming a; forthcoming b) implies that there are two ways of coming to know. In cases of knowledge generation, S comes to know in the way described by traditional virtue-theoretic accounts: i.e. S forms a true belief attributable to her own virtuous intellectual agency. In this sense, generated knowledge constitutes an individual achievement by the knower. In cases of knowledge transmission, S comes to know by mean of virtuous cooperation with a knowledgeable speaker. In this sense, transmitted knowledge constitutes a joint achievement grounded in virtuous joint agency.

8.8 Conclusion

A virtue-theoretic approach to knowledge and Gettier cases is initially plausible, but faces objections from various directions. Most notably, a persistent criticism has been that the approach cannot preserve its diagnosis of Gettier cases while at the same time accommodating the kind of social dependence that is characteristic of testimonial knowledge. Virtue epistemologists have defended various responses, and in doing so have developed the approach in significant ways. In particular, thinking about Gettier cases has inspired substantive positions regarding the nature and scope of intellectual virtue and intellectually virtuous agency.

9   Knowledge and Wisdom

Ernest Sosa

9.1 Introduction

We begin modestly by focusing on the wisdom of wise *conduct*. The wisdom
of a whole life lived wisely will stay beyond our horizon, as will that of a state
wisely ordered. Wisdom as a power or faculty can of course be present though
not manifest in wise conduct. But we first focus more narrowly on the latter,
on the wisdom of the conduct. We thus target issues of performance
normativity.

   The following aims to generalize from Gettier phenomena in epistemology.
How should we understand the failure of Gettiered beliefs to constitute
knowledge? Suppose, as is increasingly plausible, that the key to understanding such phenomena is the concept of a certain kind of luck. On this approach,
such beliefs fall short of knowledge because they attain correctness only
through a distinctive sort of luck, in ways that remove credit or reduce it
excessively. A question then arises about that long and complex literature.
Suppose that Gettier phenomena are special cases of something much more
general. Are they cases where a belief succeeds (in attaining correctness) but
just by a sort of luck that removes *epistemic* credit or reduces it excessively?
And are there cases of such epistemic luck that differ importantly from the
cases featured in the early Gettier literature? In what follows, it will be argued
that we should answer these questions in the affirmative. And we will thus be
led to a sort of *epistemic wisdom*.

9.2 What Are Performances?

Performance can be taken in a broad sense, so that even hearts and thermo-
stats are allowed to perform well or poorly. Performances need not be
episodic. They can be extended and stable, as with those live statues that
one sees at tourist sites. We here restrict ourselves to performances with an
aim, however, leaving it open whether performances could ever be aimless.

Our focus will be on human aimings, on endeavors, or endeavorings. One endeavors to attain an objective O by doing something or other in particular, by A1-ing. One does A1 *in the endeavor* to attain one's objective O. One succeeds in this endeavor when one does attain O by A1-ing. Multiple such nestings are then possible: thus, one might in turn A1 by A2-ing in the endeavor that one A1; and so on.

9.3 Performance Normativity

9.3.1 The Sweet Smell

Here is a sample thesis of performance normativity, one that will later be of use:

Success is better. It is better to succeed than to fail. Success through competence, moreover, is better yet, and more creditable than success by luck.

This seems undeniable, in *some* sense, but what does it mean? Take someone who is bent on murder. Is it better that he succeed than that he fail?

A distinction is pertinent here, between having *more final value* and being *preferable to the agent*:

Success has more final value. The success of an agent's endeavor would always be to that extent better intrinsically, or finally, or for its own sake, than its failure, other things being equal (*pro tanto*, *prima facie*). Success through competence, moreover, would be even better, and more to the credit of the agent.

Success is preferable to the agent. An agent would always prefer the success of his endeavor to its failure, and properly so, other things being equal. And he would prefer even more his success through competence.[1] (Of course, the preferability here is relative or hypothetical; in this sense even a vicious assassin properly prefers that he succeed.)

These are inequivalent. The second seems more plausible, if it says only the likes of this: that any agent endeavoring to attain a certain objective would

---

[1] Arguably, in aiming to attain O one automatically aims to *bring about* one's attainment of O, to be *responsible* for doing so, which in turn would seem to require that, in so doing, one manifest one's competence to do so. But if one aims to manifest competence in attaining O, then it is not just the attaining of O that one automatically prefers; it is also one's manifesting competence in doing so. Tucked into the near-trivial claim that it is better to succeed than to fail would be the further claim that it is better to manifest competence in succeeding than to succeed unaided by competence.

prefer success to failure, other things being equal; and, moreover, that this preference is appropriate, again other things being equal. But is this not to say that his success *is* better than his failure (provided that other things *are* equal)? How could the agent's preference be appropriate if what he prefers is not in fact better?

Well, compare the claim that, for any given thing that one believes, one would properly believe that, in so believing, one believes something true. This might just mean that *if* one believes that p, then, relative to that, one would properly believe that one's belief that p is a true belief. In other words, given that one believes p, if one is asked whether one's belief is true, one has three choices: assent, denial, and suspension, of which assent seems clearly the required choice, at least from the perspective constituted in part by one's belief that p.

Similarly, if I aim to attain O, and endeavor accordingly, then if asked whether I prefer that my endeavor succeed, I have those same three choices, and assent seems again the required choice. After all, in so aiming I already evince a preference for attaining O, and the preference that one succeed in that aim seems indissolubly linked with one's already-present preference for attaining O. Aiming to attain O does not cohere well with a preference for failure in that endeavor. Similarly, one's aiming to attain O coheres ill with suspension of preference on whether one succeeds or fails.

That success has greater final value is not obvious, but may well be true. After all, when the pursuit is trivial, the value could be minuscule, easily overridden. Nevertheless, there is some sense, or some way, in which knowledge *would* be obviously better than mere true belief. The obviousness of this fact clashes, however, with how uncertain it is that knowledge would always have final value. When the knowledge is utterly trivial, at least, I am uncertain that it does nonetheless have some objective, final, or intrinsic value. Nevertheless, if it *does* have such value, then of course we would like our account of performance normativity to accommodate this fact.

In any case, the thesis that success is always better from the agent's point of view, other things being equal, seems far more plausible. Accordingly, it would be good for our account to accommodate this more plausible thesis, *and its degree of plausibility*. Whether it does so or not remains to be seen.

We shall return in due course to these theses of performance normativity.

9.3.2 The AAA Structure

On its way straight to the target, Diana's arrow is diverted by a gust so that, without further intervention, it would miss. A second gust puts the arrow back on course, however, and Diana kills her prey. Here the shot is accurate: it does hit the target. And it is adroit: it manifests archery skill, and would have hit the target had there been no wind. Although the shot manifests skill, however, its accuracy does not. The shot is not accurate *because* adroit; it hits its target, rather, because of that second gust.

Diana's skill does contribute causally to the accuracy of her shot. Her skill is manifest in the arrow's direction and speed as it leaves her bow. Because of this direction and speed, along with the two intervening gusts, the shot hits its prey. The skill contributes to the initial direction and speed, therefore, which along with the two gusts accounts for the shot's accuracy, to its hitting the target. Nevertheless, we do not attribute the shot's success to Diana's skill. Although the shot's success owes causally to her skill, the first gust precludes its manifesting that skill.

A shot is apt only if its success *manifests* the relevant competence (the skill, or adroitness) of the archer.

What is such manifestation? What is it indeed more generally for a *disposition* to be manifest in behavior by its host? As we have seen, the answer cannot be just that the disposition is causally relevant to that behavior. Although we cannot here take up that question, fortunately no answer is required for proper use of the concept in an account of aptness and knowledge. Such use of *manifestation* no more requires a prior account than does the similar use of *truth* or of *belief*.[2]

9.3.3 Aptness Versus Meta-Aptness

In the archery hunt, judgment is required for properly picking one's shot. Diana might manifest superb archery skill in hitting a fast-moving distant prey in twilight while the wind blows. The shot is a great shot in that way. But it may still be a shot that she should never have attempted. It may show terrible judgment. So, a shot can be apt, a success manifesting great skill, without being "meta-apt," because it derives from poor target selection and

---

[2] The concept of truth invoked in epistemology is that of the truth of a belief. The concepts of truth and of belief have provoked much thought and dispute. What it is to manifest a power or a disposition is no easier to explicate. Still, we may be able to throw light on matters epistemic by use of such concepts, while leaving it to others – metaphysicians, philosophers of mind, philosophical logicians – to help us to understand all three in due course.

risk management. It might be a low-percentage shot, way too low, a poor use of her relevant resources – of her available time, energy, materials, attention, etc.

Contrariwise, a shot can be meta-apt without being apt. Thus, Diana might know it to be a high-percentage shot at a worthy target (a standing deer well within her range at cloudless noon in a windless open field), and yet her shot might still miss. It might be the rare occasion when her great archery skill fails her.

Finally, a shot is *fully* apt when its aptness manifests its meta-aptness, when it succeeds aptly under the guidance of the agent's relevant good judgment.

9.3.4 Risk and Meta-Aptness

What determines whether the hunting-relevant risk is appropriate? This turns out to be surprisingly obscure. For one thing, *is* there such a thing as *hunting-relevant* appropriateness of risk, something distinguishable from appropriateness of risk in general? Well, *are* there ends inherent to the domain of hunting, relative to which we can assess the risk of failure, even when we bracket other ends or interests of the hunter, or of his tribe, or of humanity at large?

Surely there are such ends, however imprecise. Hunters can assess a hunt, *as a hunt*, regardless of whether it promotes bonding among the hunting party, or influences a rich uncle to make one his heir, or is successful in any other such hunt-external respect. The content of a hunt's success will of course vary in different ways – with respect to whether it was a hunt for ducks, for example, or for a rare Himalayan tiger. We can understand what makes a particular hunt successful, as a hunt, moreover, even when we passionately condemn the whole activity as an immoral abomination.[3]

9.3.5 Gettier Problems

In a Gettier scenario, one's belief is correct only through a kind of accident. Extending that notion, we can take Diana's shot to be Gettiered by the compensating gusts. It is then accurate and adroit without being apt. But it

---

[3] Protecting epistemology from pragmatic encroachment requires ends proper to epistemology, relative to which assessments can be properly epistemic. A tennis shot is not a better tennis shot (in the sense of being better as a tennis shot) because it impresses a friend up in the stands, or because it kills the deadly insect otherwise likely to bite someone. Similarly, a belief is not better epistemically because of its pragmatic advantages. There are, of course, more subtle forms of pragmatic encroachment, which require more careful treatment. Protection here will still require ends distinctively proper to a domain of epistemology, no doubt, analogous to the ends distinctively proper to other domains of human endeavor, such as tennis or hunting.

is also Gettiered if a nearby wind could too easily divert her shot on the way to the target, *and* Diana is negligent or reckless not to take that into account. In that case she no longer knows that she retains her competence. Therefore, the accuracy of her shot is not meta-apt, nor fully apt. Its success is hence, in a different way, due to luck. Both Gettier scenarios deprive Diana's shot of full aptness. One scenario does so by depriving the shot of aptness. The other does so by depriving it not of aptness but of meta-aptness.

9.4 Wisdom

Where in such a structure is wisdom to be found? Unwisdom we have found already in Diana's ill-judged shot. Wisdom would be found toward the other end of that spectrum, that of fine judgment. When Diana assesses her competence and situation correctly, when she judges herself to be competent enough and well enough situated to make that shot worth taking (relative to the ends proper to the hunt), then her shot can manifest good judgment, and thereby wisdom. Of course, this wisdom is that proper to a huntress. That then is one place for wisdom within performance normativity, as a particular factor that helps to make a performance wise, one that is *hunt-specific*. And we shall find others in due course. Nevertheless, if the shot is pretentious, greedy, or defiant, if it breaks a solemn promise, it can also manifest poor judgment, and can be unwise *on the whole*.

We turn next from performance normativity in general to virtue epistemology more specifically.

9.5 Knowledge: Animal and Reflective

The tripartite AAA structure of an archery shot's normativity consists of its accuracy, its adroitness, and its aptness. Let us zoom in on the second of these.

Dictionaries generally define "competence" in a broad, primary sense in terms of power or ability, as in "the ability to do something well or effectively." In that sense, a thermostat can be competent as a thermostat. But this is ambiguous between, first, inner, constitutional competence, and, second, complete competence, which may require not only proper constitution but also proper situation.[4]

---

[4] We should distinguish true, narrow, *core* competence not only from the fuller competence that requires proper situation, but also from the fuller competence that requires the subject to be in good enough "shape." There is an innermost competence for driving a car that you do not lose even when drunk. The same of course goes for other competences.

Consider a thermostat in a display room. It might be a perfectly good thermostat, with the ability to control temperature, even if not then situated so as to be able to perform suitably or effectively in controlling the temperature of any space. It enjoys constitutional competence, as a thermostat, to control temperature, even though it lacks the full competence required to control any actual room's temperature. The latter would require that it be appropriately positioned relative to that room.

Consider performances generally, or at least those with an aim. We can now generalize from our thermostat example, distinguishing between two sorts of competence to attain success (defined as attaining the aim of the performance). This distinction gains plausibility when we juxtapose the case of the thermostat with other examples.

(a) It can be true to say of a working thermostat that it is competently able to control the temperature of a room even though in another sense it will be able to do so only once properly connected.

(b) An athlete in his prime has the ability, or the competence, to perform well, and in one sense retains that ability even when he is drugged, tied down, or in the dark.

(c) Someone can be said to be a good driver, and this can remain true even when he is hopelessly drunk. We thus distinguish his constitutional competence as a driver from the complete competence removed by his inebriation.

These examples prompt us to generalize from our distinction between *constitutional* ability or competence, and a competence or ability that is *complete*. The latter, complete competence, would include not only constitutional competence but also the agent's being properly situated and in adequate "shape," so that he *would* probably enough perform successfully if thus constituted, situated, and shaped.[5]

A first-order performance is *meta-apt* provided that the performer's concurrent judgment that it is (and would be) an apt performance is itself apt.

A first-order performance is *fully apt* provided that, in addition to being apt and meta-apt, its aptness derives from its meta-aptness. In order for a performance to be fully apt, its success must manifest a reliable enough first-order competence of the performer. It must do so, moreover, under the

---

[5] It is also required, however, that no more specific situation S', one that the subject is in, and one to which the performance should be sensitive, is such that her performances within S' would fall below the proper threshold of reliability.

guidance of that subject's second-order competence to assess when his relevant first-order competences would be apt.

Animal knowledge that *p* is truth-apt belief that *p*, belief that hits its mark of truth and in so doing manifests the believer's first-order epistemic competence. Knowing full well is having a fully apt belief – that is, a belief whose aptness derives from the believer's meta-aptness.[6]

9.6 Two Platonic Problems

The *Meno* poses the problem of how knowledge is distinctively valuable when compared with its corresponding true belief. Does knowledge of how to get to Larissa improve on true belief? How could it? Won't mere true belief get you there equally well? Such questions have puzzled some more recently as "the value problem."

A second Platonic problem is posed when the *Theaetetus* inquires into the nature of human knowledge. A contemporary variant of this problem long held center stage in epistemology as a form of "the Gettier problem."

We are now in a position to offer a solution for both problems: two solutions, in fact. This is because we can distinguish between two sorts of knowledge: animal knowledge and reflective knowledge.

Animal knowledge is apt belief. That is its analysis and its nature. Apt belief is better than the corresponding merely true belief that is not apt, moreover, which is a special case of the fact that apt performance is better than the corresponding merely successful performance. This ostensibly solves both Platonic problems for animal knowledge.

Reflective knowledge goes beyond animal knowledge in requiring not only the aptness of its constitutive belief, but also the believer's awareness of the aptness of that belief. Knowing full well requires in addition the full aptness of one's belief. Such fully apt belief is better than the corresponding merely true belief, moreover, this being a special case of the fact that fully apt performance is better than the corresponding performance that is successful, or even apt, without being meta-apt.

These solutions for the Platonic problems, both as regards animal knowledge and as regards reflective knowledge, are thus in line with our theses of performance normativity: that it is better to succeed than to fail, better to

---

[6] If Diana judges competently that she is completely competent to shoot at a given target, but decides by a coin toss whether to shoot, then her shot falls short of full aptness, even if it is both apt and meta-apt.

succeed aptly than merely to succeed, and better yet to succeed with full aptness.

Setting the problems of epistemology within our framework of performance normativity throws further light on the Gettier problem, which we can now see to have two quite different forms. When one deduces a truth from a justified falsehood, with no other access to that truth, one's belief is not knowledge, since it is not even apt. It does not qualify for so much as animal knowledge. Compare, however, the fake-barns case (see Goldman 1976). Seeing a barn 25 yards away at cloudless noon may call forth an apt belief that it is a barn, through ability to sort such objects based on their appearances. In fake-barn country one arguably still exercises that competence. But one no longer knows oneself to retain that competence, no longer knows oneself to be situated as required. Too easily now might one have gone wrong by trusting appearances. One's belief is apt but not meta-apt, and hence not fully apt: it qualifies as knowledge on the animal but not on the reflective level. Anyone powerfully enough attracted by the intuition that the fake-barns subject does not know might reasonably require for knowledge some level of meta-aptness, and of full aptness, some degree of reflective knowledge. All knowledge would thus be reflective to some degree. "Animal knowledge" might then be viewed as just metaphorical, as is presumably the attribution to a supermarket door of "knowledge" that someone is approaching.

In more recent work, however, I argue for an alternative virtue-epistemological solution that still gives a crucial place to fully apt performance. That further development also makes room for default assumptions within our competences generally, including the epistemic. These default assumptions correspond to background conditions for the exercise of a given competence, conditions that must hold and must be assumed competently to hold even when they need not be known to hold, nor need they even hold safely, in order to stand fast and support our relevant knowledge corpus. These have key features attributed by Wittgenstein (1969) to his "hinge propositions."

I now find compelling a conception of competences that allows their possessors to make such default assumptions in their proper exercise, as explained in the last chapter of my *Epistemology* (2017). More recently my *Epistemic Explanations* (forthcoming), I defend that approach. A key example is that of athletes in a night game, the quality of whose performance is not affected by the fact that the lights are nearly certain to fail. If the lights did fail, *that* would affect the quality of performance, but the mere *danger* that they will fail has no such effect, no matter how high the danger. Of course, the athletes implicitly assume that the lights will not fail. But in our imagined example the athletes make that assumption quite properly even when it is far from something they know. Nor is it even a safe assumption. Yet it is a proper default assumption, despite being so unsafe and not nearly known to be true. In order to sustain the quality of athletic performance on that field, that default assumption need only be *true* and *appropriate or competent*. Once the idea is extended to epistemology, it enables a compelling response to the skeptic's use of the fake-barns example. It also casts light on the appeal to "relevant alternatives" and on the place in epistemology of the "hinges" in Wittgenstein's (1969) *On Certainty*.

9.7 The Place of Wisdom in Epistemology

Consider the *aptness* of a second-order judgment concerning one's first-order aptness or competence. The aptness of such a meta-judgment must manifest meta-competence, the ability to form such judgments reliably. The subject must be able to know whether he has the relevant first-order *complete* competence. By being manifest in the success of the first-order performance, this first-order competence secures the aptness of that performance.

The competences or virtues constitutive of such meta-competence, those involved in relevant risk management, help to provide a kind of *wisdom*, one crucial for the reflective and rational attainment of first-order success. Such wisdom goes beyond mere meta-aptness and even beyond full aptness, and it comes in degrees.

Wisdom to the first degree requires competence to judge the risk attendant on one's first-order performances. And it involves also the discipline and control to proceed accordingly (at least as far as the subject's mind is concerned, including his character and will power). A first-order performance gains by being not only apt but also wise to that degree.[7]

In addition to the competences pertinent to a range of aimed performances, and to the primary virtues proper to a first degree of wisdom, there are also

---

[7] Alternatively, we might require more for even the lowest degree of wisdom. Such perceptiveness of risk, and such discipline and control, may be said to provide conditions necessary for wise action, but sufficient only for a kind of proto-wisdom. True wisdom in *action* (as opposed to mere forbearance) may plausibly be said to require more than that. Nevertheless, our perceptiveness, discipline, and control provide at least a first degree of wisdom.

secondary virtues. It helps to have good judgment, prospectively and con-currently, as to whether one's pertinent competence and situational condi-tions are likely to be present, and likely enough to deliver successful, apt performance. But it helps also to have the virtues required for *securing* and *sustaining* the relevant competence and situation. These secondary virtues still fall within the relevant domain.

Diana, for example, knows how to secure and sustain her full competence (constitutional and situational). She knows to avoid too much wine, knows how to position herself favorably for a shot at a prey, how to find the prey and to approach it with stealth, and so on. Diana has thereby important competences proper to a huntress. These competences are important even if they are virtues whose direct manifestation is *neither* the successful archery kill, *nor even* the assessment of how likely one is to succeed. They help to constitute rather a second degree of wisdom. One is the wiser as a hunter by exercising compe-tences that properly enhance one's competence and situation for successful hunting. And one's apt shots can manifest this second degree of wisdom, which goes beyond the competence to assess risk and act accordingly.

9.8 Three Dimensions of Virtue

Three such dimensions relevant to performance normativity can thus be explained as follows, all with respect to a given performance (such as taking a shot at a prey), where "manifestation" will be short for "direct manifestation."

Tertiary virtues are those whose manifestation (individually or jointly) aptly help to position one to perform aptly, by providing something required for apt performance: the constitutional competence, for example, or the situation or "shape" needed for its proper exercise.

Secondary virtues are those whose manifestation enables one to tell aptly (whether concurrently, retrospectively, or prospectively) that one is (or was, or will be) competent to perform aptly, that one enjoys the complete compe-tence whose manifestation would be the apt performance.

Primary virtues are those whose manifestation would be the success of one's performance, the success that attains its primary or basic aim.

9.9 Three Varieties of Credit

Here again we need distinctions. A dastardly deed earns moral *dis*credit by being *credited* causally to the performer as an apt performance, one that manifests his competence in attaining his abominable aim. Think of the hired assassin of a good political leader.

Of the several variations and aspects of that general theme, we are focusing on the sort of credit that pertains to a restricted domain: a particular sport, say, or a performance art. Assignment of credit to someone within a domain admits three varieties. The performance might be a particular shot, or a particular passage or cadenza, or it might spread over a whole match, or a whole concerto. Whatever its length, however complex, that performance is then evaluable by the standards proper to that domain. It can be more or less successful as a performance. And it might then manifest some level of mastery by the performer. At this primary level, we consider the credit proper to the apt performance, whose success manifests competence and not just luck.

Beyond that, we consider also the judgment of the performer in assessing his limits. He may or may not be competent to tackle that particular performance. This applies with special plausibility and frequency to the particular tennis shot – or the particular operatic cadenza or the particular ballet pas – and how it is attacked. What is justifiably judged by a virtuoso to be within his competence may be so judged *un*justifiably by a lesser pianist, who might *still* happen to be fully competent to attack that particular passage in the demanding way he chooses for that important concert. He *happens* to be competent, by luck, but shows poor judgment nonetheless. He overreaches in his choice of how to play under the circumstances, relative at least to what he can reasonably expect. He deserves primary credit, therefore, but not second-ary credit. His performance is apt, but it is not even meta-apt, much less fully apt. He earns credit of the first degree, but not of the second degree. Credit-reducing luck enters at that higher level.

Even a performer who has credit on both the first and second dimen-sions can fall short on a third dimension, for he may have done little of what he properly should have done in order to attain a fullness of competence well within his reach. While gifted with the genius to perform superbly at will, he is unwilling or unable to cultivate his talent or to enhance his situation or shape with respect to the target perfor-mance. He may even degrade his full competence with poorly timed drink. Despite deplorable negligence, he performs successfully, in a way that is both apt and meta-apt. He both manifests his great gift, and also knows that he is then completely competent to do so. Since it is successfully guided by this latter knowledge, moreover, his performance is also fully apt. Nevertheless, he has no credit on the third dimension. He neglects his talent and fails to enhance his shape and position so as to approach levels of performance attainable by him.[8]

All three dimensions of credit, and all three corresponding dimensions of virtue, can be domain-specific. They can all lie within the domain of tennis, say, or of the archery hunt, or within the domain of one of the performance arts, such as the ballet or the concert violin. Someone can be a wise dean, or baseball manager, even while his personal life is a wreck. Dimensions of credit, and of virtue, can be defined abstractly for performances generally, as I have tried to do. Instances would then be found in specific domains, such as particular sports, or performance arts, etc., and in their characteristic lines of endeavor.

9.10 Epistemology

That all applies in particular to *epistemic* domains, where the central performance is the judgment or belief. Here again three dimensions of virtue are distinguishable. First comes the primary: the competence that is manifest directly when one discerns the true from the false. Next comes the secondary: the competence to discern when one does enjoy full primary competence on a question in the domain, and to guide one's first-order performances accordingly. Third, finally, we have the tertiary: the competence to attain and sustain full competence on questions in that domain.

Corresponding to those three dimensions of virtue are three dimensions of credit. A discovery earns credit in the first dimension for the epistemic agent who attains that success aptly, manifesting his epistemic competence to discern the true from the false. In addition, it might earn him credit in the second dimension if he not only attains the truth aptly, but does so through a first degree of wisdom – does so in and through the knowledge of his complete competence on the question at issue. Finally, he might deserve credit in the third dimension, depending on how responsible he is for his attainment of that competence.

---

[8] It might seem arbitrary to stop with tertiary virtues. Is there not a potentially infinite hierarchy here? There is indeed, I agree, but higher-order levels soon lapse into insignificance through human limitations. Not only are they levels that humans rarely or never reach, it is also doubtful that they are levels we *ought* to reach, given relevant forms of the principle that *ought implies can*.

9.11 A Fourth Dimension of Virtue and Credit

Wise performance requires also competent target selection. An aimed performance is assessable by whether the performer selects wisely a target of appropriate value that he is likely enough to hit.

As we have seen, a first-order performance is *wise* to the extent that (a) it is fully apt, (b) the performer also judges aptly that it is likely to fit about as successful a pattern within that domain as any then open to him, or to the larger social unit as a member of which he then performs, and (c) the performance is based properly on judgments (a) and (b). It thus manifests good judgment, the hallmark of wisdom.

A performance also manifests wisdom to the extent that its success derives from the agent's ability to manage his relevant competence and to situate himself properly for such performance.

9.12 Guidance of Attention and Pursuit

In addition, there is, in a fourth dimension, the quaternary virtue pertinent to proper guidance of attention and aim. Not all matters are worthy of our attention; not all aims are worth pursuing. That varies with the practical circumstances, with the aptitudes, background, and situation of the agent. For a given agent, with his particular aptitudes, background, and situation, not all matters are worth attention or pursuit, either at a given moment or over longer spans. Quaternary virtue enables proper guidance of attention and of pursuit. Such guidance need not be consciously explicit or voluntary. Wisdom in this fourth dimension can operate subconsciously. It can subliminally guide attention and receptivity to certain domains and questions, so that over time the agent's picture of his nature and situation improves in its capacity to provide better control, prediction, and understanding. And this might lead in turn to changes in life situation, opening possibilities for new learning that in turn enhances the agent's picture.

Such interplay between virtue, picture, and situation exemplifies a more general phenomenon, admitting other forms of feedback. Proper guidance of attention, for example, depends on apt discerning of what deserves attention, which requires the exercise of primary virtues – indeed of those most primary, our basic cognitive faculties. And it can depend also on one's aptly discerning that what is deserving of attention does deserve such attention, that it is relevant, that it bears, and how it bears. The full array of virtues of various levels and the span of degrees of credit will pertain to such questions, as to any other.[9]

9.13 Epistemic Wisdom

The distinctions and ideas considered – concerning dimensions of virtue and credit – apply to aimed performances generally. Beliefs and judgments are cognitive performances most often aimed at truth (though often aimed at other things in addition, or instead). These are hence a special case of the structure laid out, in ways we have begun to explore.

Our distinctions apply to cognition as a special case. *Epistemology* is a broad discipline, with two main parts. *Theory of knowledge* mainly involves primary and secondary virtues, and the correlated degrees of credit. *Intellectual ethics* goes beyond that, and concerns also tertiary and quaternary virtues, and the degrees of credit that go with these dimensions. This is the main realm of epistemic wisdom.

---

[9] *Imagination* gives us questions relevant to our endeavor; *understanding* gives us considerations pro or con regarding how to answer those questions, with respective degrees of plausibility; and *judgment* enables us to weigh those considerations and to arrive at answers. When we endeavor to answer a question (correctly), good judgment will help us to succeed.

10   The Gettier Problem and the Program of Analysis

Patrick Rysiew

10.1 Introduction

A central task of mid-twentieth-century epistemology was "the analysis of knowledge," understood as an attempt to state necessary and sufficient conditions for the correct application of the concept of knowledge. Gettier's (1963) paper marked a crucial moment in this tradition's history: on the usual telling (see note 4), it awoke "justified true belief" (JTB) theorists from their dogmatic slumbers, showing the received analysis of knowledge to be inadequate. Just as importantly, for many, the subsequent (perceived) failure of attempts to solve the problem, with ever more complex analyses succumbing to counterexample, called into question the value and/or feasibility of analyzing knowledge. The Gettier problem has thus prompted important methodological questions about the epistemological enterprise. Most obviously, is it realistic to think that providing an analysis – or "definition" – of knowledge, understood along classical lines, is worthwhile, or that it's even possible? If, as many now seem to think, it is not, why not? And – just as pressing – what might we put in its place?

This chapter reviews some of the most prominent answers to such questions. Following a brief discussion of the aim and method of conceptual analysis in its classical form (Section 10.2), we will review (Section 10.3) some possible reasons for skepticism about either its prospects or value, at least as applied to knowledge. We will then turn (Section 10.4) to a consideration of some suggestions as to a plausible successor to the program of classical analysis, and some further potential reasons for pessimism about the latter. As we'll see, some of the latter proposals are quite revisionary, and others less so, with little consensus and much lively debate about the appropriate methodological moral to draw from the Gettier problem.

10.2 Classical Analysis

The search for classical analyses or "definitions," including of central episte-mic subjects, is at least as old as Plato; and, as has been said, "[t]he rules of the game have changed very little over the last 2500 years" (Stich 1992, p. 247). In the *Theaetetus*, for example, in response to Socrates' query "What is knowledge?," Theaetetus tries out a number of answers, with it being pointed out in each case that there are examples running counter to the proposal. Such counterinstances lead to refinements of the proposed definition, which is then subjected to further testing.

This familiar instance illustrates the typical goal and method of conceptual analysis, as classically conceived. The goal is to identify the features that all and only cases of the target have in common. That is, where knowledge is our *analysandum* or *definiendum* (the thing that we want to analyze or define), in attempting a *classical analysis* we are seeking a satisfactory completion of the following schema,

S knows that p if and only if ("iff") _____,

where what appears on the right-hand side (in the *analysans* or *definiens*) are conditions that are individually necessary (any instance of knowledge must satisfy them) and jointly sufficient (when all of them are satisfied, the subject knows). An analysis fails when it is found that there is a case of knowledge in which one or more of the supposedly necessary conditions does not obtain (in which case, the account is too "narrow" or "strong"), or an instance of the supposedly jointly sufficient conditions obtaining that we wouldn't count as knowledge (in which case, the account is too "broad" or "weak").

As to method, the type of investigation that we're considering is usually taken to be *a priori*, not empirical. This is connected with the fact that the investigation is in some good sense conceptual: we are trying to find necessary and sufficient conditions for the correct application of the *concept* of knowl-edge; otherwise put, we are trying to identify necessary and sufficient condi-tions for someone's knowing that p as determined solely by the concept in question, and the biconditional as a whole is meant to express a conceptually necessary truth. This, in turn, is why the method permits the use of merely hypothetical, and sometimes rather "far out," cases: the conditions that we are seeking are intended to be conceptually necessary and sufficient; and a merely possible case, however unrealistic, is enough to refute a claim of conceptual necessity or sufficiency (Lycan 2006, p. 151).

Part of the appeal of demanding a traditional analysis is that it promotes the ideals of clarity and rigor to which analytic philosophy aspires, and encourages the testing of theories. But we also want to increase our understanding of the relevant phenomena. Thus, it is because it is wholly uninformative that "S knows that p iff S knows that p," while perfectly clear and testable, and while expressing a necessary truth, is a poor analysis (Lehrer 1990, pp. 6–8; Neta 2002, p. 663; Ichikawa and Steup 2018, Intro.). (It is circular, of course, but its utter uninformativeness seems to be the more fundamental failing.) So, even the extensional equivalence of *analysandum* and *analysans* across possible worlds, and hence a necessarily true biconditional, doesn't suffice for a good analysis.[1] Different suggestions have been made about the kind of information that a good analysis provides – for example, an account of how ascriptions of knowledge are made true by other facts (Jackson 1998, pp. 28–30); an explanation of "how a person knows that her information is correct and how her knowledge claims are justified" (Lehrer 1990, p. 8); guidance in the application of epistemic terms to particular cases; or help in solving certain puzzles concerning knowledge (e.g. Neta 2002). But there is general consensus in prohibiting circularity, vagueness, ad hoc, or "merely negative" conditions, and the appeal to items more obscure or complex than what we're trying to understand (Zagzebski 1999, p. 98; Earl n.d., sec. 3c).

As others have noted (e.g. Williamson 2011; Ichikawa and Steup 2018), within this general framework an analysis is sometimes undertaken as a metaphysical investigation into the *nature* or *essence* of knowledge – as a search for a "real definition," in Locke's sense (Zagzebski 1999; cf. Earl n.d., sec. 1). At other times, it is undertaken as an analysis of concepts, breaking them down into their simpler components, or of the meanings or truth-conditions of certain sentence types. And often the matter is just left unclear.[2] ("Conceptual analysis" is itself syntactically ambiguous: it might refer to the object of analysis or to its distinctive means or mode.)

Insofar as philosophers in many cases fail to show much concern with distinguishing between the metaphysical and conceptual (or linguistic)

---

[1] Compare Kvanvig's (2017, p. 155) concern that the search for a "real definition" – for "whatever is fundamental to knowledge" – "doesn't fit well with the language of necessary and sufficient conditions," since not everything necessary for someone's having knowledge reveals something about its nature. Kvanvig sees Williamson (see Section 10.4) as stressing this distinction between logical and metaphysical relations.

[2] Such variability – and, at times, unclarity – is evident in and across the papers collected in Roth and Galis (1970), for example.

projects, one reason might be that these are assumed to be closely related. For instance, those who focus on concepts or words tend to think that theirs isn't a purely psychological or linguistic investigation – the relevant concept/word refers to something real, and an analysis of the former reveals something about the nature of the latter (e.g. MacIver 1958, p. 1; Weatherson 2003, pp. 16–17; Hacker 2013, p. 452; cf. Jenkins 2014, pp. 105–6). Likewise, those whose aims are expressly metaphysical may be seen as employing the concept, and "the method of possible cases" (Jackson 1998, p. 28), in an attempt to articulate truths about the natures of the relevant worldly epistemic phenomena (e.g. Ichikawa and Jarvis 2013, pp. 228–9; Hetherington 2016a, pp. 128–9); and, insofar as our judgments about whether someone knows are guided by our concepts, the former can reveal things about the latter (e.g. Goldman and Pust 1998; Jackson 1998, pp. 31–3). (As we'll see, such a happy complementarity has been challenged: some, such as Kornblith (2002, 2007), hold that we should investigate knowledge itself *rather than* our concepts, the latter being prone to error and of no real philosophical interest.)

Second, whether their stated target is metaphysical or conceptual (/linguistic), all parties within the tradition in question seem committed to providing analyses of the sort described above – that is, lawlike biconditional statements, subject to testing by a consideration of actual and merely possible cases (Shope 2004, p. 285; Ichikawa and Steup 2018, Intro.).[3] Thus, as Shope notes, an example showing that a statement of the form "S knows that p only if q" or "If r, then S knows that p" is false would challenge any analysis suggesting otherwise, regardless of the specific form that it took. "Perhaps," he says, "this is why so many philosophers leave ambiguous which of the above types of analyses they are pursuing" (2004, p. 286).

10.3 Analyzing Knowledge: Some Reasons for Skepticism?

As we've seen, while the specific aim and target of those attempting an "analysis of knowledge" have varied, the shared assumption is that an analysis should provide a noncircular and informative set of necessary and sufficient conditions that survives the method of possible cases. The definition of knowledge as justified true belief is "perhaps the most famous example" of a classical analysis in this vein (Beaney 2016, sec. 6). This, it is often said, is the conception of knowledge with which epistemologists since Plato had been

---

[3] Zagzebski calls this "the method of truth condition analysis" (1999, p. 96).

operating, often implicitly, and in many cases without using the language of "justification," until Gettier (1963) showed that there are situations in which the three conditions are satisfied though we balk at granting knowledge.[4]

In response, and just as Theaetetus had done in the face of Socrates' probing, epistemologists modified the account: adding a fourth condition (e.g. a defeasibility, no false lemmas, anti-luck, safety, or sensitivity requirement); less often, replacing the justification condition (causal views, some reliabilist accounts); or, more rarely still, advocating a view of justification whereby it entails truth, thereby undermining one of the assumptions made in setting up Gettier cases – namely, that one can be justified in believing a falsehood.

It's no part of the present chapter to scout and evaluate such proposals. For present purposes, the important point is that none has won universal, even general, acceptance: each has been confronted with further purported counterexamples and/or charges of vagueness, ad hocery, and so on. Of course, it could be that some such account is correct, or that the correct account has yet to be discovered. After all, while it's plausible that we each have practical mastery of the relevant concepts, there's no reason to think that a correct explicit analysis of them should therefore be easy to obtain or recognize. But the lack of any consensus, and perhaps even of any significant progress, after fifty-plus years of intense theorizing, has dampened many philosophers' enthusiasm for pursuing an analysis of knowledge that survives Gettier cases. Meanwhile, and for reasons beyond the just-noted recent history, a number of philosophers have questioned whether it is worthwhile or possible to provide a reasonably neat set of noncircular and informative necessary and sufficient conditions for knowing.

One reason for disaffection with the program of analysis concerns not its prospects but its value. For example, Mark Kaplan argues that "we simply have no use for a definition of propositional knowledge" (1985, p. 363). As an inquirer, having carefully weighed the evidence and formed the belief that p, there is nothing to be gained from asking, "But do I *know* that p?" The question does nothing to advance or clarify the proper conduct of inquiry. Hence, whatever the prospects for a solution to the Gettier problem, it's just not clear what even a widely accepted solution to it would be "good for" (1985, p. 363). Other, related, complaints about the worth of the attempt to provide an analysis of knowledge concern its failure to engage with radical

---

[4] For reasons to doubt whether JTB really was the "going view" prior to Gettier, see MacIver (1958, p. 4), Shope (1983, pp. 12–17), Kaplan (1985), Antognazza (2015), and Dutant (2015).

skepticism (Williams 1978) or to explain the distinctive *value* of knowledge (see Williamson 2000, p. 31; Greco 2015, p. 429). No doubt, it is in part because it is seen as failing to engage with such questions that the analysis of knowledge is sometimes derided.[5] However, even granting the relevant points, they seem not to expose any fatal defect in the program of analysis itself. An analysis or account, of whatever form, is always relative to some objective (Lehrer 1990, p. 5; Zagzebski 1999). We shouldn't expect that an account that serves one epistemological aim will thereby accomplish others. Thus, that the analysis of knowledge does not address certain other issues does not mean that its typical goal of helping us better understand its target is not worthwhile (Conee 1988). Nor is it clear that a better understanding of what knowledge is, or what the concept entails, couldn't at least help in clarifying its value, promoting its acquisition, or addressing other long-standing epistemological issues.

Of course, all of this assumes that the project of analyzing knowledge can be satisfactorily carried out. And many now doubt that it can. One argument that might seem to suggest such a conclusion is presented by Linda Zagzebski (1994). According to her, for any proposal whereby knowledge is true belief meeting some further condition, x (justification, or justification plus some additional requirement[s]), so long as x is logically independent of truth, we can construct a Gettier case: imagine that condition x is met, but that unluckily S's belief is false; then alter the case slightly, so that a further element of luck results in S's belief's being true after all. Importantly, Zagzebski herself does not conclude from this that knowledge cannot be analyzed. Instead, she infers that "there must be a necessary connection between truth and [x]" (1999, p. 102) – in particular, that the concept of an act of intellectual virtue, which she sees as closing the gap between (true) belief and knowledge, is truth-entailing (1999, p. 111). Many worry that any such solution to the Gettier problem comes at too high a cost, ruling out most ordinary cases of knowing and casting most intuitive epistemic judgments as simply mistaken (e.g. Lycan 2006, pp. 160–1). But Zagzebski does not. Meanwhile, others have argued that incorporating an anti-luck condition into one's account, for example, short-circuits Zagzebski's argument: x need not be truth-entailing in order to avoid the existence of cases having the structure that she describes

---

[5] Beaney, for example, speaks of "idle cog-spinning or epicycling, or Gettier games played for their own sake" (2013, p. 27). It is not clear whether the perceived detachment from such extradefinitional matters, any more than the apparent failure to have come up with a reasonably neat, noncircular (etc.) analysis that's widely regarded as satisfactory, explains the scorn often directed at "the Gettier industry." See Lycan (2006).

(see Leite 2010, p. 373). It's an open question, of course, whether the imagined type of account satisfies other standard *desiderata* for a classical analysis mentioned earlier – for example, whether it avoids unacceptable vagueness or circularity.[6] In general, however, whether Zagzebski's argument provides grounds for pessimism about the prospects for a satisfactory analysis of knowledge is controversial.

A second possible reason for skepticism about the likelihood of finding a (good) classical analysis of knowledge has more metaphysical roots (see Zagzebski 1999, sec. 2). As we saw earlier, one common aim in pursuing such an analysis is to improve our understanding of the *nature* or *essence* of knowing. Natural kinds such as *gold* or *water* might be thought to be amenable to such Lockean real definitions. But is knowledge a natural kind? Perhaps the category of knowledge is more like *refreshing water*, or *offside* (Williams 2015), which seem not to carve nature at the joints. Or perhaps it is like *jade*, constituting no single kind of its own but, rather, different types that we happen to have grouped together. The ontological status of knowledge is an important matter to consider. However, two things bear noting here. First, it's not obvious what the correct stance on the issue(s) just posed is – this is no more clear and settled than is the question of whether we should be optimistic about the prospects for an analysis of knowledge, on which, it was implied, the present considerations might shed light. Second, it's not clear how neatly a given stance on the issue(s) just posed lines up with a specific view as to the prospects for a successful classical analysis anyway. Some of the staunchest critics of the latter project (e.g. Kornblith 2007) think that knowledge *is* a natural kind. Further, even if asking after the nature or essence of knowledge really does involve the presumption that this must be given by nature, as we saw above, not everyone who undertakes such an analysis views it as a metaphysical investigation. Goldman, for example, is among the most vocal defenders of the idea that epistemologists must engage in some conceptual investigation of a broadly traditional sort; any doubts that he has as to the prospects for a classical analysis (see Section 10.4) have their source in something other than skepticism – which he in fact shares (e.g. 2005; 2015) – about whether knowledge is a natural kind.

---

[6] Zagzebski (1999, p. 103) and Ichikawa and Steup (2018, sec. 8), for example, raise such concerns – concerns that might apply to Zagzebski's own proposal, which she grants "is vague and needs more extensive analysis" (1999, p. 112). Sorensen argues that the vagueness of typical fourth conditions supports the view that "know" itself is vague, and that this raises doubts about the prospects for a definition of knowledge (1987, pp. 770–2). See, too, Hetherington (2005b, sec. 14) and Earl (n.d., sec. 4c).

We've just fended off some reasons for pessimism about either the value of, or the prospects for, a classical analysis of knowledge. But is there any good reason to expect that such an analysis is possible in the first place? As Keith Lehrer observes, "the finest monuments of scientific achievement mark the refutation of claims of impossibility" (1990, p. 6). Even so, it's plausible that not every concept (or word) can be analyzed, on pain of regress. And, not least because of the already-noted absence of clear progress in solving the Gettier problem, current epistemology tends to be less focused on the attempt to analyze knowledge than it was even a generation ago. At the same time, a number of alternatives to the program of analysis have been suggested. In the next section, we consider the more prominent among these, as well as some further alleged reasons for doubt about the viability or interest of a classical analysis of knowledge.

10.4 Some Proposed Alternatives

One influential recent alternative to the program of analysis is the knowledge-first approach to epistemology. "Knowledge first" refers not to a specific thesis, but rather to a number of more or less closely related themes and commitments.[7] Chief among these is the idea that knowledge should be treated as fundamental in at least a couple of senses, each of which contrasts with an assumption of the tradition in which epistemologists sought to analyze knowledge. First, on the traditional view, knowledge is seen as a hybrid state – that is, as a composite of mental and nonmental factors. (Belief and truth, respectively; whether and to what extent justification is regarded as mental depends on one's theory.) On the knowledge-first approach, by contrast, knowledge is seen both as noncomposite and as mental through-and-through. Second, and relatedly, on the traditional approach knowledge is treated as a, or even *the*, central *explanandum*, with things like evidence, justification, and belief being recruited to help us better understand it. The knowledge-first approach reverses this priority: knowledge is a kind of "unexplained explainer" (Williamson 2000, p. 10); knowledge, or our concept thereof, is used to help us understand such things as justification, evidence, and belief, and/or the corresponding concepts.[8] Thus, for example, it has been

---

[7] For discussion of the latter, and of the relations among them, see Williamson (2011), McGlynn (2014), and Ichikawa and Jenkins (forthcoming).

[8] As in the program of analysis, there is occasional unclarity about whether what's at issue is the relevant concepts or, instead, that to which they refer (McGlynn 2014, p. 17; Ichikawa and Jenkins forthcoming). Cook Wilson provides a clear and recent precedent for this type of approach (see

suggested that a subject's evidence is constituted by what s/he knows ("E = K") (Williamson 2000, ch. 9); that belief "aims at knowledge," with mere believing being "a kind of botched knowing" (2000, p. 47); and that, by "the knowledge rule for belief," "only knowledge constitutes justified belief ... there are no justified false beliefs" (Williamson 2011, p. 214) – which, as we've seen, is an idea with obvious application to the Gettier problem.

Clearly, if this approach is correct, knowledge is not analyzable in anything like the usual sense: if knowledge is not composite, it cannot be broken down into simpler elements, and so cannot be given the sort of decompositional (or "reductive") treatment that classical analysis attempts. Thus, the lack of any clear solution to the Gettier problem, with each successive attempt to provide a satisfactory analysis of knowledge "succumbing to the same pattern of counterexamples and epicycles" (Williamson 2000, p. 31), is exactly what the knowledge-first approach predicts. And, indeed, the (perceived) failure of post-Gettier epistemology is often stressed by proponents of the knowledge-first approach and taken to provide strong inductive support for it (e.g. Bird 2007, p. 82; Williamson 2011, p. 209; Kelp 2016, pp. 78–9).[9]

Importantly, however, there are alternative explanations of the (supposed) insolubility of the Gettier problem, ones that don't single out the knowledge-first approach. For example, it is plausible that the program of classical analysis presumes a view of concepts that is now widely discredited (Ramsey 1992; Kornblith 2007). According to the "classical theory of concepts," a lexical (roughly, "word-sized") concept is a structured representation; it is composed of simpler concepts that express just what a classical analysis seeks – individually necessary and jointly sufficient conditions for something to fall under the concept's extension (see Laurence and Margolis 1999; Earl n.d.). In spite of its long history and obvious attractions, the classical theory has fallen into disrepute.[10] One reason for this coincides with a major source of skepticism about the Gettier project: while some concepts yield easily to an analysis (a *bachelor* is an *unmarried male*), most resist the attempt. Just as importantly, the classical theory fits poorly with various empirical findings.[11] Prominent

Marion 2016, sec. 4). According to some, Plato, for example, constitutes a much earlier one (see the works cited in note 4).

[9] Williamson (2000, p. 31n4) also cites Fodor's (1998) discussion of "the demise of definition."

[10] Murphy, for instance, says that "[t]o a considerable degree, it has simply ceased to be a serious contender in the psychology of concepts" (2002, p. 38); more bluntly, he calls it "a total flop" (2002, p. 483).

[11] For reviews, see Smith and Medin (1981) and Murphy (2002).

among the latter are *typicality effects* – that is, the fact that in various tasks subjects treat apples, for example, as more typical or representative fruits than plums, though there's no room for one kind of fruit to *better satisfy* the presumed definition.

The psychology of concepts is itself the focus of intense debate, and even if the classical theory is rejected it's not clear what to put in its place (Murphy 2002; Laurence and Margolis 1999). So, it's not obvious how we should think of the concept of *knowledge*, if not along the lines suggested by the classical theory. In response to certain knowledge-first arguments, both Adam Leite (2005, p. 168) and Elizabeth Fricker (2009, pp. 44–5) have suggested that it may be an "open texture" or "familiar resemblance" concept, possessing semantic complexity, but none capturable by any set of (noncircular) necessary and sufficient conditions.[12] Current theories of concepts congenial to the latter idea include the prototype and exemplar views.[13] Perhaps predictably, the latter views tend to excel where their chief rivals falter, and vice versa; and a similar combination of strengths and weaknesses attends other views (e.g. the "theory" or "knowledge" approach and "neoclassical" theories).[14] For our purposes here, however, the important point is that, as Leite puts it, "it is implausible to claim that if a concept of a certain state or condition cannot be provided with informative[15] necessary and sufficient conditions for its application, then we do not conceive of that state or condition as a complex involving different kinds of factors" (2005, p. 168). And if there *is* complexity there, there is the opportunity for analysis, whether or not it is undertaken with the expectation that it will result in a set of neat and noncircular necessary and sufficient conditions. Thus, for example, we find Goldman (2015) suggesting that the discovery of typicality effects, and the consequent

---

[12] Lycan (2006: 158–9) argues that *knowledge* does not possess a "family resemblance" structure in particular. Hacker (2013, ch. 4, App.) rejects the latter model for *knowledge*, too, suggesting instead that it is a "multi-focal" concept best treated via a connective analysis. (On the latter notion, more later in this section.)

[13] Briefly, a *prototype* is a collection of properties often present in instances of the concept, weighted by frequency or perceptual salience; an *exemplar* is a specific instance of the kind in question that the cognizer has in mind (Goldman 1993, pp. 128–9; Earl n.d., sec. 2d).

[14] For instance, while prototype and exemplar theories seem well-suited to accommodating typicality effects, they are said by some (e.g. Fodor 1998) to struggle with compositionality.

[15] The qualification is important. As we saw above, uninformative such conditions are all-too-easy to provide. In terms of the prototype theory, for example, "being sufficiently similar to the relevant prototype is necessary and sufficient for being a bird" (Jackson 1998, p. 61; cf. Weatherson 2003, pp. 18–19). As Kornblith says, then, "[a]ny account of concepts will give necessary and sufficient conditions for application of the concept, including prototype and exemplar accounts" (2007, p. 41n10; cf. Goldman 2007, p. 23).

implausibility of the classical theory of concepts, calls for a *refinement* of the usual approach to philosophical analysis, rather than its abandonment:

> I see no problem in principle here. There should be ways to incorporate into the structure of concepts a weighting scheme that assigns different "strengths" to different properties. Cognitive science can and should be used to improve the kind of investigations that traditional philosophers engage in. However, as far as I can see, this would not imply a thorough debunking or abandonment of methods that use hypothetical examples and intuitive classifications thereof. (Indeed, the finding of typicality effects relied on just such intuitive classifications.)

While Goldman is speaking here in defense of key components of "the standard practice of conceptual analysis" (2015) – specifically, the use of hypothetical examples and intuitive classifications thereof – it should be noted that knowledge-first epistemologists employ such methods too, and that they do so in service of claims and theories that often look a lot like the products of traditional conceptual analysis. According to Aidan McGlynn, "the knowledge first literature is no less full of attempts to state informative necessary and sufficient conditions than the rest of the post-Gettier literature" (2014, p. 17). Relatedly, that literature contains familiar post-Gettier examples and patterns of argument. For example, Christoph Kelp (2016) argues that various other knowledge-first accounts of justification fall prey to Gettier counterexamples, whereas his does not; Williamson's claim that "only knowledge constitutes full justification" (2011, p. 215) recalls views (like Zagzebski's) on which what must be added to true belief to yield knowledge is truth-entailing, and is subjected to similar criticisms (e.g. Cohen and Comesaña 2013, pp. 15–16); and familiar counterexamples, such as barn cases, are used against various knowledge-first theses, prompting refinements, alternatives, and new distinctions (McGlynn 2014, p. 173).[16]

All of this might lead one to wonder whether knowledge-first epistemologists aren't themselves engaged in something *like* old-fashioned analysis. It is important to note, then, that

---

[16] McGlynn writes (2014, pp. 172–3): "If the pattern of counterexamples found in the post-Gettier literature were a symptom of the pursuit of a bad research programme – the pursuit of analyses – then we would expect to find that abandoning that research programme would result in a break in the pattern. [But . . .] this hasn't happened. On the contrary, the approach has been plagued by apparent counterexamples, often running into problems with the very examples that cropped up in the Gettier literature."

Williamson is also careful to emphasize that rejection of the project of analyzing knowledge in no way suggests that there are not interesting and informative necessary or sufficient conditions on knowledge. The traditional ideas that knowledge entails truth, belief, and justification are all consistent with the knowledge first project. And Williamson (2000, p. 126) is explicit in endorsement of a safety condition on knowledge. (Ichikawa and Steup 2018, sec. 11)

Knowledge-firsters hold that such conditions reflect important "structural features" of knowledge (Williamson 2009, p. 306) and contribute to a "reflective understanding" of the concept (Williamson 2000, p. 33). What they deny is that agreement on such conditions represents progress toward a reductive account of knowledge, wherein it is broken down into simpler components – something, they think, that cannot be done.[17] Still, as we've seen, the energies of those working within the program of analysis tend to be focused on such conditions themselves – getting *those* right – rather than on the question of whether knowledge, or our concept thereof, is composite. At least in that sense, then, there may be greater kinship of goal and method between that program and the knowledge-first approach than one might have thought – especially since, as we'll see shortly, some traditional "belief first" theorists adopt the methods of classical analysis while sharing the knowledge-first epistemologist's skepticism that it will yield a neat, noncircular, and exceptionless *analysans*. So, too, those who regard knowledge as composite, but who are nonetheless skeptical about the prospects for providing a classical analysis of it, are of course free to investigate its structural features, as Williamson calls them, and/or to pursue a reflective understanding of the concept.

Hilary Kornblith has put forward another alternative to the program of analysis. According to him, not only does traditional philosophical analysis require a thoroughly discredited theory of concepts (viz. the classical theory), but the *concept* of knowledge is of virtually no philosophical interest anyway: it is no more a worthy target of epistemological theory than the *concept* of aluminum is a worthy target of inquiry for a metallurgist. Kornblith himself thinks that knowledge is a natural kind. But even if it is not – even if it is, say,

---

[17] A favorite example of Williamson's in support of this point is the following (2000, p. 3; cf. 2011, p. 210, and note 1 in this chapter): "Although being coloured is a necessary but insufficient condition for being red, we cannot state a necessary and sufficient condition for being red by conjoining being coloured with other properties specified without reference to red. Neither the equation 'Red = coloured + X' nor the equation 'Knowledge = true belief + X' need have a non-circular solution."

a socially constructed category – there is no assurance that our "folk" concept of knowledge, or even the epistemologist's, characterizes it correctly. And when we realize that our epistemic concepts "may fail to characterize the categories they are concepts of, the philosophical interest of our concepts thereby wanes" (2007, p. 37). Instead, we should simply study knowledge itself.

As to methodology, Kornblith's proposal is that epistemology should be thoroughly empirical: taking their cue from our imagined metallurgist, epistemologists should proceed by examining apparently clear cases of knowledge, looking to find what they have in common. Very likely, this process will involve reclassifying examples, deciding that some aren't cases of knowledge after all, and that other, previously excluded, examples are. Out of this process will emerge a picture of the true nature of knowledge. Specifically, Kornblith thinks, what will emerge is a picture of knowledge as reliably produced true belief, with the latter being "instrumental in the production of behavior successful in meeting biological needs and thereby implicated in the Darwinian explanation of the selective retention of traits" (2002, p. 62).

In response to the foregoing line of argument, one concern is that it moves too quickly from the possibility that our concepts incorporate error to their being of no theoretical interest: "The fact that there is a 'gap' between 'concept and category' is no more worrying than the fact that there is a 'gap' between how things *look* or *sound* to us and how they actually are" (Jenkins 2014, pp. 106–7). A second concern is that, without *some* reliance on our pretheoretic concepts, the empirical study that Kornblith recommends could not get off the ground: "a prior method is needed to pick out which set of extra-mental events in the world should be the target of a Kornblithian empirical investigation" (Goldman 2015; cf. MacIver 1958, p. 2; Jackson 1998, pp. 30–1, 41–2; Weatherson 2003, pp. 15–16).

According to Goldman, the needed prior method is an analysis of our concepts, as grounded in our intuitive classifications of various cases, actual and hypothetical. In a couple of respects, however, the type of analysis that Goldman advocates departs importantly from the classical model. First, while in earlier work (e.g. 1986) Goldman seemed to regard conceptual analysis and the consulting of intuitions as an *a priori* method, more recently (1999; 2005; 2007; Goldman and Pust 1998) he has suggested that the conceptual work characteristic of epistemological theorizing is a form of *a posteriori* empirical investigation: a sample case is presented, and the subject's classificational intuitions constitute quasi-observational data revealing features of his/her epistemic concepts (2005, pp. 408–9).[18] Second, in part because of typicality effects and the consequent discrediting of the classical theory of concepts, Goldman doubts that a subject's concepts should be represented as specifying informative and noncircular necessary and sufficient conditions (e.g. 1986, pp. 38–9; 2007, p. 23; 2015).[19] (As we saw above, he suggests that those engaged in conceptual analysis should find a way of including a weighting scheme that assigns different "strengths" to different properties.) At the same time, however, Goldman insists that, in addition to including all (philosophically significant) necessary conditions, an adequate account of a given concept should at least be *tested* in the usual way for sufficiency. If it fails, then "either there is some *sufficient* condition that has not yet been identified or . . . one or more *necessary* (but insufficient) conditions have been *omitted*" (2009, p. 75). In this way, the methods of classical analysis are retained, and even regarded as essential tools of the epistemologist, though there is no presumption that the investigation will yield a neat, noncircular, and exceptionless classical *analysans* (cf. Beaney 2016, sec. 6), or one expressing a necessary truth (see Zagzebski 1999, p. 96, including n12).[20]

Still another alternative to the program of analysis is defended by Edward Craig (1990). While he is skeptical about the prospects for solving the Gettier problem, his more fundamental concern with the program of analysis is that even if we had an extensionally adequate account of knowing, it might not connect with the concept's "intuitive intension" – that is, with our intuitions

---

[18] A further reason for skepticism about conceptual analysis stems from work within "experimental philosophy" ("X-phi") purporting to show that there is significant diversity in the epistemic intuitions on which such analyses rely. Such intuitions are said to vary both within individuals (Swain et al. 2008) and between groups, including "along such epistemically scary fault lines" (Nagel 2012, p. 495) as ethnicity (Weinberg et al. 2001) and gender (Buckwalter and Stich 2011). The interpretation and significance of the relevant data are controversial. Further, more recent studies (Nagel et al. 2013; Kim and Yuan 2015; Seyedsayamdost 2015) have failed to replicate the results in question. And, in his most recent work on the subject, Stich – along with his coauthors (see Machery et al. 2017) – has argued for the cross-cultural *robustness* of certain epistemic intuitions, including about Gettier cases.

[19] Compare Chalmers and Jackson's view that conceptual analysis "proceeds at least in part through consideration of a concept's extension within hypothetical scenarios, and noting regularities that emerge" (2001, p. 321), where it is not assumed that such consideration involves definitions – that is, "finite expressions in the relevant language that are a priori equivalent to the original terms, yielding counterexample-free analyses of those terms" (2001: 320).

[20] Goldman's views here resemble Zagzebski's. Zagzebski has doubts about whether it's possible to satisfy all the requirements for a good definition simultaneously, and she favors "retaining the method of truth condition analysis but without letting the aim to make the definition counter-example-free dominate the list of desiderata" (1999, p. 104). Plantinga (1993b, p. 20) and Lycan (2006, p. 158) are two others who employ the methods of classical analysis while granting that central epistemic concepts might not fully yield to them.

about *why* certain cases do, or do not, qualify as knowledge (1990, p. 1). More generally, even a successful analysis might fail to engage with such questions as those of why knowledge is worth caring about, and why the concept enjoys such widespread use (1990, p. 2).

We encountered such concerns in Section 10.2, and denied that they exposed any problems with the project of analyzing knowledge per se. Even so, Craig argues, given the difficulties of post-Gettier epistemology, it's surely worthwhile to approach the concept of knowledge via a different method altogether (1990, p. 1). Specifically, he suggests that, instead of fixing directly on the concept and trying to analyze it, we should ask "what knowledge does for us, what its role in our life might be, and then ask what a concept having that role would be like" (1990, p. 2). According to Craig, a conspicuous general fact about the human situation is that we must rely on others as sources of information (1990, p. 11). So we need some way to pick out *good* informants, and Craig's hypothesis is that our concept of the knower is the highly "objectivized" notion of a good informant, where the latter is someone who is likely to have a very high degree of reliability on the matter in question (1990, p. 91).

Such a "practical explication"[21] of the concept of knowledge might help to explain some of the attractions of the JTB conception, since a typical good informant may satisfy those three conditions (1990, pp. 69–70). (At the same time, that there may be good informants who *don't* satisfy one or more of those conditions presents no objection to Craig's account, since it doesn't aim at supplying necessary and sufficient conditions for knowing.) So, too, that epistemologists have proposed "truth-tracking," causal, and reliabilist analyses of knowledge is hardly surprising, since these focus on features plausibly associated with a person's being likely to be correct on some matter. However, Craig argues, there is no property, X, such that its satisfaction by the subject guarantees that s/he has a high probability of being right about p. For "there will always be something else which we could come to believe (call it Y),

---

[21] A Craigian "practical explication" differs from Rudolph Carnap's method of explication. Whereas a practical explication, like a classical analysis, aims for descriptive adequacy (Craig 1990, p. 8), Carnapian explication is normative – it involves "making more exact a vague or not quite exact concept used in everyday life or in an earlier stage of scientific or logical development, or rather of replacing it by a newly constructed, more exact concept" (Carnap 1947, pp. 7–8). While this new, more precise, concept should be similar to the original, it should also be simple and theoretically fruitful, connecting easily with extant concepts and laws and facilitating the formulation of universal statements. A recent application of Carnap's method to *knowledge* and the Gettier problem is by Olsson (2015). According to Olsson, failure to give the right intuitive result in Gettier cases can be offset by other theoretical virtues, and so does not itself threaten a given explication. For related ideas and arguments, see Weatherson (2013).

such that $(X$ and $Y)$ doesn't lend much probability to 'S is right as to whether p'" (1990, p. 52); as with other proposed analyses, sufficiency can be achieved only by requiring something too strong to be necessary (1990, p. 81). So it is not surprising either that the Gettier problem remains unsolved.

Craig's practical explication of *knowledge* can be seen as one instance of a more general alternative to the program of classical analysis – what *p*. F. Strawson calls the method of "connective analysis" (1992, ch. 2). When tasked with elucidating some concept, one option is indeed to employ the "reductive or atomistic" method (1992, p. 21) of "dismantling" it, identifying its simpler elements, and specifying necessary and sufficient conditions for its application. A "more realistic and fertile" approach (1992, p. 19; see, too, Hacker 2013, App.), Strawson suggests, is to undertake a *connective analysis*, which involves articulating the connections between a given concept and others with which it is associated (in Craig's case, between the concept of *knowledge* and that of a *good informant*). There is no presumption that, as we elucidate a complex concept by tracing its connections with others, there will be a movement toward either greater simplicity or anything resembling a classical *analysans* (1992, pp. 22–3). Nor should we be surprised or troubled if, "in the process of tracing connection from one point to another of the network [of concepts], we find ourselves returning to, or passing through, our starting point" (1992, p. 19). Such a "circular" path may well be illuminating, improving our understanding of the target concept.[22]

According to John Greco, Craig's approach also illustrates a more general shift in epistemological methodology that has occurred post-Gettier. As Greco sees it, "Gettier-era epistemology" was driven by "intuitionism" – the idea that epistemological theories should be evaluated "according to how well they preserve our pretheoretical intuitions about particular cases" (2015, p. 426). "[T]he method of counterexample" – and, more generally, of possible cases – that's characteristic of classical analysis "is in fact the method of intuitionism" (2015, p. 426). There are worries about such a method, however, some of which we encountered above – for example, that it tends to promote merely extensionally adequate theories, rather than genuinely illuminating ones (2015, p. 426); relatedly, that two (or more) theories might do equally well in accommodating intuitions about particular cases, in which case we would need some further basis for choosing between them (2015, pp. 426–7);

---

[22] Strawson's notion of a connective analysis is anticipated in A. C. Ewing: see Beaney (2016, sec. 8). It also recalls Ryle's (1949) notion of a "logical geography" of concepts. On the similarities and differences between connective analysis and Williamson's knowledge-first approach, see Cassam (2009, pp. 24–5) and Williamson (2009, pp. 285–90).

and, once again, that the method has failed to generate any significant consensus post-Gettier (2015, p. 423).[23]

Yet, in spite of all this, "epistemology in the early part of the twenty-first century is alive and well, even flourishing" (2015, p. 434). What explains this? The fact that epistemologists have moved away from mere "intuitionism," incorporating new methodological constraints on an adequate theory of knowledge. Specifically, they've begun to demand that such a theory explain such things as the distinctive value of knowledge, its close connection with both assertion and action, the social role of the concept, and the point and purpose of epistemic evaluations more generally (Craig 1990; Henderson and Greco 2015).

No doubt, the general shift in methodology that Greco describes is real. It is important to stress, however, that it is a *shift*, rather than the swapping of an old method for a new one.[24] For example, the above-noted demand (Section 10.2) that a good analysis be *informative* is an acknowledgment within the program of analysis of the insufficiency of mere extensional adequacy, and so of the importance of considerations beyond mere conformity to intuitions about particular cases. Likewise, the broader methodology that Greco describes includes epistemologists' making liberal use of our epistemic intuitions about particular cases and the method of counterexample – and so, in Greco's terms, of the method of intuitionism. In general, whatever the prospects for an analysis of knowledge – in its classical form, or in the modified form that, say, Goldman envisages – there is no reason to think that the methods employed therein can't be peacefully and productively used alongside, or within, the broader methodological framework that Greco describes. The same point applies to Strawsonian connective analysis, and – once again – to the knowledge-first epistemologist's similarly nonreductive focus on "structural features" of knowledge: they too afford useful means of approaching the relevant concepts while promoting clarity and rigor and improving our understanding of epistemic subjects. Employing them does not require that one take the concept of *knowledge* not to be analyzable, or knowledge itself not to be composite; it no more requires this than using the method of possible cases and attempting to state informative conditions on knowing requires that one think that they *are*.

---

[23] Greco also cites experimental philosophy and the doubts that it might raise about "the evidential quality of our intuitions about cases" (2015, p. 428). As he notes, the relevant results and their interpretation are contentious, even within X-phi; see note 18.

[24] I don't mean to suggest that Greco sees things otherwise.

10.5 Conclusion

The Gettier problem is often seen as casting a shadow over recent episte-mology. But it has had the welcome effect of encouraging greater reflection on epistemological methodology. As we've seen, there is little consensus about either the value of seeking an analysis of *knowledge* or whether there are principled reasons why the attempt is bound to fail. More generally, there is plenty of lively debate about the appropriate methodological moral to draw from the Gettier problem. Whatever the correct position is to take here, an increased awareness of the methodological issues needing to be addressed, and of the options available to us while moving forward, is surely a good thing.

11   Intuition in the Gettier Problem

Elijah Chudnoff

11.1 Introduction

Gettier's paper "Is Justified True Belief Knowledge?" is widely taken to be a paradigm example of a certain kind of philosophical methodology. Circumscribing the methodology is somewhat difficult. It was prominent in late-twentieth-century analytic philosophy. But it can also be found in Plato's Socratic dialogues. Counterexamples to proposed analyses of concepts, such as the analysis of the concept of knowledge as the concept of justified true belief, figure in it. But not all practitioners pursue the negative task of refutation, and not all practitioners see analyzing concepts as particularly central to philosophy. One often finds talk about intuitive judgments in instances of the methodology, but, as we will see, what intuitive judgments might be and whether they really play a central role in the methodology are contested issues. The methodology incorporates thought experiments, but just what doing so amounts to also remains a contested issue.

Here is one thing that I think we can say with confidence. Gettier's paper is widely taken to be a paradigm example of the kind of philosophical methodology exhibited in works that take his paper and other works such as Kripke's *Naming and Necessity*, Putnam's "The Meaning of 'Meaning,'" Burge's "Individualism and the Mental," Thomson's "A Defense of Abortion" and "The Trolley Problem," and Jackson's "Epiphenomenal Qualia" as research landmarks. This is the kind of methodology people who have been discussing philosophical methodology in the recent literature have been most concerned with. For convenience, in this chapter I'll just call it philosophical methodology, without any qualification. My characterization of the methodology isn't intended to help just anyone, no matter how unfamiliar with it, to understand what I have in mind; here I am simply locating my topic for those already somewhat familiar with it.

Gettier doesn't talk about intuitive judgments in his paper. Instead, after a bit of preliminary discussion, he describes two familiar cases, the first in which Smith forms a belief in (e), and the second in which Smith forms a belief in (h):

(e) The man who will get the job has ten coins in his pocket.
(h) Either Jones owns a Ford, or Brown is in Barcelona.

With respect to the first case, Gettier (1963, p.122) writes: "In our example, then, all of the following are true: (i) (e) is true, (ii) Smith believes that (e) is true, and (iii) Smith is justified in believing that (e) is true. But it is equally clear that Smith does not *know* that (e) is true"; with respect to the second case, Gettier writes: "Smith does *not* know that (h) is true, even though (i) (h) *is* true, (ii) Smith does believe that (h) is true, and (iii) Smith is justified in believing that (h) is true." On the basis of these judgments about the cases, Gettier concludes that justified true belief is not sufficient for knowledge.

There is a standard view about the philosophical methodology of which Gettier's paper is supposed to be a paradigm. On this view, Gettier's judgments about his cases are *intuitive* judgments, and reflection on the role they play in his discussion prima facie motivates the following four theses about such intuitive judgments and the philosophical methodology in which they figure:

(A) Intuitive judgments form an epistemically distinctive kind.
(B) Intuitive judgments play an epistemically privileged role in philosophical methodology.
(C) If intuitive judgments play an epistemically privileged role in philosophical methodology, then their role is to be taken as given inputs into generally accepted forms of reasoning.
(D) Philosophical methodology is reasonable.

It is difficult to deny the prima facie motivation. (A) Gettier's judgments about his cases do seem to be epistemically different from other kinds of judgments. They are not obviously perceptual, introspective, or based on memory, testimony, or inference. (B) The judgments do seem to drive his argument: it is in light of them that he motivates his main thesis, that justified true belief is not sufficient for knowledge. (C) It seems that Gettier takes his judgments as givens. He does not argue *for* them. Rather, using standard logical reasoning, he argues *from* them. Logically, it just can't be that both justified true belief is sufficient for knowledge and Gettier's judgments about his cases are true. (D) Gettier's paper is very convincing. It convinced almost everyone who read it that justified true belief is not sufficient for knowledge, and this consensus is on its face a reasonable one.

So, we have what I'll call the standard view of philosophical methodology and its motivation by taking Gettier's paper as a paradigm. The standard view has come under criticism from a number of different directions in recent years. Williamson (2004; 2008; 2013) has criticized (A). Cappelen (2012) and Deutsch (2010; 2015) have criticized (B). Negative experimental philosophers have criticized (D) (here I take Swain et al. 2008 to be representative). (C) has been something of a fixed point, however. If (C) is true, then the reasonableness of philosophical methodology depends on the quality of intuitive judgments as given inputs into generally accepted forms of reasoning. Negative experimental philosophers make a "garbage in, garbage out" argument. Defenders of the standard view, such as Bealer (1998), Goldman and Pust (1998), Ludwig (2007), Sosa (2007a; 2007b), Nagel (2012), and Bengson (2013), respond by denying the "garbage in" step.

My own view is that (C) is mistaken. I will discuss that in due course. But first I want to explore some of the arguments against the other pieces of the standard view of philosophical methodology. I will suggest that these pieces of the standard view hold up under scrutiny, though our understanding of them will have to shift somewhat in light of the rejection of (C). Here is how I will proceed. I will discuss (A) and (B) in order, first setting out the negative experimental challenge to (D) as a framework within which to see recent challenges to them. Then I will come to my own worries about (C), which will suggest an alternative account of how to defend (D) in response to work by negative experimental philosophers.

11.2 The Negative Experimental Challenge

Experimental philosophy now encompasses many different projects. Here, I am interested in what's called negative experimental philosophy. This is the kind of experimental philosophy that mounts challenges to philosophical methodology on the basis of data about the results of surveys posing the sorts of thought experiments figuring in that methodology to their participants. The data are supposed to provide a basis for challenging philosophical methodology because they suggest that intuitive judgments about philosophical thought experiments are biased by factors such as cultural background, socioeconomic status, emotional state, and order of presentation that are philosophically irrelevant.

Consider, for example, what Swain et al. (2008, pp. 140–1) say, in light of their own and others' experimental results from surveys:

> To the extent that intuitions are sensitive to these sorts of variable they are ill-suited to do the work philosophers ask of them. Intuitions track more than just the philosophically-relevant content of the thought-experiments; they track factors that are irrelevant to the issues the thought-experiments attempt to address. The particular socio-economic status and cultural background of a person who considers a thought experiment should be irrelevant to whether or not that thought-experiment presents a case of knowledge. Such sensitivity to irrelevant factors undermines intuitions' status as evidence.

Nothing I say will hinge on details about the surveys or the experimental methods that negative experimental philosophers have employed. My interest is in the reasoning that proceeds from data about the results of the surveys to the conclusion that philosophical methodology is flawed, and here I will take Swain et al.'s discussion to be representative. It will be useful to zoom in a bit and reveal some of its fine structure, however.

One of the main novelties in experimental philosophers' own methodology is that they do not just survey the judgments of professional philosophers. They survey the folk. So, the first phase in their reasoning focuses on folk judgments and folk intuitions, where I use "folk judgments" to mean the answers folk give to the surveys and "folk intuitions" to mean the intuitions whose contents those answers are supposed to express. We might render the first phase in negative experimental reasoning as follows:

(1) Surveys show that folk judgments about thought experiments are influenced by factors that do not track the truth about their subject matter.
(2) If folk judgments about thought experiments are influenced by factors that do not track the truth about their subject matter, then this is because folk intuitions about thought experiments are influenced by factors that do not track the truth about their subject matter.
(3) So folk intuitions about thought experiments are influenced by factors that do not track the truth about their subject matter.

Some defenders of philosophical methodology critique the negative experimental challenge at this first phase. They might reject (1) by criticizing the experimental support for it (Sosa 2007a; 2007b; Nagel 2012). Or they might reject (2) and (3) by arguing that patterns of judgments in surveys are not good guides to patterns of intuition (Ludwig 2007; Bengson 2013; Chudnoff 2013; but see also Weinberg and Alexander 2014).

The aim of negative experimental philosophy is to pose a challenge to philosophers, not the folk. So, there needs to be some bridge connecting the conclusion about folk intuitions to a claim about philosophers' intuitions. This is the second phase:

(4) Folk intuitions and philosophers' intuitions are subject to the same influences.
(5) So philosophers' intuitions about thought experiments are influenced by factors that do not track the truth about their subject matter.

Some defenders of philosophical methodology object to this second bridging phase. They think that philosophical training and practice protects philosophers' intuitions from the biases that influence folk intuitions. This is at least one aspect of the so-called "expertise defense." Early proponents include Kauppinen (2007), Ludwig (2007), and Sosa (2007a; 2007b). Nado (2014) is a helpful review of further developments.

Finally, while claims such as (3) about folk intuitions and (5) about philosophers' intuitions are interesting in themselves, the result of the negative experimental challenge should be about philosophical methodology, not intuitions. Hence the third phase of the negative experimental reasoning:

(6) If philosophers' intuitions about thought experiments are influenced by factors that do not track the truth about their subject matter, then it is unreasonable to accord intuitive judgments expressing them an epistemically privileged role in philosophical methodology.
(7) Philosophers' intuitive judgments about thought experiments are accorded an epistemically privileged role in philosophical methodology.
(8) So philosophical methodology is unreasonable.

Some defenders of philosophical methodology object to the third phase of the negative experimental reasoning. Their criticisms of negative experimental philosophy are radical, however, in that they derive from criticisms of what I've been calling the standard view of philosophical methodology. The strategy is to undermine the negative experimental challenge by rejecting the standard picture of philosophical methodology that it presupposes.

One form that this strategy takes is to deny (B) in that picture (cf. Deutsch 2010; 2015; Cappelen 2012). This is the claim that intuitive judgments play an epistemically privileged role in philosophical methodology. If this is untrue, then the negative experimental challenge breaks down at (7) since philosophers' intuitions about thought experiments in particular are not accorded an epistemically privileged role in philosophical methodology. A second form that the strategy takes is to deny (A) in the standard picture (cf. Williamson 2004; 2008; 2013). This is the claim that intuitive judgments form an epistemically distinctive kind. If (A) is untrue, then the negative experimental challenge breaks down at (7) once again, but for a different reason: there is no epistemically distinctive class of judgments that might or might not be accorded an epistemically privileged role in philosophical methodology. Philosophers do rely on their judgments about thought experiments. But since there is nothing epistemically distinctive about these judgments, there can be no grounds for skepticism about them that do not disastrously generalize to grounds for skepticism about our judgments in general (cf. Williamson 2004; 2008).

In the next two sections I consider these radical defenses of philosophical methodology, focusing first on Williamson's challenge to (7) via a challenge to (A), and second on Cappelen and Deutsch's challenge to (7) via a challenge to (B).

11.3 The Nature of Intuitive Judgments

What are intuitive judgments? There is a traditional answer. Suppose we ask "What are perceptual judgments?" The natural answer is that they are judgments formed by taking a perceptual experience at face value. Say that you look out your window and see a palm tree. You have a visual experience as of a palm tree. Suppose you have no reason to doubt the veracity of your visual experience, so you simply acquiesce in its portrayal of your surroundings. That is, you take your visual experience at face value. In doing so you now not only have an experience as of it being the case, but also make a judgment that there is a palm tree about. This judgment is a perceptual judgment.

The traditional view about intuitive judgments is that they are analogous to perceptual judgments. There are intuition experiences. They portray matters more abstract than those concerning your surroundings, such as those concerning mathematics, metaphysics, and morality. And intuitive judgments are those judgments that you form when you take such intuition experiences at face value. Here is a characteristic expression of this traditional view (Descartes 1991, p. 331):

You will surely admit that you are less certain of the presence of the objects you can see than of the truth of the proposition "I am thinking, therefore I exist." Now this knowledge is not the work of your reasoning or information passed on to you by teachers; it is something that your mind sees, feels and handles; and although your imagination insistently mixes itself up with your thoughts and lessens the clarity of this knowledge by trying to clothe it with shapes, it is nevertheless a proof of the capacity of our soul for receiving intuitive knowledge from God.

Descartes expresses the idea that bits of intuitive knowledge (i.e. intuitive judgments that amount to knowledge) are based on experiences analogous to perceptual experiences (e.g. experiences of seeing, feeling, and handling), but which provide us with a kind of access to reality that is different from the kind that we get through reasoning, testimony, or sensation.

Few current defenders of the standard picture of philosophical methodology outlined in the Introduction would follow Descartes very far in how he thinks about intuitive judgments and intuition experiences. Most would go as far as claim (A), however. This is the claim that intuitive judgments form an epistemically distinctive kind. Just *what makes* intuitive judgments epistemically distinctive is a contested issue. It seems to be fairly common ground, however, that Descartes was correct in thinking that, no matter what accounts for this fact, it is indeed a fact that intuitive judgments are not based on sensory experience. They are epistemically distinctive in that they are, in some reasonable sense, *a priori*.

Williamson has long opposed various more or less specific ways of demarcating a special class of intuitive judgments that are supposed to play an epistemically privileged role in philosophical methodology (Williamson 2004; 2008). Here I will focus on his most recent onslaught (Williamson 2013), which cuts to the core by purporting to show that *a priority* itself is not an epistemically significant feature of judgments.

Williamson invites us to consider the following two truths, the first *a priori* and the second *a posteriori*:

(1) All crimson things are red.
(2) All recent volumes of *Who's Who* are red.

He describes the details of how a person, Norman, might come to know each. Roughly: Norman imagines crimson things and recognizes them to be red; Norman imagines recent volumes of *Who's Who* and recognizes them to be red. The psychological processes are very similar. And this is what suggests to Williamson that the *a priori/a posteriori* distinction is "epistemically shallow" (2013, p. 296):

> The problem is obvious. As characterized earlier, the cognitive processes underlying Norman's clearly a priori knowledge of (1) and his clearly a posteriori knowledge of (2) are almost exactly similar. If so, how can there be a deep epistemological difference between them? But if there is none, then the a priori–a posteriori distinction is epistemologically shallow.

It would be mistaken to reason solely from the premise that two processes are psychologically similar at some level of description to the conclusion that they are epistemically similar (cf. Malmgren 2011). But Williamson supplements the above line of argument with supporting epistemological considerations.

Reflection on the roles of Norman's previous sensory experiences of crimson things and recent volumes of *Who's Who* suggests to Williamson that they are both "more than purely enabling but less than strictly evidential" in grounding his knowledge of (1) and (2). They are supposed to be more than purely enabling because they affect the reliability of the psychological processes resulting in Norman's judgments. They are supposed to be less-than-strictly evidential because they need not be preserved – by memory, say – in a form that enables Norman to cite them as considerations in favor of (1) and (2), but might instead retain their significance precisely because of how they shaped the psychological processes resulting in those judgments.

The fact that something impacts the reliability of the psychological processes resulting in a judgment, however, does not show that it does more than merely enable that judgment. The quantity of oxygen in the room in which you are contemplating a question affects the reliability of the psychological processes resulting in your judgment about that question. But the quantity of oxygen in the room does no more than merely enable you to make that judgment. One might complain that the quantity of oxygen in the room is not of the right category for us to even ask whether it is more than merely enabling a judgment. I agree. But there remains the question of why not, if having an impact on the reliability of psychological processes resulting in judgments is our test.

Better tests for whether something does more than merely enable a judgment should focus on properly epistemic dependencies, such as those revealed by epistemic defeat. Suppose, for example, that Norman learns that all his previous sensory experiences as of crimson things were hallucinations. He never genuinely saw anything crimson. Does that undercut the justification he has for believing (1), and therefore make it that he does not know (1)? No. It does not matter whether his previous sensory experiences as of crimson things were hallucinations. Suppose Norman learns that all his previous sensory experiences as of recent volumes of *Who's Who* were hallucinations. He never genuinely saw any recent volumes of *Who's Who*. Does that undercut the justification he has for believing (2), and therefore make it that he does not know (2)? Yes. It does matter whether his previous sensory experiences as of recent volumes of *Who's Who* were hallucinations.

These considerations do not just show that Norman's justification for believing (2), but not his justification for believing (1), is open to empirical defeat. Plausibly, both are open to empirical defeat of some sort or another (cf. Casullo 2003). My observation concerns a specific form of defeat – namely, undercutting rather than overriding defeat. The information that Norman acquires does not just outweigh the justification he has for believing (2) but fail to outweigh the justification he has for believing (1). Rather, the information that Norman acquires makes it that he no longer has any justification for believing (2) but fails to make it that he no longer has any justification for believing (1). Contrast cases in which Norman learns that experts say that not all crimson things are red or that not all recent volumes of *Who's Who* are red.

There is a variant on the above case that is worth noting. Suppose that in fact Norman's previous sensory experiences as of crimson things and as of recent volumes of *Who's Who* were hallucinations – but he does not learn this. Plausibly, the mere fact neither undercuts the justification he has for believing (1) nor undercuts the justification he has for believing (2). Still, the mere fact does make a difference with respect to what he knows. Even if it is a fact that Norman's previous sensory experiences as of crimson things were hallucinations, still he knows (1). One might lend support to this judgment by noting that hallucinations suffice to enable one to ascertain various color relations – such as similarity and relative brightness (cf. Johnston 2004). But if it is a fact that Norman's previous sensory experiences as of recent volumes of *Who's Who* were hallucinations, then Norman does not know (2). Here we find the presence of another epistemic dependence on previous experience that is absent in Norman's judgment of (1).

The foregoing gives us reason to reject Williamson's claim that Norman's previous sensory experiences are playing a "more than purely enabling but less than strictly evidential" role in grounding his knowledge of both (1) and (2). With respect to (1), Norman's previous sensory experiences are no more than purely enabling, as is shown by the irrelevance of whether they are hallucinations and the irrelevance of whether Norman knows that they are hallucinations. The epistemic qualities of the previous experiences do not make a difference to the epistemic qualities of Norman's judgment of (1). Further, with respect to (2), one might argue that Norman's previous sensory experiences are *no less than strictly evidential.* This is suggested by the relevance of whether they are hallucinations and the relevance of whether Norman knows that they are hallucinations. The epistemic qualities of the previous experiences do make a difference to the epistemic qualities of Norman's judgment of (2). There remains the question of how the experiences can be no less than strictly evidential, since they need not furnish Norman with considerations that he can cite in favor of (2). But it might be that one possesses and relies on lots of evidence that one cannot cite in the form of considerations (cf. Chudnoff 2018).

The fact that Norman's judgment of (1) is *a priori* marks at least two epistemically deep features of it: it cannot be defeated by calling into question the veridicality of Norman's previous sensory experiences; and the appropriate connection to the facts that its status as knowledge demands is independent of whether Norman's previous sensory experiences appropriately connected him to his surroundings.

What does this tell us about Gettier's judgment to the effect that Smith's justified true belief in (e), say, does not amount to knowledge? About *this* judgment, not much. But I am inclined to think that this is not a good example of an intuitive judgment anyway. This can sound perverse. But if we aim to learn something about Gettier by reflection on Norman, then we shouldn't do so by comparing Gettier's judgment about Smith with Norman's judgment of (1). Rather, we should introduce another of Gettier's judgments and another of Norman's judgments and consider a total of four judgments:

(G1) Gettier's judgment that Smith's belief in (e) does not amount to knowledge.

(G2) Gettier's judgment that justified true belief is not sufficient for knowledge.

(N1) Norman's judgment that this imagined instance of crimson is red.

(N2) Norman's judgment of (1), that all crimson things are red.

(N1) is one of the judgments that Norman makes during the imaginative endeavors that enable him to make judgment (N2). (N2) is Norman's *a priori* – and, we might add, intuitive – judgment. Analogously, (G1) is a judgment that Gettier makes during the imaginative endeavors – the thought experiments – that enable him to make judgment (G2). Its etiology and epistemology are obscure. Perhaps much of what Williamson says about it – e.g. that it results from exercising capacities to apply epistemic concepts to real cases along with capacities to apply concepts we can apply to real cases to imagined cases – is correct. Either way, I think that (G2) is clearly among Gettier's *a priori* and intuitive judgments. It is *a priori* and intuitive in just the way that one's judgment that true belief is not sufficient for knowledge is, when one considers cases of lucky guesses, or in the way that one's judgment that belief is not sufficient for knowledge is, when one considers cases of false beliefs. These are the sorts of judgment about which Descartes is talking in the passage quoted above.

I think it is a good idea to understand thought experiments such as Gettier's as being analogous to imaginative endeavors such as Norman's. Both can be compared to the use of pictures in grasping mathematical truths. Here is an example:

Sum of the first n numbers
$$1+2+3+4+5+\ldots+n=n(n+1)/2$$

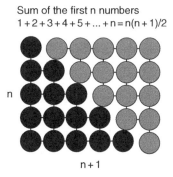

n

n + 1

Figure 11.1 Sum of the first n Numbers.

Seeing or imagining such a picture helps you to grasp intuitively and to know *a priori* the fact that the sum of the first n numbers is n(n + 1)/2. In the course of the endeavor, you might make other judgments, such as that the black array and the gray array contain the same number of dots. Similarly, imagining – or perceptually encountering, as Williamson has emphasized – Gettier cases helps you to grasp intuitively, and to know *a priori*, the fact that justified true belief is not sufficient for knowledge. In the course of the endeavor you might make other judgments, such as that Smith's belief in (e) does not amount to knowledge.

Williamson might accept the analogy and argue that this just shows that the *a priority* and intuitiveness of the mathematical judgments are also shallow. But that is plausible only if what he says about Norman is plausible, and I've already given reasons for thinking it is not. The intent of my analogy is not to add anything to that discussion. Rather, it is to locate just which judgment of Gettier's we should regard as the paradigmatically epistemically distinctive one. In my view it is the judgment that justified true belief is not sufficient for knowledge.

11.4 The Centrality of Intuitive Judgments

The title of this section is drawn from Cappelen's target in his book *Philosophy Without Intuitions* (2012, p. 3), namely:

> Centrality (of Intuitions in Contemporary Philosophy): Contemporary analytic philosophers rely on intuitions as evidence (or as a source of evidence) for philosophical theories.

Developing ideas from an earlier paper (2010), Deutsch has also written a book-length criticism of a similar thesis (2015, p. 36):

> (EC1) Many philosophical arguments treat the fact that certain contents are intuitive as evidence for those very contents.

My claim (B) says that intuitive judgments play an epistemically privileged role in philosophical methodology, and plausibly, to "rely on intuitions as evidence" and to "treat the fact that certain contents are intuitive as evidence" are two ways of according intuitive judgments epistemic privilege. But I've intentionally left vague the notion of epistemic privilege. The core idea, which can be developed in different ways, is that intuitive judgments play a role in philosophical methodology that reflects their epistemically distinctive features – features of the sort discussed in the previous section. My own preference is to say that, just as we make justified perceptual judgments on the basis of perceptual experiences, so we make justified intuitive judgments on the basis of intuition experiences. This is something that Cappelen and Deutsch deny.

Before getting to the main business of this section, I should make two preliminary points. First, Cappelen and Deutsch devote a good deal of space to discussing what philosophers say or do not say when using terms such as "intuition," "intuitive," "intuitively," and the like. I'm not going to focus on this part of their challenge to (B). I'm going to focus on what they say about examples of philosophical practice, and in particular about our paradigm example of that practice – Gettier's paper. Second, Cappelen and Deutsch take Gettier's intuitive judgments to include the judgment that Smith's belief in (e) does not amount to knowledge. As noted in the previous section, I think that this is not the best example. In my view, one should focus on more general claims, such as that justified true belief is not sufficient for knowledge. For the purposes of this section, however, I will set this point aside and will follow Cappelen and Deutsch in focusing on Gettier's judgments about Smith.

Above, I quoted some of what Gettier says about Smith and (e) in his ten-coins case. The passage, however, extends beyond what I quoted. Here is a fuller excerpt, with the additional text in bold (1963, p. 122):

> In our example, then, all of the following are true: (i) (e) is true, (ii) Smith beliefs that (e) is true, and (iii) Smith is justified in believing that (e) is true. But it is equally clear that Smith does not *know* that (e) is true; **for (e) is true in virtue of the number of coins in Smith's pocket, while Smith does not know how many coins are in Smith's pocket, and bases his belief in (e) on a count of the coins in Jones's pocket, whom he falsely believe to be the man who will get the job.**

Cappelen and Deutsch interpret the text in bold as an argument for Gettier's intuitive judgment that Smith's belief in (e) does not amount to knowledge. Deutsch writes (2015, p. 82):

> The fact that this argument is present in Gettier's very short paper refuting the JTB theory, which is supposed to be one of the clearest examples we have of a piece of analytic philosophy that depends on taking intuitions as evidence – and, indeed, as the *only* evidence – for judgments about thought experiments, shows that the view of the nature of analytic philosophy that takes it to rely heavily on intuitions as evidence is almost certainly mistaken. If there are arguments for intuitive judgments about thought experiments in Gettier's paper, then they are bound to be found in many other papers in analytic philosophy besides.

Cappelen (2012, p. 194) makes a similar point about Gettier's paper, after making the case that such arguments for intuitive judgments about thought experiments can indeed be found in many other papers – in fact, in no fewer than ten classics of analytic philosophy.

Here, then, are two theses:

Intuition. Gettier and his readers make a justified judgment that Smith's belief in (e) doesn't amount to knowledge, on the basis of an intuition experience.

Inference. Gettier and his readers make a justified judgment that Smith's belief in (e) doesn't amount to knowledge, on the basis of an inference from supporting considerations.

According to Cappelen and Deutsch, *Inference*, but not *Intuition*, is true here and analogues of *Inference*, but not analogues of *Intuition*, are true elsewhere with respect to analogous moments in philosophy, and this fact gives us good reason to reject Centrality, (EC1), (B), and the like. As Cappelen (2014) and Deutsch (2016) have already acknowledged, however, the mere *presence* of supporting considerations does not by itself settle that *Inference*, but not *Intuition*, is true. The supporting considerations might be present precisely to enable the intuition experience (cf. Koksvik 2013; Bengson 2014). How might we decide?

Contrast the following cases.

Table 11.1 Intuition versus Inference

Considerations Enabling an Intuition	Considerations Constituting an Inference
The sum of the first n numbers is $n(n + 1)/2$. Consider the sum of the first 5 numbers. You can write it going from 1 to 5 or from 5 to 1: $$1 + 2 + 3 + 4 + 5$$ $$5 + 4 + 3 + 2 + 1$$ Notice that if you add the first representation of the sum to the second, then the result is $6 + 6 + 6 + 6 + 6$. That is, twice the sum of the first 5 numbers is 5×6, and so the sum of the first 5 numbers must be $(5 \times 6)/2$. Clearly we can do this for any number and in general the sum of the first n numbers is $n(n + 1)/2$.	The sum of the first n numbers is $n(n + 1)/2$. Take 0. The sum of the first 0 numbers is $n(n + 1)/2$, since $0(0 + 1)/2 = 0$. Now take some arbitrary number n and suppose the sum of the first n numbers is $n(n + 1)/2$. It follows that the sum of the first $n + 1$ numbers is $[(n + 1)(n + 2)]/2$, for if the sum of the first n numbers is $n(n + 1)/2$, then, by familiar algebraic manipulations: $n + (n + 1) = n(n + 1)/2 + (n + 1) = [n(n + 1) + 2(n + 1)]/2 = [(n + 1)(n + 2)]/2$. So the proposition is true for 0 and if the proposition is true for n, it is also true for $n + 1$. It follows by mathematical induction that in general the sum of the first n numbers is $n(n + 1)/2$.

I've given two ways of talking someone through to the claim that the sum of the first n numbers is $n(n + 1)/2$. I claim that the first way illustrates considerations enabling an intuition and the second way illustrates considerations constituting an inference. Here is a key difference between them:

Different Constitution. If you infer c from $p_1 \ldots p_n$, then your justification for believing c is constituted by your justification for believing $p_1 \ldots p_n$. Say that your justification for believing in the principle of mathematical induction is constituted by the testimony of a textbook. Then, in the inference case, your justification for believing the formula is partly constituted by testimony. If consideration of $p_1 \ldots p_n$ enables your intuition that c, then your justification for believing c need not be constituted by your justification for believing $p_1 \ldots p_n$. Rather, it is constituted by your intuition. Say that your justification for believing that $4 + 2$ is 6 is constituted by the testimony of a textbook. You learned this in school and just haven't thought about it since. Nonetheless, in the intuition case your justification for the formula need not be partly constituted by testimony.

A number of different hallmarks of inference are consequent on or closely related to this key distinguishing feature.

First, inferences do not have a very flexible construction. If you infer c from $p_1 \ldots p_n$, then your justification for believing c is different from the justification that you would have for believing c, were you to take into account alternative considerations $p_1^* \ldots p_n^*$. So, if the argument in the inference case invoked different algebraic manipulations or a variant on the principle of mathematical induction, your justification for believing the formula would be different.

Second, the justification you have by inference is no stronger than the justification you have for the supporting considerations. If you infer c from $p_1 \ldots p_n$, then your justification for believing c is no stronger than your justification for believing $p_1 \ldots p_n$. So, if you are shaky on mathematical induction, then your justification for believing the formula might be rather weak.

Third, the justification you have by inference inherits the defeasibility conditions of the justification you have for the supporting considerations. If you infer c from $p_1 \ldots p_n$, then whatever defeats your justification for believing one of $p_1 \ldots p_n$ defeats your justification for believing c. If a recognized authority plays a trick on you and tells you that mathematical induction is illegitimate, then this will weaken your inferential justification for believing the formula.

Fourth, the constitution of your justification for a judgment is, at least in many cases, reflected in the phenomenology of your experience of making that judgment. In many cases, what it feels like to infer c from $p_1 \ldots p_n$ reflects the fact that you take $p_1 \ldots p_n$ to support c. And in many cases what it feels like to intuit c, on the other hand, reflects the fact that you see, or at least seem to see, into the truth of c on its own merits.

Now consider Gettier's judgment that Smith doesn't know (e), and the consideration he points out to the effect that Smith's belief isn't based on an encounter with the fact in virtue of which it is true. Does the consideration fit into a structure of considerations with the hallmarks of inference? Arguably, no. First, it could just as well have been replaced by an anti-luck consideration without making much of a difference to the nature of the justification that Gettier's discussion gives us for thinking that Smith doesn't know (e). Second, the justification we have for thinking Smith doesn't know (e) seems to be a lot stronger than the justification we have for thinking that, say, knowledge of a fact requires some kind of encounter with that fact. Indeed, and third, whatever justification we might have had for believing in such an encounter condition on knowledge has been defeated by the subsequent Gettier literature, but nothing in that literature defeats the justification that readers of Gettier's paper have for thinking that Smith doesn't know (e). It is not as if, every time that a proposed condition on knowledge is refuted, participants in the discussion lose their justification for thinking that Smith doesn't know (e), until they regain it by consideration of another condition. Fourth, the phenomenology of judging that Smith doesn't know (e) just isn't much like the phenomenology of making an inference, even when we are extra attentive because we have been altered to the possibility that we are making an inference. Rather, at least in my own experience (though I suspect that this is true of many others as well), the considerations that Gettier cites in his discussion of the judgment simply help to make it vivid in itself that Smith doesn't know (e).

Earlier, I suggested that reflection on Gettier's paper prima facie motivated the idea expressed in (B), that intuitive judgments play an epistemically privileged role in philosophical methodology. Cappelen and Deutsch can concede the prima facie motivation. But their view is that further reflection on Gettier's practice shows that it does not really support (B), or related claims such as Centrality and (EC1). I believe that the foregoing casts doubt on their view. The mere presence of supporting considerations in Gettier's paper does not establish that his discussion of his thought experiments rests on inference rather than intuition. And indeed that discussion is much more naturally assimilated to one that provides considerations aimed at enabling an intuition rather than to one that provides considerations that constitute an inference. Whether the point generalizes to other instances of philosophical methodology is a nice question.

11.5 The Place of Intuitive Judgments in Philosophical Methodology

In his "Emendation of the Intellect," Spinoza clarifies how he understands intuitive knowledge, by contrasting different ways of figuring out what number x stands in the same ratio to c as b does to a (1992, p. 238):

> Three numbers are given; a fourth is required, which is to the third as the second to the first. Here tradesmen generally tell us that they know what to do to find the fourth number, for they have not forgotten the procedure which they merely learned without proof from their teachers. Others formulate a universal axiom from their experience with simple numbers when the fourth number is self-evident, as in the case of the numbers 2, 4, 3, 6 ... But mathematicians, because of the force of the demonstration of Proposition 19 of Book 7 of Euclid, know what numbers are propositional to one another from the nature and property of proportion, which tells us that the product of the first and fourth numbers is equal to the product of the second and third. However, they do not see the adequate proportionality of the given numbers, and if they do see it, they see it not by the force of that proposition but intuitively, without going through any procedure.

Spinoza's picture is similar to Descartes': when, for some a, b, and c, you find x intuitively this is because you see into the truth of $a/b = c/x$ on its own merits, without following rules passed on by testimony or derived by reasoning or suggested by previous experience. With respect to this kind of knowledge, Spinoza also writes (1992, pp. 238, 239):

> By the same kind of knowledge we know that two and three are five, and that if two lines are parallel to a third line, they are parallel to one another, and so on. But the things that I have hitherto been able to know by this kind of knowledge have been very few.

And:

> Now that we know what kind of knowledge is necessary for us [i.e. intuitive knowledge], we must describe the way and method by which

we may come to know by this kind of knowledge the things that are needful to be known.

The key point that I want to draw attention to here is that Spinoza thinks of intuitive knowledge as something we work toward not work from. Hitherto we haven't had much of it to work from. And what we need is a way and method by which we can work toward it. Philosophical inquiry does not start with intuitive knowledge and build theories on the basis of it. Rather, philosophical inquiry has intuitive knowledge as its goal.

I do not find Spinoza's view of the place of intuition in philosophical inquiry to be particularly idiosyncratic. It is not idiosyncratic in two ways. First, it is quite common in the history of philosophy. But I will not try to make that case here. Second, even if the view itself is not one that is commonly endorsed by analytic philosophers – by practitioners of "philosophical methodology" in the sense stipulated in Section 11.1 – still it is a view of the place of intuition in philosophical inquiry that, I believe, holds true of what those practitioners actually do, at least to a significant extent. If that is correct, then the piece of the standard view of philosophical methodology that has to go is (C) – the claim that if intuitive judgments play an epistemically privileged role in philosophical methodology, then their role is to be taken as given inputs into generally accepted forms of reasoning.

I am not able to make a full case against (C) here. My aims in the balance of this section are threefold. First, I will clarify why (B) in the standard picture of philosophical methodology does not on its own force us to accept (C). Second, I will explain how endorsing (B) while rejecting (C) provides a satisfying framework within which to read Gettier's paper. Third, I will briefly explore the bearing that this framework has on the negative experimental challenge to (D), the claim expressing the reasonableness of philosophical methodology.

The standard picture of philosophical methodology combines two ideas: (B) that intuitive judgments play an epistemically privileged role in philosophical methodology, and (C) that if intuitive judgments play an epistemically privileged role in philosophical methodology, then their role is to be taken as given inputs into generally accepted forms of reasoning. It is tempting to think that (C) just spells out what the sort of epistemic privilege (B) ascribes amounts to. The temptation, I believe, derives from the – in my view, largely correct – idea that the supposed epistemic privilege at least partly consists in being immediately, or – if, as also seems correct to me, the two can come apart – at least noninferentially, justified. Philosophers reason in favor of philosophical theories, and their reasoning bottoms out in intuitive judgments which have to be taken as given. But this is a confusion.

Epistemic immediacy is different from methodological immediacy. Suppose that intuitive judgments are justified – and, for simplicity, *immediately* justified – by intuition experiences and that this is their epistemic privilege. So, (B) is true. It doesn't follow that intuitive judgments are judgments with which we have to start. It doesn't follow, because it could be that various intuition experiences are ones that are available to us only *after* philosophical reflection and reasoning. This idea is commonplace in discussions of mathematical intuition. Responding to Hans Hahns's (1980) popularization of challenges to the reliance on intuition in mathematics deriving from supposedly counterintuitive results of late-nineteenth and early-twentieth century analysis, Mandelbrot (1983, p. 150) writes: "This Essay demonstrates that Hahn is dead wrong. To tame his own examples, I find it necessary to train our present intuition to perform new tasks, but it does not suffer any discontinuous change of character. Hahn draws a mistaken diagnosis, and suggests a lethal treatment." The training that Mandelbrot has in mind involves substantive mathematical reflection and reasoning, such as drawing mathematical distinctions, considering mathematical examples, clarifying the meanings of mathematical terms, isolating guiding mathematical principles, exploring helpful mathematical metaphors, working through mathematical arguments, building up mathematical theory, etc. There is no reason to think that intuition is any different in philosophy. In philosophy, however, the relevant intuition experiences largely depend on philosophical reflection and reasoning, such as drawing philosophical distinctions, considering philosophical examples (or thought experiments), clarifying philosophical meanings (maybe via conceptual analysis), isolating guiding philosophical principles, exploring helpful philosophical metaphors, working through philosophical arguments, building up philosophical theory, etc. The starting points in all this need not be justified judgments, and even less need they be intuitively justified judgments. Suppose that they are hunches instead. If the result is a new body of intuitively justified judgments, then our overall body of judgments can come to be justified via eventual connections to them.

We can see this in Gettier. The fact that justified true belief does not suffice for knowledge had already been recognized here and there in guiding thoughts to the effect that knowledge requires a connection to reality that reasonableness and fortune cannot guarantee – thoughts, perhaps, that motivated various theological and idealist intrusions into epistemology. Gettier's achievement was to make the fact intuitively clear. He did this in two ways. First, he clarified the relevant notion of reasonableness – or "being justified," "having adequate evidence," having "the right to be sure." This part of his paper hasn't figured much in recent discussions of philosophical methodology, but to my mind it is crucial. This is the part in which Gettier says that there can be justified false beliefs and that justification can be transmitted by deduction. Second, Gettier presented his famous examples which, once one is clear about the nature of justi-fication, make it intuitively clear that there can be justified true beliefs that do not amount to knowledge. It is worth briefly mentioning another paradigmatic instance of philosophical methodology for comparison – Kripke's (1980) *Naming and Necessity*. Kripke's presentation and subse-quent discussion of his own famous thought experiments about reference have come under much recent scrutiny. What I want to point out is the glaringly indisputable fact that the thought experiments themselves only enter the picture in the second lecture, after a whole first lecture in which Kripke engages in precisely those practices that tutor our intuition: he draws distinctions, gives examples, clarifies meanings, enunciates some guiding principles, discusses good and bad metaphors, assesses arguments, and, though he demurs from essaying a theory himself, he makes important critical contributions to the project of theory building. After working through that lecture, it is very difficult not to share Kripke's intuitions about his example cases. Gettier's preliminary discussion is clearly less involved than Kripke's. But both seem to me to serve the same end – namely, to enable us to have the right intuition experiences.

    And this brings us to the negative experimental challenge. Let us assume for the sake of argument that the first and second phases are sound. So, philosophers' intuitions about thought experiments are influenced by factors that do not track the truth about their subject matter. The third phase, recall, goes like this:

(6) If philosophers' intuitions about thought experiments are influenced by factors that do not track the truth about their subject matter, then it is unreasonable to accord intuitive judgments expressing them an epistemically privileged role in philosophical methodology.

(7) Philosophers' intuitive judgments about thought experiments are accorded an epistemically privileged role in philosophical methodology.

(8) So, philosophical methodology is unreasonable

Cappelen, Deutsch, and Williamson criticize (7) on the basis of radical departures from the standard picture of philosophical methodology. Perhaps the departure I am recommending also counts as radical, though I would rather think of it as taking us back to the longer tradition of theorizing about philosophical methodology, one that includes Spinoza. Either way, it provides a basis for keeping (7) but rejecting (6), and so blocking the inference to (8).

Being a philosopher might not make your intuitions immune to influences that do not track the truth about their subject matter. But it does subject your intuitions to influences that, we have reason to think, do track the truth about their subject matter. These are the influences contained in the large body of philosophical literature in which relevant distinctions are drawn, examples presented, clarifications made, principles enunciated, metaphors explored, arguments assessed, and theories constructed. We have reason to think that these influences track the truth about their subject matter, because these are just the sorts of activities in which good thinking consists across disciplines.

Here is a worry. Influences on intuition incorporated into philosophical practice might guide us toward better intuitions, but . . . they might not: they might guide us toward worse intuitions. This is always a possibility. But it is no more a ground for skepticism about philosophical practice than is the fact that it is always a possibility that empirically based methods in other disciplines might very well be leading us to adopt false views about the world. A variant on the worry is that it is not just that the influences on intuition incorporated into philosophical practice *might* guide us toward worse intuitions, but that we have no way of telling whether or not they are. Perhaps this is part of what Weinberg (2007) has in mind when he calls philosophical practice hopeless. I do not agree, however, that we have no way of telling. It is true that there is no simple test that applies across the board. Sometimes there are relatively simple tests that apply to limited domains. For those areas of philosophy that are closely connected to other areas of inquiry tests for coherence with the well-supported results of those areas are examples of such tests. By and large, however, checks on the course of philosophical inquiry are more holistic. You try to put the pieces together – the pieces from different areas of philosophy, the pieces from other disciplines – and you see whether the result is coherent and intellectually satisfying. This does not look much like the kinds of tests that we have for filtering out bad observational data. But the thrust of my argument here has been that, even if intuitions are epistemically akin to observations, their methodological position in inquiry is quite different.

12   Experimental Epistemology and "Gettier" Cases

John Turri

12.1 Gettier's Cases

Edmund Gettier's 1963 paper, "Is Justified True Belief Knowledge?," was explicitly concerned with evaluating "various attempts" that had "been made in recent years to state necessary and sufficient conditions for someone's knowing a given proposition." Gettier claimed that those "attempts have often been such that they can be stated in a form similar to" a definition stating that *you know that p* just in case *you have a justified true belief that p*. Gettier claimed, furthermore, that the latter was insufficient for the former, providing two examples to support his claim. Here is one of Gettier's original examples (1963, pp. 122–3: "Case II"):

> Let us suppose that Smith has strong evidence for the following proposition:
>
> (f) Jones owns a Ford.
>
>   Smith's evidence might be that Jones has at all times in the past within Smith's memory owned a car, and always a Ford, and that Jones has just offered Smith a ride while driving a Ford. Let us imagine, now, that Smith has another friend, Brown, of whose whereabouts he is totally ignorant. Smith selects three place-names quite at random, and constructs the following three propositions:
>
> (g) Either Jones owns a Ford, or Brown is in Boston;
>
> (h) Either Jones owns a Ford, or Brown is in Barcelona;
>
> (i) Either Jones owns a Ford, or Brown is in Brest-Litovsk.

For helpful feedback and discussion, I thank Stephen Hetherington and Angelo Turri. This research was supported by the Canada Research Chairs Program and the Social Sciences and Humanities Research Council of Canada.

Each of these propositions is entailed by (f). Imagine that Smith realizes the entailment of each of these propositions he has constructed by (f), and proceeds to accept (g), (h), and (i) on the basis of (f). Smith has correctly inferred (g), (h), and (i) from a proposition for which he has strong evidence. Smith is therefore completely justified in believing each of these three propositions. Smith, of course, has no idea where Brown is.

But imagine now that two further conditions hold. First, Jones does *not* own a Ford, but is at present driving a rented car. And secondly, by the sheerest coincidence and entirely unknown to Smith the place mentioned in proposition (h) happens really to be the place where Brown is. If these two conditions hold then Smith does *not* know that (h) is true, even though (*i*) (h) *is* true, (*ii*) Smith does belief that (h) is true, and (*iii*) Smith is justified in believing that (h) is true.

One leading philosopher labeled Gettier's paper as "Gettier's survey" (Jackson 2011, pp. 480–1), which "invited" philosophers "to agree with his intuition" that the examples were not cases of knowledge (Jackson 1998, p. 28). Evidence from surveys on whether people attribute or deny knowledge in specific cases is "highly relevant to what their concept of knowledge is," so the contribution of Gettier's paper was to provide "empirical, a posteriori" evidence that "so many readers agreed with Gettier that the cases he presented were not cases of knowledge" (Jackson 2011, pp. 476–7). Literature reviews claim that "most" philosophers who consider such cases agree with Gettier (e.g. Turri 2012a, p. 215; Hetherington 2016a, p. ix).

Several critical points should be made immediately about such claims and Gettier's cases. First, it is not actually known whether "many" or "most" philosophers agree about such cases, because no empirical study of philosophers' judgments of Gettier's cases has ever been published. Accordingly, any claim about the relevant proportions is speculative and ought to be treated as such. Second, the description of Gettier's paper as a "survey," even in an attenuated and extended sense, is inaccurate and misleading. Gettier did not "invite" philosophers to share his intuition. Instead, he used language apt to prime attributions of ignorance: Smith is described as selecting propositions "at random," accepting them despite having "no idea" regarding principal facts implicated by the propositions, and also ending up with a true belief "by the sheerest coincidence" for reasons "entirely unknown" to him. Gettier did not probe for judgments. Instead, he confidently and unqualifiedly inserted his own verdicts into the description of the case. Despite the unnaturalness and pointlessness of Smith's inferences, Gettier tells us that Smith is "completely justified" in making them, and that "Smith does not know" the relevant proposition despite having a justified true belief. Third, and relatedly, when judged as survey instruments intended to probe for knowledge judgments, Gettier's cases are miserably constructed. In addition to being "contrived and artificial" (Dancy 1985, p. 26), they are long, stilted, tendentious, multiply confounded, and not paired with relevant controls.

For these reasons, even if one tested Gettier's cases and found that people unanimously judged that "Smith doesn't know," it would provide little if any information about "our folk theory" of knowledge, contrary to what some have suggested (e.g. Jackson 1998, p. 31). Similarly, if one thought that the concept of knowledge at issue in the contemporary literature was "a philosophers' artifact" unconnected to "anything possessed by ordinary people" (Lycan 2006, p. 165), testing Gettier's cases would provide negligible information about the standards implicit in professional philosophers' judgments. In short, Gettier's cases are completely unsuitable for any serious or worthwhile attempt to gain evidence regarding people's knowledge concept. In particular, they do not "prov[e] that justified true belief is insufficient for knowledge" (Jacquette 1996, pp. 115–16), according to any knowledge concept.

As if this were not bad enough, adding to this embarrassment of contemporary epistemology, much simpler cases had long existed that are better suited to teach the lesson supposedly learned from Gettier's cases, as prominent philosophers have pointed out for decades (e.g. Goldman 1967, p. 357n1; Matilal 1986, pp. 135–7; Chisholm 1989, pp. 92–3). Moreover, there is no evidence that the view targeted by Gettier's cases – the "justified true belief" or "JTB" theory of knowledge – was ever held by historically influential philosophers (Kaplan 1985; Plantinga 1993a, pp. 6–7; Dutant 2015), let alone any evidence for the wildly irresponsible claim that it was "the most widely accepted definition of (propositional) knowledge in the history of philosophy" (Jacquette 1996, p. 115).

The serious defects undermining Gettier's original cases are not limited to those particular cases. Another influential case from early in the literature also focused on car ownership (Lehrer 1965, pp. 169–70). The agent in this example, Keith, has an "honest and reliable" friend named "Mr. Nogot." Nogot gets out of a new Ford, walks into Keith's office, tells Keith that he has "just purchased the car," and – weirdly – "shows [Keith] a certificate that states that he owns the Ford." On this basis, Keith believes, reasonably, that "Mr. Nogot, who is in my office, owns a Ford." Then Keith deduces that

"Someone in my office owns a Ford." We are told that Keith is "completely justified" in making this inference, despite its unnaturalness and apparent pointlessness. We are then told that Mr. Nogot has "deceived" Keith and does not own a Ford. We are left to guess why Mr. Nogot, honest and reliable friend that he is, would do this. Nevertheless, Keith also sees another person in his office, "Mr. Havit," who does own a Ford. But Keith has "no evidence that [Mr. Havit] owns a Ford." Thus, it is true that someone in Keith's office owns a Ford. However, we are told, Keith does "not know that it is true." Again, a weirdly contrived scenario is described using tendentious language, and all of the relevant verdicts are confidently inserted into the case's description.

Here is another, recent example of a "Gettier" case offered in apparent seriousness, although it might be more accurately labeled a "chain linked Gettier" case because it consists of two parts: one that explains how an agent is "Gettiered," and another that then attempts to embed the first part into a more complicated situation (Church 2013, p. 174, pp. 175–6):

> (*Expert botanist*) David is an expert botanist, able to competently distinguish between the over 20,000 different species of orchid. David is presented with an orchid and asked to identify its species. Using his amazing skill, he can clearly tell that this particular orchid is either going to be a *Platanthera tescamnis* or a *Platanthera sparsiflora* (which look quite similar), and upon even further expert analysis he comes to the conclusion that it is a *Platanthera tescamnis* orchid, which it is. However, Kevin, David's nemesis and an expert botanist in his own right, decided the night before to disguise the *Platanthera tescamnis* orchid to look like a *Platanthera sparsiflora* orchid. Thankfully, however, Alvin, David's other expert botanist nemesis (who is conveniently not on speaking terms with Kevin), decided to try to trick David in the same way – arriving shortly after Kevin left, perceiving that the orchid was a *Platanthera sparsiflora*, and disguising Kevin's disguise to look like a *Platanthera tescamnis*, which it happens to actually be.

> (*Orchid guessing*) Ruth, Dave, Shelly, and Bob are playing a guess-the-species-of-orchid game – a game where they are presented with various types of orchid and asked to identify the species. Ruth is an expert botanist. When she is presented with an orchid she is able to use her immense skills as a botanist to narrow down the over 20,000 possibilities to the one right answer. Dave too is an expert botanist; indeed, he is every bit as knowledgeable as Ruth. Using his amazing skill he can clearly tell that the orchid

before him is either going to be a *Platanthera tescamnis* or a *Platanthera sparsiflora* (which look quite similar), and upon even further expert analysis he comes to the conclusion that it is a *Platanthera tescamnis* orchid, which it is. However, after narrowing down the over 20,000 possibilities to just *Platanthera tescamnis* and *Platanthera sparsiflora*, Dave is Gettiered about these final two options. Thirdly, Shelly is presented with an orchid. She knows almost nothing about botany; however, she is something of an idiot savant – having memorized the names of every single species of orchid. She has no idea what species is before her, so she simply picks a species at random and just happens to get it right. Finally, Bob is presented with an orchid. He knows absolutely nothing about botany. He doesn't even know the names of any species. When he goes to hazard a guess; however, he chokes on a burp and just so happens to utter the name of the species before him.

Afterward – in the main text, after presenting the cases and while stipulating verdicts about them – the author of these examples clarifies that Dave's "circumstances are just like David's in the case of Expert Botanist" (Church 2013, p. 176). Again we are confronted with a long, complicated description of an exceedingly contrived situation. (Or is it two situations?) Despite the length, some critical details are omitted, and are later stipulated elsewhere. Tendentious language abounds – "knows almost nothing," "is Gettiered" (!), "has no idea," "guessing," "picks [an answer] at random and just happens to get it right," "knows absolutely nothing," "goes to hazard a guess," "just so happens to utter the name of the species." I leave it to others to speculate on the significance of the fact that some professional philosophers believe that we advance our understanding of anything by considering whether an agent's intellectual performance is "on a par with Bob's choked-on burp" (Church 2013, p. 176).

Arguably, we can detect an underlying structure in some of these poorly constructed cases (Zagzebski 1996; Jacquette 1996; Feldman 2003). It involves a person with imperfect but potentially good evidence for thinking that a specific proposition is true. This person notices that this first proposition entails a second proposition, which he concludes is true. And it is true. However, the impressive evidence with which he began turns out to be misleading and he never detected that the first proposition is true. In fact, the first proposition is false. In a proper study of judgments about the case, we would now decide two things. On the one hand, does the person have a justified true belief that the second proposition is true?

On the other hand, does the person know that the second proposition is true? If the central tendency is for our answers to be "yes" and "no," respectively, then we are committed to denying that knowledge is equivalent to justified true belief.

Researchers have recently made serious, unbiased attempts to test cases structured in this way, to which we turn next. In what follows, I distinguish between *Gettier's cases*, which I have already discussed, and *"Gettier" cases* (always with scare quotes). The former come from Gettier's original paper, but the latter are merely a nominal category with no underlying unity (Turri 2016a). For reasons already discussed, no serious study of knowledge judgments would use Gettier's cases because the results could not be meaningfully interpreted. As the theoretical literature developed over the decades, a bewildering array of cases have been carelessly labeled "Gettier" cases. Based on the disappointingly uncritical reception of Gettier's cases, it is perhaps not surprising that philosophers have been injudicious in keeping track of whether and how new "Gettier" cases differ from Gettier's cases or from each other, and whether such differences are important. By contrast, in just a few years, the experimental research discussed below has made significant progress in identifying factors affecting central tendencies in knowledge judgments. Of course, once a case's structure is clarified, serviceable stimuli are constructed, and appropriate controls are included, the study has the potential to be informative regarding knowledge judgments. Whether we call it a "Gettier" case is immaterial.

12.2 Experimental Research on "Gettier" Cases

The first study of "Gettier" cases of which I am aware was motivated by psychological research suggesting important cultural differences in reasoning styles and moral judgments (Weinberg, Nichols, and Stich 2001). Researchers tested a story about car ownership on US undergraduates from a variety of cultural backgrounds. The story was similar to some cases from the early Gettier literature, but it was phrased much more naturally and unbiasedly (2001, p. 429):

> Bob has a friend, Jill, who has driven a Buick for many years. Bob therefore thinks that Jill drives an American car. He is not aware, however, that her Buick has recently been stolen, and he is also not aware that Jill has replaced it with a Pontiac, which is a different kind of American car. Does Bob really know that Jill drives an American car, or does he only believe it?

Approximately 25 percent of those reporting Western cultural backgrounds attributed knowledge, but more than half of those reporting east-
ern or southern Asian backgrounds attributed knowledge. The results fit
nicely with prior cross-cultural work on other sorts of judgment. Follow-up
work on knowledge judgments has not consistently replicated these
cultural differences when using the same materials on undergraduates in
the United States (Kim and Yuan 2015), when using slightly modified
materials on lay populations in the United Kingdom (Seyedsayamdost
2015), when using modified materials and procedures to test residents of
the USA and India (Turri 2013, sec. 7), or, on some ways of probing for
knowledge judgments, when using different materials to test residents of
Brazil, India, Japan, and the United States in their native languages
(Machery, Stich, Rose, Chatterjee et al. 2017). This follow-up work has
observed consistently low rates of knowledge attribution, typically around
20 percent. Some of this work included minimally matched control conditions where people attributed knowledge.

Nevertheless, at least three separate studies have found a statistically
significant difference whereby people with Asian cultural backgrounds
attribute knowledge at higher rates than "Westerners" do in such cases
(Weinberg, Nichols, and Stich 2001; Kim and Yuan 2015, p. 356n3 [unfor-
tunately relegating this finding to a footnote in a paper entitled, "No cross-
cultural differences in Gettier car case intuition"]; Machery, Stich, Rose,
Chatterjee et al. 2017). Another cross-cultural study, by far the most wide-
ranging one on knowledge attribution in "Gettier" cases to date, found
substantial agreement in knowledge judgments across seventeen languages,
with one group, Israeli Bedouins, diverging radically from the rest. So, at
this point, the balance of evidence supports the conclusion that there is
a cross-culturally robust central tendency to deny knowledge in some
"Gettier" cases on some ways of probing. At the same time, there is also
some evidence that other, seemingly simpler, ways of probing erase and
potentially even reverse that tendency, and there is a nontrivial chance that
some cultural variation exists in these matters.

At present, the evidence also suggests that participants' biological sex
and age have little, if any, effect on knowledge judgments about "Gettier"
cases (e.g. Starmans and Friedman 2012; Turri 2013; Kim and Yuan 2015;
Machery, Stich, Rose, Alai et al. 2017; Turri 2017b). Recent evidence
suggests that individual differences, such as personality traits, might affect
such judgments. A large cross-cultural study found a negative correlation
between conscientiousness and denying knowledge in a "Gettier" case

(Machery, Stich, Rose, Alai et al. 2017). That is, the more conscientious a participant was, the more likely the participant was to attribute knowledge in a "Gettier" case. By contrast, neuroticism and openness to new experiences correlated positively with denying knowledge. These tantalizing results are likely to spark debate and speculation, which is natural and appropriate, but, as the researchers themselves admirably emphasize, further research is needed before drawing confident conclusions about these matters. In other words, a theory should not get too far ahead of the data.

Researchers have investigated whether questioning procedures affect the rate of knowledge attribution in "Gettier" cases. For example, participants are less likely to attribute knowledge in a "Gettier" case when the scenario is broken up into multiple parts on three separate screens, rather than being presented all at once on a single screen, and when participants are asked questions that make certain features of the case salient (Turri 2013; 2016b, experiment 4). At present, it is unclear why this happens. To take another example, when participants read the case about Bob's car (see above), researchers observed a significantly lower rate of knowledge attribution when the response options were "really knows/only believes" than when they were "knows/does not now" (Cullen 2010, p. 288; Turri 2016b, experiment 4). Other researchers first probed for knowledge attributions with the options "Yes, he knows/No, he doesn't know," followed by (within-subjects) "He knew/He thought he knew but he did not actually know" (Machery, Stich, Rose, Chatterjee et al. 2017; Machery, Stich, Rose, Alai et al. 2017; compare Nagel, Mar, and San Juan 2013). Knowledge attribution was much higher for the "Yes/No" option, a pattern that is cross-culturally robust. Interpreting this last finding is complicated, however, by the fact that the verbal difference between the pairs of options was confounded with order, length, and complexity, as well as by other intervening questions about the case. For instance, maybe the mere fact that people are being asked about knowledge *again* leads them to attribute it less, or maybe they are less likely to answer affirmatively for longer or more complex response options. Nevertheless, overall the evidence clearly shows that questioning procedures can affect the psychological processing involved in producing or recording knowledge judgments, perhaps by triggering slightly different knowledge concepts, by causing the same concept to be construed in different ways, or by changing the way in which participants interpret the task. Further research is required to investigate the matter.

Arguably the most important study of "Gettier" cases to date distinguished between *apparent* and *authentic* evidence (Starmans and Friedman 2012). Apparent evidence is "evidence that appears to be informative about reality, but is not really," whereas authentic evidence is, roughly, evidence that makes the belief true when based on it (2012, p. 280). To illustrate the difference, consider two versions of a story about Corey, who collects coins in his piggy bank. One day, Corey looks at a quarter that he is putting into his bank, and notices that it looks pretty old. He checks the date and reads "1936." In the authentic-evidence version of the story, the coin is from 1936. In the apparent-evidence version, it is from 1938 and part of the date has rubbed off. In each version, there is already a 1936 quarter buried deep in the piggy bank, but Corey isn't aware of this other quarter. Then he takes a short nap, during which his roommate comes home, takes the quarter that Corey just deposited in the bank, and leaves. Corey wakes up soon after and does not realize what his roommate did. Here is the complete text of both versions:

> (*Apparent evidence*) Corey has been collecting coins in his piggy bank for years. One day he is about to put a quarter in his piggy bank, and notices that it looks pretty old. Though he's never paid attention to dates before, he reads the date and sees that it's from 1936. However, he doesn't realize that the date has partially rubbed off and it is really from 1938. There is already a quarter dated 1936 buried deep in his piggy bank, but Corey isn't aware of this. He deposits the quarter and goes to take a nap. Corey's roommate Scott comes home, and needs some change for the bus. He shakes the piggy bank and the quarter Corey just put in falls out. Scott takes it and leaves. Corey wakes up after a 10-minute nap, and doesn't realize that Scott was there.

> (*Authentic evidence*) Corey has been collecting coins in his piggy bank for years. One day he is about to put a quarter in his piggy bank, and notices that it looks pretty old. Though he's never paid attention to dates before, he reads the date and sees that it's from 1936. However, he doesn't realize that 1936 is the year his grandmother was born. There is already a quarter dated 1936 buried deep in his piggy bank, but Corey isn't aware of this. He deposits the quarter and goes to take a nap. Corey's roommate Scott comes home, and needs some change for the bus. He shakes the piggy bank and the quarter Corey just put in falls out. Scott takes it and leaves. Corey wakes up after a 10 minute nap, and doesn't realize that Scott was there.

When Corey wakes up from his nap, does he "really know" or does he "only believe" that there is a 1936 coin in his piggy bank? People who read the authentic-evidence version tended to attribute knowledge, but people who read the apparent-evidence version tended to deny knowledge. The basic finding that people tend to deny knowledge in apparent-evidence cases has been replicated (e.g. Turri 2013, sec. 2), and so has the finding that people tend to attribute knowledge exceeding chance rates in authentic-evidence cases (e.g. Nagel, San Juan, and Mar 2013, using very different questioning procedures; for important discussion and corrections regarding the statistical analyses, see Starmans and Friedman 2013, p. 664; see also Powell et al. 2013, using a very different measure involving false recall).

Building on the apparent/authentic distinction, more recent work has shown that the structure of "Gettier" cases differs in at least three important ways (Turri, Buckwalter, and Blouw 2014; 2015). First, many differ in whether the agent *initially perceives* a state of affairs that makes his or her belief true (a "truth-maker," for short). In some examples, the agent perceives a truth-maker, but in others the agent perceives a convincing fake or something that seems to entail that the relevant proposition is true. Second, many examples differ in whether the agent's perceptual relation *remains intact* throughout. Sometimes, the agent perceives a certain truth-maker and events threaten to disrupt that truth-maker, but the threat ultimately fails. At other times, the threat succeeds in disrupting the original truth-maker, which is then replaced by a "backup" truth-maker. Third, many examples differ in *how similar* the perceived truth-maker and backup truth-maker are. Sometimes they very closely resemble one another, while at other times they differ greatly.

Current evidence suggests that all three differences affect knowledge judgments (Turri, Buckwalter, and Blouw 2015). In one study, participants read one of seven versions of a story. One version was a "knowledge control," intended to elicit very high rates of knowledge attribution. Another version was an "ignorance control," intended to elicit very low rates of knowledge attribution. The other five versions combined different permutations of the three structural variables noted above. The basic storyline featured an agent, Emma, admiring jewelry in a fancy department store. She purchases a stone from the diamond display, puts it in her pocket, browses for another minute, then leaves the store. The different versions of the story vary as to whether the stone is a real diamond or a fake, whether there is a threat to the stone remaining in Emma's pocket, whether the threat fails or succeeds, and whether any other stone also ends up in Emma's pocket. In the terminology introduced above, the different versions manipulated whether Emma *detects* an initial truth-maker for her belief that there is a diamond in her pocket as she leaves the store, whether Emma's truth-detection is saliently *threatened*, whether the threat *succeeds* in disrupting the initial truth-maker, and whether the backup truth-maker is highly *similar or dissimilar* to the initial one.

In all versions, Emma purchases a stone from a jewelry store, puts it in her pocket, and soon walks out of the store. In all the stories that involve detection, the stone she purchases is a diamond. In all the stories that do not involve detection, the stone is a fake. In all the stories that involve similar backup truth-makers, the backup truth-maker is that, one way or another, a diamond is put into Emma's pocket before she leaves the store. In all the stories that involve dissimilar backup truth-makers, the backup truth-maker is that a real diamond was secretly sewn into Emma's pocket by a previous owner long ago. Table 12.1 summarizes the seven versions of the story.

Table 12.1 Description of the seven versions of the story (from Turri, Buckwalter, and Blouw 2015)

Condition	Description
1. Knowledge Control	The stone Emma purchases is a diamond. She walks out of the store and nothing else happens.
2. Failed Threat	The stone Emma purchases is a diamond. A skilled jewel thief tries to steal it from her pocket before she leaves the store, but he fails.
3. Detection Similar Replacement	The stone Emma purchases is a diamond. A skilled jewel thief tries to steal it from her pocket before she leaves the store, and he succeeds. Someone secretly slips a diamond into Emma's pocket before she leaves the store.
4. Detection Dissimilar Replacement	The stone Emma purchases is a diamond. A skilled jewel thief tries to steal it from her pocket before she leaves the store, and he succeeds. Long ago, Emma's grandmother secretly sewed a diamond into the pocket of Emma's coat.
5. No Detection Similar Replacement	The stone Emma purchases is a fake. A skilled jewel thief tries to steal it from her pocket before she leaves the store, and he succeeds. Someone secretly slips a diamond into Emma's pocket before she leaves the store.
6. No Detection Dissimilar Replacement	The stone Emma purchases is a fake. A skilled jewel thief tries to steal it from her pocket before she leaves the store, and he succeeds. Long ago, Emma's grandmother secretly sewed a diamond into the pocket of Emma's coat.
7. Ignorance Control	The stone Emma purchases is a fake. She walks out of the store and nothing else happens.

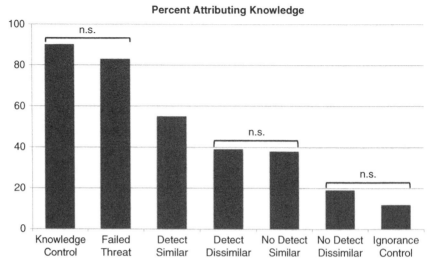

Figure 12.1 Percent of participants attributing knowledge across conditions. Except where nonsignificance is indicated, significance for all comparisons at the $p < 0.01$ level (from Turri, Buckwalter, and Blouw 2015).

By one estimation or another, stories 2–6 would all count as "Gettier" cases (e.g. Goldman 1976; Sosa 1991, pp. 238–9; Zagzebski 1996, 283–5; Pritchard 2005; Greco 2010, ch. 5). Story 2 is structurally similar to the "fake barn" case, and story 6 is structurally similar in some important ways to Gettier's original cases. But people judged the stories very differently (see Figure 12.1). Rates of knowledge attribution for story 2 were very high (over 80 percent), and did not differ from rates observed for the knowledge control story. By contrast, rates of knowledge for story 6 were extremely low (under 20 percent), and did not differ from rates observed for the ignorance control story. Rates for the other three stories fell somewhere in between. Researchers have replicated this same basic pattern of results, using different cover stories and procedures.

Of course, there is no reason to expect that the taxonomy identifies all the factors that affect knowledge judgments or all the criteria implicit in our ordinary knowledge concept. The researchers who proposed the taxonomy never made such ambitious and unsubstantiated claims, and existing research on folk epistemology clearly demonstrates that other factors also matter, including a qualitative difference between knowing positively and negatively valenced outcomes (Beebe and Buckwalter 2010; Beebe and Jensen 2012; Buckwalter 2014; Turri 2014), a qualitative difference between probabilistic information pertaining to propensities and base-rates (Turri and Friedman 2014; Friedman and Turri 2015; Turri in press), a qualitative difference between different informational sources (Turri 2015a; 2015c), a qualitative difference between knowing affirmations and negations (Turri 2017a; manuscript), and the relationship between knowledge and actionability (Turri, Buckwalter, and Rose 2016; Turri and Buckwalter 2017). Researchers are fully aware that further work remains to be done (Blouw, Buckwalter, and Turri 2018). Instead, the value and purpose of the taxonomy is that it systematically identifies several factors that affect knowledge judgments, whose significance the theoretical literature has failed to consistently and explicitly reflect, and which, at this point, will inform any responsible treatment of "Gettier" cases. Hopefully, future research advances to the point where the taxonomy is surpassed and no longer generates further research questions in this area.

In the meantime, the taxonomy just discussed can be used to catalogue and even to predict results from other studies of "Gettier" cases. For example, stories 3 ("detect similar") and 5 ("no detect similar") are structurally similar to the "authentic evidence" and "apparent evidence" scenarios, respectively, that were previously tested by researchers. Based on how the taxonomy classifies these cases, the prediction is that, other things being equal, people will tend to attribute knowledge in authentic-evidence cases and to deny knowledge in apparent-evidence cases. As noted earlier, this is exactly what researchers observed. Also, earlier I mentioned that story 2 ("failed threat") is structurally similar to "fake barn" cases, which researchers had already begun studying. In the epistemology literature, theorists have claimed, without providing evidence, that "we would be strongly inclined" not to attribute knowledge in such cases (Goldman 1976; see also Sosa 1991, pp. 238–9; Neta and Rohrbaugh 2004, p. 401; Pritchard 2005, pp. 161–2; Kvanvig 2008, p. 274). And philosophers have relied on this verdict in order to evaluate or motivate theories of knowledge. However, based on how the taxonomy classifies this case, the prediction is that, other things being equal, people will tend to attribute knowledge (Swain, Alexander, and Weinberg 2008, pp. 154–5):

> The first study of judgments regarding a "fake barn" case used this scenario:
>
>> Suzy looks out the window of her car and sees a barn near the road, and so she comes to believe that there's a barn near the road. However, Suzy doesn't realize that the countryside she is driving through is currently

being used as the set of a film, and that the set designers have constructed many fake-barn façades in this area that look as though they are real barns. In fact, Suzy is looking at the only real barn in the area.

Participants then rated the statement "Suzy knows there is a barn near the road" on a 5-point Likert scale ("strongly disagree" = 1, through "strongly agree" = 5). Researchers found that participants tended to attribute knowledge, with the mean rating (= 3.6) exceeding the neutral midpoint (= 3) and came close to the mean rating observed for what the researchers judged to be a "clear case of knowledge" (= 3.9) (2008, pp. 143, 146). However, the "clear case of knowledge," involving a chemist, was very different from the "fake barn" case, so interpreting this comparison is difficult. Another study tested the same "fake barn" case involving Suzy, but used a dichotomous measure for the knowledge attribution. Again, researchers failed to detect a central tendency to deny knowledge, and rates of knowledge attribution reached nearly 60 percent in some conditions, even though the same participants tended to deny knowledge for other cases (Wright 2010).

The primary purpose of those first two studies of "fake barn" cases, it should be noted, was to look for order effects on knowledge attributions, so they used a within-subjects design, and they did not include control comparisons for the "fake barn" case specifically. No order effects were detected for the "fake barn" case (Swain, Alexander, and Weinberg (2008), p. 146; Wright 2010, p. 494, reporting $p = 0.086$ for the relevant comparison, which, contrary to what is suggested by the summary of results in the study's discussion section, is not statistically significant by conventional standards of interpretation). Several subsequent studies were designed to investigate knowledge judgments in "fake barn" cases specifically, and these studies included closely matched controls. The results have consistently shown that people tend to attribute knowledge to agents in such cases.

For example, one research team tested a case involving an agent, Gerald, who sees many things, including a cow and a real house amidst a large number of "house façades" (Colaço et al. 2014). Participants then rated their agreement with a knowledge attribution on a 7-point Likert scale. In the control condition, participants rated whether Gerald knows that "he saw a cow." (The story did not mention anything about "fake cows.") In the experimental condition, participants rated whether Gerald knows that "he saw a house." The mean score was higher in the control condition than in the experimental condition, indicating that the presence of façades depressed knowledge attribution. Nevertheless, mean response in the experimental condition was significantly above the scale's midpoint, indicating that people tended to attribute knowledge.

In another series of studies, people tended to attribute knowledge that an albino "vervet monkey" was in a tree even when it "was surrounded by" visibly indistinguishable "snow monkeys" (Turri 2016c). Again results from a closely matched control condition, in which the vervet monkey was a different color, suggest that nearby, visibly similar, distractors depress knowledge attribution. Nevertheless, even when there were nearby "fakes," attributing knowledge remained the central tendency.

Researchers also recently tested this pair of cases (Turri 2016b. p. 762):

(Control/Experimental) Sarah is driving with her son down the highway. Sarah looks out the window of her car and sees a red barn near the road. Sarah doesn't realize that the countryside she is driving through is currently being used as the set of a film, and that the set designers have constructed many [cheap barns/fake-barn façades] in this area that look as though they are [expensive/real] barns. Despite all the [cheap barns/fakes] around, Sarah is in fact looking at the one [expensive/real] barn in the area. Sarah's son points to the barn and says, "Mom, I have to do a report on barns for my social studies class. Is that a barn?"

Participants selected from one of four options that "best describes Sarah":

She knows that it's a barn, and she should tell her son that it's a barn.
She knows that it's a barn, and she should not tell her son that it's a barn.
She does not know that it's a barn, and she should tell her son that it's a barn.
She does not know that it's a barn, and she should not tell her son that it's a barn.

(All options were randomly rotated and participants never saw numerical labels.) The overwhelming majority selected "She knows that it's a barn, and she should tell her son that it's a barn," in both the control (94 percent) and the experimental (83 percent) conditions, with no statistically significant difference between them. This same basic finding was replicated using a 7-point Likert scale to collect knowledge judgments on their own (i.e. without being paired with assertability ratings in a series of conjunctions) (Turri 2017b).

Participants continued to attribute knowledge even when Sarah was explicitly described as incorrectly classifying four structures as barns before correctly classifying a fifth structure (Turri 2017b). That is, even in a "multiple-iteration fake barn case" where the agent first repeatedly encounters and misclassifies the first "fakes" that she sees, people tend to attribute knowledge when the agent correctly classifies the real barn she sees.

Interestingly, in a closely matched control condition that did not mention the existence of fakes or any other factor that would cause the agent to misidentify a non-barn as a barn, an importantly different pattern was observed: people tended to deny knowledge when the agent correctly classified the real barn on the fifth try. In other words, the presence of nearby fakes could actually prevent iterated errors from depressing knowledge judgments. Regression and causal-search analyses suggested that this effect was due to participants making different inferences about whether the agent was able to detect barns in the two conditions. When the errors were plausibly due to the fakes, people still thought that the agent was able to detect barns, and, when she got the correct answer through that ability, they attributed knowledge (compare Turri 2016d). By contrast, when no information presented could plausibly explain the errors, participants inferred that the agent lacked the relevant perceptual ability, so they did not attribute knowledge.

At this point, it is clear that there is a central tendency to attribute knowledge in "fake barn" cases. Thus, a founding assumption of this episode in professional epistemologists' fascination with "Gettier" cases – namely, that there is no such tendency – is false. One might conjecture that this is an instance where "trained professionals" tend to have very different intuitions than do untrained laypeople. But the evidence does not support that, either: when researchers tested epistemologists' judgments about cases with a "fake barn" structure, most attributed knowledge (Horvath and Wiegmann 2016).

12.3 Conclusion

Despite a potential bright spot here or there, the theoretical literature on Gettier's cases, "Gettier" cases, and "the Gettier problem" is an embarrassing, confusing, and unproductive mess, for several reasons. Many of the cases proposed in the literature, including Gettier's originals, are unsuitable to provide useful information because of their poor construction and prejudiced presentation. The theory that the cases supposedly undermine – the allegedly "traditional" theory of knowledge as "justified true belief" – was not the traditional theory and, in fact, might not have been held by any influential philosopher before the mid-twentieth century. Moreover, prior to Gettier, many philosophers had proposed simpler, clearer, and therefore better cases apt to teach the same lesson that Gettier's cases allegedly taught, so the intense focus on Gettier's later, inferior, cases is both counterproductive and unfair. Additionally, philosophers have made unsupported empirical claims about how people tend to judge "Gettier" cases, and they have relied on these claims to motivate and evaluate theories, but empirical research has shown that some of those empirical claims are false. Philosophers are also apparently misinformed about how philosophers tend to judge some "Gettier" cases, with recent studies finding that most epistemologists attribute knowledge in cases that were allegedly intuitive cases of ignorance. Relatedly, perhaps, philosophers have incompetently curated the genre of thought experiments variously counted as "Gettier" cases: experimental studies have shown that knowledge attribution in different "Gettier" cases varies from lower than 20 percent to higher than 80 percent.

If judgments about "Gettier" cases vary this widely – from patterns resembling paradigmatic ignorance to patterns resembling paradigmatic knowledge – then "Gettier case" is a theoretically useless category. The fact that something is a "Gettier" case is consistent with its being both overwhelmingly judged knowledge and overwhelmingly judged ignorance. Such findings demonstrate the importance of including control conditions and tight manipulations using closely matched stimuli. Doing these things allows us to make meaningful comparisons and responsibly interpret results, which in turn sanctions (defeasible) inferences about features of people's knowledge concept. It can also prevent us from grouping wildly heterogeneous cases into theoretically useless categories.

So, instead of dwelling at length on "the Gettier problem" and trying to "radically" adjust our views about what the "distinctive" feature of Gettier's cases was (Hetherington 2016a), and instead of trying to "vindicate the tradition [*sic*] by showing JTB to be *almost* right" (Turri 2012b, p. 257), a much better way forward would be for epistemologists, individually and collectively, to stop crediting Gettier for an idea that was not originally his, to stop repeating lies about the historical importance of the theory he criticized, to stop ignoring the irredeemable faults of his original cases, and to be much more discerning and humble about curating genres of thought experiment, identifying central tendencies in judgments about particular cases, and drawing theoretical conclusions based on such (alleged) tendencies. In short, end the malpractice.

Additionally, in light of the fact that mainstream philosophical research in this area has been guilty of grave shortcomings for so long, we should not take seriously vague, self-flattering worries about whether ordinary people can "competently assess" various cases, where the supposed standard of competence is the alleged central tendency in philosophers' judgments about the matter (Turri 2013). Philosophers should be more careful before proclaiming consensus on an issue, and more mindful of the possibility that they lack unproblematic transparent access to their intuitions and attitudes about cases, let alone to those of others. Relatedly, potentially fruitful lines of research in the psychology and sociology of philosophy could explore the extent to which an appearance of disciplinary "consensus" results from mechanisms of, at the very least, dubious intellectual legitimacy, such as thought-experimenter bias, gatekeeper effects, selection effects, false consensus effects, conformism, and motivated reasoning (for references and further discussion, see Turri 2016a).

Accordingly, I propose that after decades of generating much heat and little if any light, we should close the book on this long and sad chapter of contemporary anglophone theoretical epistemology. In the aftermath, if for some unexpected reason, revisiting Gettier's cases or "the Gettier problem" merits our attention, then, by all means, let us do so, but this time much more seriously and honestly.

By contrast, in just a few short years, experimental work on "Gettier" cases has generated a range of informative and replicated results, which have begun answering questions about the ordinary knowledge concept. It is a good bet that further progress lies in this direction, so this sort of work should be welcomed and encouraged. The fact that previous results pertained to "Gettier" cases is incidental, however, because that is not a meaningful category. We would be better off simply dropping the eponymous labeling, and instead focusing on the underlying factors that actually affect knowledge judgments, such as perceptions of ability, luck, deception, or interference, to name just a few.

Some philosophers might be tempted to insist that empirical results are irrelevant to their research project, which is "pursing only the minutiae of a concept possessed" by "English-speaking philosophers" but not by other people (Lycan 2006, p. 165). Philosophers should resist this temptation because it is an empirical question which concepts philosophers possess. To the extent that they do succumb, philosophers should not be surprised when people stop ignoring their navel-gazing only to malign it.

Of course, studying a knowledge concept is not the only project in which one might be interested. Instead, one might wish to study knowledge itself, a real cognitive relation that often obtains between minds and facts, which our concepts could mischaracterize. In this chapter, I have not concerned myself with this other project because, based on the methodology they utilize, it is perfectly clear that neither Gettier's paper nor most philosophical writings addressing "the Gettier problem" provide serious evidence about the nature of knowledge. They study thought experiments and argue about implications of stipulated verdicts for artificially precise definitions of knowledge; they do not study minds, mental states, or cognitive processes that actually generate, store, transmit, or utilize knowledge. It is equally clear, it should be added, and would be happily acknowledged by researchers working in the field, that the experimental research reviewed here is informative regarding only a small fraction of what occurs in people's minds, namely that pertaining to their knowledge concept and the processing of knowledge judgments in relation to a limited set of factors.

13   The Gettier Problem's Explicability Problem

Stephen Hetherington

13.1 Introduction

This chapter derives a limitative result for post-Gettier epistemology. This result is a surprising and potentially substantial constraint upon how such epistemology can proceed. It is a result relevant to all epistemological attempts that could in principle be devised with the aim of understanding knowledge in light of Edmund Gettier's (1963) influential challenge. The result should also be seen as a *problem* for most of the theories of knowledge that have actually been developed by epistemologists seeking either to build upon or to defuse Gettier's challenge. I will speak, therefore, of *the explicability problem* – and of its bearing upon what epistemologists have long designated as "the Gettier problem."

William Lycan (2006) talked of "the Gettier Problem problem." This was seemingly the high hurdle of ascertaining why no clear solution to the Gettier problem had emerged, in spite of so much epistemological energy being directed since 1963 toward meeting Gettier's challenge. This chapter offers at least a partial possible answer to Lycan's question. Maybe at least part of the reason why there has been no widely accepted solution to the Gettier problem is that the pertinent post-Gettier theories of knowledge that have gained currency have been vulnerable to this chapter's limitative result. Has there been only insufficient meta-epistemological self-monitoring accompanying attempts to explicate and defuse Gettier's challenge?

An even larger meta-epistemological question is implicit in that concern: are epistemologists ever meta-epistemological enough?[1] But this chapter will discuss just Gettier's challenge. The chapter enjoins philosophers to be more cautious when saying what the correlative Gettier problem is in the

---

[1] See Hetherington (1992; 2010) for some skeptical meta-epistemological arguments, questioning whether epistemologists ever have justification or knowledge for their claims and theories.

first place – even when introducing it to readers and students in what might feel like "intuitive" terms. We should likewise be more cautious when proposing epistemological lessons to be learned from the Gettier problem – ideas about how we need to describe knowledge if we are to surmount Gettier's challenge.

13.2 Gettier's Knowledge-Fallibilist Question

Gettier introduced his counterexamples with two epistemic principles, intended to highlight and justify both the structure and the interpretive reach of those counterexamples. This section describes the important interpretive role played within Gettier's counterexamples by one of those two principles.[2]

His first principle was a traditional form of fallibilism about what is being allowed by knowledge's supposedly required justification component (1963, p. 121): "in that sense of 'justified' in which S's being justified in believing P is a necessary condition of S's knowing that P, it is possible for a person to be justified in believing a proposition that is in fact false." [3] We may leave aside the question of whether, ultimately, knowledge would best be understood as needing to include infallible justificatory support (if it must include justificatory support at all)[4] – justification that somehow eliminates even the possibility of the belief in question being false. My immediate aim is merely interpretive. Even in this respect, we must tread carefully when presenting Gettier's thinking, since it was *not* overtly part of an argument in support of an infallibilism about knowledge's justificatory component. Even if we wish to use Gettier's thinking to ground a consequent resolve to embrace knowledge-infallibilism,[5] we must begin more restrainedly when trying merely to explicate – to understand – his challenge on its own terms.

---

[2] I will not rehearse those counterexamples here. This chapter presumes that readers are familiar with the content of Gettier's two cases, as well as with the main moves that have been made by epistemologists in response to those cases and to the many others that have followed his two. For more details of this history, see Shope (1983), Lycan (2006), and Hetherington (2016a, ch. 1; 2016b). Section 13.6 will discuss briefly one well-known Gettier case.

[3] What other forms of such a fallibilism might there be? See Hetherington (1999; 2005a; 2016c; 2018) and Dougherty (2011).

[4] On the possibility of knowledge's not needing to include justificatory support at all, see Hetherington (2001, ch. 4; 2011a, ch. 4; forthcoming).

[5] A knowledge-infallibilism was advocated by Linda Zagzebski (1994), for example, in response to Gettier's cases.

After all, Gettier offers no sign that he was trying to argue that no fallibly justified true belief is knowledge. Notably, he says nothing about everyday or normal justified true beliefs; he discusses only what are presumably some justified true beliefs that are somehow quite exceptional or unusual in how each blends its being true, its being justified, and its being a belief. So, consider a more everyday justified true belief – such as a true belief, formed on the basis of apparently normal evidence in normal circumstances, that one is seeing a tree. One's justification in this case is normal; it is also fallible, still in a normal way. Gettier was not aiming to show that even a (fallibly) justified true belief like this would not be knowledge. More precisely, his intention was at least not to deny that such a belief is knowledge purely because its justificatory component is providing only fallible support for its being true.

Nonetheless, we should acknowledge that he was aiming to show something pertaining even to such normal justified true beliefs. He aimed to show that – even for an everyday (fallibly) justified true belief such as this one – to mention merely a belief's being true and (fallibly) justified is not yet to have said enough about why that belief is knowledge, even if it is. We might parse this as one's not yet having said enough to convey an epistemological understanding of the belief's being knowledge. "Tell us more about why this belief is knowledge," we could say, prompted by Gettier's challenge: mindful of Gettier's counterexamples, we recognize a need to elicit further epistemological details before allowing that our interlocutor understands knowledge's nature – even the nature of just a particular belief's being knowledge. If we are to understand some belief's being (fallibly justified) knowledge, then – Gettier was implicitly asking – what must philosophers say other than simply that it is (fallibly) justified and true? What further (fallibilist) details need to be mentioned if we are to be explicating a particular belief's being (fallible) knowledge?

So, the moral in Gettier's challenge is meant to be quite general. Until we can describe enough such details even for a single case (no matter if it is an unusual case), we are left with a challenge that arises for every case (including usual cases). Until we can describe enough such details even for a single case, we are left with what has turned out to be too generic a conception to constitute real understanding of knowledge and its precise conceptual boundaries. If our conception remains the generic "knowledge = justified true belief," then – according to the usual epistemological acceptance of Gettier's challenge as successfully falsifying that conception – we remain vulnerable to our conception's having to allow at least some justified true beliefs to be knowledge even when in fact they are not knowledge. This possibility is what Gettier made manifest for philosophers with his counterexamples.[6] By describing sufficiently detailed situations where a belief would satisfy that generic conception – "knowledge = justified true belief" – even while failing to be knowledge, Gettier *showed how* this could happen. Post-Gettier epistemology was then spurred onwards by the question of which further details – either directly fallibilist themselves, or at least not clashing with fallibilism – need to be mentioned if we are to understand or explicate, in what many have called a *Gettier-proof* way, how a fallibly justified true belief is to be knowledge.

Post-Gettier epistemology has also generalized that question, beyond the generically fallibilist conception of knowledge with which Gettier himself was engaging. His challenge has persisted, *mutatis mutandis*, even when – as has happened often since 1963 – epistemologists have offered details intended to constitute more informative conceptions of knowledge than the generic "knowledge = justified true belief" equation that Gettier was overtly discussing. This prolonged persistence of the general idea behind Gettier's specific challenge has been due to most epistemologists having thought, time after time, that further details are still needed even after some have been provided by this, or by that, proposed theory of knowledge: no post-Gettier theory of knowledge has ever, it still seems to most epistemologists, said quite enough in this respect. Counterexamples in the same spirit as Gettier's own two have apparently remained available – indeed, available for each of these suggested (and less generic) fallibilist conceptions of knowledge.

13.3 An Explicative Aim

Gettier's challenge was centered upon his two counterexamples. These gave to epistemology the idea of (what others soon referred to as) a *Gettier case*. A Gettier case is any actual or possible situation relevantly akin to the two that were articulated by Gettier. Many such cases have enlivened post-1963

---

[6] Two possible analogies come to mind. (i) Did Gettier do this in a way that was akin to how an analytically minded short-story writer could make manifest some rare emotional state's permutations, for instance? (ii) Was Gettier's focus on unusual cases – in effect, saying that we do not understand even what usual knowledge is until we understand such unusual cases – akin to what seems to have been a long-standing emphasis by psychologists upon seeking to understand mental health by understanding first and foremost unhealthy emotions, rather than by pursuing "positive" psychology at the outset? On the latter, see Seligman (2002), for instance.

philosophical discussions of knowledge. Can we render more precisely the idea of a Gettier case?

Care is needed here, because it is not unusual for an epistemologist, from the outset, to build into her description of Gettier cases what is actually a contestable theoretical slant or a covertly interpretive move, perhaps presented as being "intuitive." Hopefully, the following description avoids that failing while still incorporating the standard epistemological view that, always, the belief at the core of a Gettier fails to be knowledge:

> Any Gettier case includes an epistemic agent or subject with a belief that is true and (fallibly) justified while also failing to be knowledge. This failure is due somehow, and to some degree, to the obtaining of an odd or abnormal circumstance in the situation. (The belief is, we may say, *Gettiered*, in virtue of its being true, its being and justified, and the obtaining of this odd circumstance.)

As to the odd circumstance, in his own two cases Gettier (1963, pp. 122, 123) highlighted the fact that the person with the belief has no knowledge of the actual circumstance that (as we might say, although Gettier did not talk in this metaphysical way)[7] happens to make his belief true. In gaining the evidence and forming his belief (noted Gettier), the person is aware instead of other aspects of the setting. We are meant, it seems, to regard the odd – and overlooked – circumstance as playing a pivotal role in why the case's central belief fails to be knowledge.

What role might that be? The usual epistemological aim now becomes one of explication or understanding. Why is that belief not knowledge? Sometimes, a pithier version of that introductory description-cum-interpretation might be used. It will say that *any Gettiered belief fails to be knowledge*.[8] A word of caution is needed, however, about speaking in this way when trying to understand Gettier's challenge. Through habituation, it seems, some philosophers now treat "Gettiered" as conceptually encompassing "not knowledge." So much so that, for them, "Any Gettiered belief fails to be knowledge" is true both intuitively and analytically. But we need to avoid

---

[7] It is metaphysical, with its talk of truthmaking; as to which notion, see Armstrong (2004). Gettier mentioned some specific circumstances within the case, ones of which – as he observed – the epistemic agent or subject had no knowledge. Presumably, readers were meant to take this as either evidence for, or explanatory of, the belief's not being knowledge – which interpretation of the belief Gettier did offer, in the same breath.

[8] I treat the term "Gettiered" as applying, first of all, to beliefs. Sometimes we say that a person is Gettiered. This is fine, so long as we remember that a person is Gettiered only secondarily: she is Gettiered only insofar as she has a belief that is Gettiered.

making such an assumption about Gettiered beliefs at this stage of the discussion. As we will see, if this chapter is correct then many apparently tempting epistemological attempts to explicate or understand "[a]ny Gettiered belief fails to be knowledge" cannot actually succeed; in which case, there is at least a possibility that this thesis – that a belief's being Gettiered precludes its being knowledge – should never have received such unquestioning acceptance by epistemologists. I am not arguing here that the thesis in question ("No Gettiered belief is knowledge") is not true[9] However, the question remains of why it is true, if it is.

In accord with Section 13.2's analysis of the meta-epistemological challenge being posed by Gettier's cases, the previous paragraph's question – Why is no Gettiered belief knowledge? – can be treated as this one:

> How must we describe, with further details, what is needed if a belief that is already described as being true and (fallibly) justified is to be described also as knowledge – given that (as Gettier cases show or display) something's being described as a true and (fallibly) justified belief is not enough to describe it as knowledge?

Note, though, that we can also treat the main question being posed by Gettier's cases as this one:

> How may we describe, with further details, what would suffice for a belief. that is already described as being true and (fallibly) justified not to be described nonetheless as failing, in virtue of being Gettiered, to be knowledge?

To answer either of those questions would be to provide an explication – even if the two questions would be eliciting, respectively, different forms of explication – of post-Gettier epistemology's guiding thesis. I call that thesis *Gettierism*. Again, it is the thesis that *being Gettiered precludes being knowledge*.[10] In general, epistemologists have tried to understand it by engaging just with the first of the above two questions that are pertinent and available. Accordingly, that is the question on which I focus in the rest of this chapter.[11]

---

[9] I have done so elsewhere (e.g. 1998; 2001, ch. 3; 2011a, ch. 3).

[10] For a fuller articulation of it, see Hetherington (2016a, ch. 1).

[11] I mention the second question, nonetheless, because (i) epistemologists have in general overlooked its availability, (ii) I will end the chapter with the optimistic thought that, in spite of the problem outlined here, it is possible for epistemologists to explicate Gettier cases adequately, and because (iii) choosing to answer the second – rather than the usually discussed first – form of question is part of why that optimistic thought in (ii) might be true. Here, I mention this without further justification; for such justification, see Hetherington (2016a, ch. 7).

13.4 A Limitative Result

A *Gettieristic explication* (as we may call it) could take two related forms. In seeking to answer the epistemologically standard question highlighted at the end of Section 13.3 (the first of the two questions mentioned there), it could choose to talk of knowledge in general: "To be Gettiered is to have feature F; and having F precludes being knowledge." Or it might focus on a particular Gettier case (while trying to answer that same question): "This Gettiered belief has feature F, which is why it is not knowledge." In what follows, for specificity I discuss the latter – seemingly the more tractable – approach. It is the attempt to explicate a specific Gettier case by telling us why that case's central belief is not knowledge, an explication that supports or coheres with Gettierism. We will find that even this well-trodden form of Gettieristic thinking faces a significant meta-epistemological constraint.

Consider, then, a particular belief B, within some Gettier case G built around B. *As* the central belief within G, B is a Gettiered belief. B is thereby – according to Gettierism – not knowledge. But *why* is B thereby not knowledge? To answer this is to expand the epistemological story explicatively. Accordingly, let "R" be the centerpiece of our attempted explication: that is, let "R" denote and describe the reason why – according to our attempted Gettieristic explication – B within G is not knowledge. Now, "R" could be more or less complex in the description that it provides of one or more aspect of G: for example, "R" could be describing something of G's causal structuring, or some fact within G that defeats the evidence being used within G to support B, etc. No matter which of these (or other) circumstances is being denoted or described by "R," though, one detail that "R" cannot ever include in an explanatory capacity is B's ever being false, even within some other possible world. This is due to two theses (each of which comes from Section 13.3):

(1) *The factivity of being Gettiered.* It is inherent to *B's being Gettiered* that B is true. (This is simply an element of what it is to *be* a Gettiered belief. If anything is conceptually and trivially implied about the nature of Gettier cases, this is.)

(2) *The facthood of being Gettiered.* Any Gettieristic explication of *B's being Gettiered* is an understanding of a *state of affairs* – specifically, the state of affairs that is *B's being Gettiered*. (This is also – like (1) – a trivial truth, this time about any Gettieristic explicative aim. This truth is categorizing metaphysically the sort of thing of which an explication of Gettierism would be an understanding.)

Now, (2) implies that any Gettieristic explication could not be of a state of affairs that is anything other than B's being Gettiered. Hence, it could not even be of a state of affairs that is *only almost* B's being Gettiered, say. For even that would not be telling us why B, in being Gettiered, is not knowledge. So, a Gettieristic explication of what happens within G could not be of a state of affairs constituted by B and *some but not all* elements inherent in the state of affairs of *B's being Gettiered*. Hence, given (1), it cannot be part of any Gettieristic explication of G to be pointing to implications of a state of affairs where B is not true.

Let us see more fully why that is so. Any Gettieristic explication has to be of G's central belief B failing, due to its being Gettiered, to be knowledge. That is, the explication is of the failure, by the state of affairs that is B's being Gettiered, to be knowledge – the failure, more precisely, of B to be knowledge, because of its being part of the state of affairs *B's being Gettiered*. But no such explication could rely on including this (or anything that entails it):

In some possible world(s), distinct from this world, B-within-G is false.

For, given the factivity – described in (1) – of being Gettiered, in no possible world *is* B false while still within G. And, given that – as described in (2) – any explication of B's (due to its being within G) not being knowledge has to be of the state of affairs that is *B's being within G (and thereby not being knowledge)*, no such explication can be pointing to a possible world where B is false. In other words, no *Gettieristic* explication can call upon the idea of there being some possible world(s), distinct from this one, where B is present yet false while still being based on the same evidence, for example, as it is within G in this world. Yet putative Gettieristic explications do often point to there being some such possible worlds.[12] And maybe there are some such possible worlds, for a given B and a given G. But whether or not there are any such worlds is not my point. For there being some such possible worlds is not the same as those worlds including B *still within* G – that is, B *in its capacity as* the central belief within G – while also being false. On the contrary: insofar as B is false within a possible world, it is *ipso facto* not still functioning within that world as the central belief inside G. Thus, those worlds would not be ones containing the state of affairs that is B's being Gettiered in G.[13] And this entails that no such worlds can

---

[12] Section 13.6 will return to this claim, by discussing an instance of such an approach.
[13] Or – if this state of affairs is itself constituted in a transworld way – those worlds would not be helping to constitute the state of affairs that is B's being Gettiered within G.

be part of a Gettieristic explication of how, by being Gettiered within G, B fails to be knowledge.

Consequently, we have this limitative result:

No Gettieristic explication of Gettier cases can be in terms of some reason or circumstance, an essential element of which is at least the possibility of a false belief.

13.5 Did Gettier Point Us in the Wrong Explicative Direction?

Time and again, though, post-Gettier epistemology has offered us putative explications that aim to be Gettieristic (by trying to explain why some particular belief, in being Gettiered, fails to be knowledge), yet that do violate Section 13.4's result. (They are offered in apparent ignorance of that result.) This is a stark clash; something must give way. If the limitative result stands, these would-be explications have failed to provide what their proponents have claimed to be providing – namely, Gettieristic insight into why the particular belief, due to being Gettiered, is not knowledge. The fault, I believe, is with post-Gettier epistemological orthodoxy; elsewhere (2016a, chs 2, 3), I have supported this belief in detail. For now, I will gesture at how easily we might trace some of the spirit of the thinking behind such a mistake to how Gettier himself commented on his cases.

Section 13.2 explained how those cases were built around, in part, a traditional form of knowledge-fallibilism – the thesis, adopted by Gettier for at least the sake of argument, that knowledge's justificatory component could in general be allowed to be fallible in strength. So, we may apply Gettier's interpretation of his own cases to our currently representative form of Gettier case – G, featuring B. This application allows that B is justified only fallibly within G. Yet B's being justified only fallibly within G entails that, in some way or sense, there *is* a possibility of the justification provided for B within G coexisting – somewhere, in some alternative world – with B's falsity: this is a fallibilist possibility. Now, Section 13.4's limitative result entails that this fallibility as such cannot be part of the problem – in effect, the knowledge-precluding feature that is denoted and described by "R" – within a given Gettier case: it cannot be part of *why* B, in being Gettiered within G, fails to be knowledge. For argument's sake, we may say that the fallibility in question allows that any Gettiered belief – considered in those same circumstances except for the fact of its being true – is such that it might easily have not been true. That possible outcome – B's not being true within some other possible world(s) – would, when it is actual and not merely possible within some world, be a manifestation within that world of the Gettiered belief's being justified only fallibly within this world. However, that possible outcome could not thereby be a manifestation of *the Gettiered belief as such* – the state of affairs of B's being the central belief, the Gettiered belief, within G – being *able to coexist with* being false; for, once there is a false belief, that belief is *ipso facto* not Gettiered within that setting. So, the possible falsity, even if it is to be manifested only in other worlds, is not part of being Gettiered, even within this world: if we reidentify across possible worlds the state of affairs that, within this world, is *B's being Gettiered within G*, then falsity will never be present as part of that state of affairs, even within another possible world.

Well and good: a knowledge-fallibilist should want it to follow that the fallibility as such is never part of the explication of why a given Gettiered belief fails to be knowledge. But now we must ask whether the various post-Gettier theories of knowledge have done enough to ensure that they are not unwittingly allowing their explicative reactions to Gettier cases – "That Gettiered belief is not knowledge" – to be shaped, even partly, by applying a standard for knowing that reflects a knowledge-infallibilism rather than a knowledge-fallibilism.[14] That would be a methodologically inappropriate way of reacting to the cases, insofar as one is seeking to explicate them Gettieristically.

13.6 How to Misinterpret the Limitative Result

How might an epistemologist seek to evade Sections 13.4 and 13.5, while retaining a commitment to some standard – hence, a Gettieristic – way of trying to explicate Gettier cases? Here is one standard line of thought that

---

[14] On this possibility, see Hetherington (2016a, chs 5, 6). The key word here is "unwittingly." Rightly, epistemologists do not say that the fallibility is why, in their view, the Gettiered belief is not knowledge. Yet this does not entail that they are in fact being sufficiently sensitive, when reacting to a particular case, to the need to interpret Gettier cases in light of a fallibilist standard for knowing. We might well wonder where, if anywhere, is the methodological control on epistemologists' reactions to a given Gettier case – so that they know definitively (infallibly?) that their Gettieristic reaction, according to which the case's central (Gettiered) belief is not knowledge, is not misplacedly applying an infallibilist standard in its underlying motivation. An infallibilist would-be explication of B's not being knowledge would not be a Gettieristic explication, since it would have discarded or overlooked Section 13.2's interpretive constraint – the need for a Gettieristic explication to accommodate a fallibilism about knowledge's justificatory component.

might well arise, with the aim of directing our attention more to the means or method by which a specific Gettiered belief has been formed:

> The reason why B within G is not knowledge is that B is formed, not merely fallibly, but too fallibly – with this being due to the odd nature of the circumstances, hence due to the fact that G is a Gettier case. For example, B is true but only luckily so, relative to the justificatory path pursued within G in forming B.[15] It is possible – indeed, easily so – for a false belief to have been formed even while following that same justificatory path. The fact that, as it happens, B is true within G does not alter this modal point (about how easily B might not have been true, even with the same justification being used in the same way to support B). That modal point is the reason why B is not knowledge within G. Thus, we can explicate Gettierism, by considering a particular Gettier case such as G and the Gettiered belief B within it.

Such thinking has felt natural to many recent epistemologists. Let us see how it would apply to a famous Gettier case such as Roderick Chisholm's (1966, p. 23n22; 1977, p. 105; 1989, p. 93) sheep-in-the-field case. Here is a version of the case (adapted so as to be talking about you):

> You see what looks, in apparently normal circumstances, to be a sheep in a field in front of you. Accordingly, you believe that there is a sheep in that field. Your belief is true – but only because of a sheep that you do not see, hidden from your gaze, behind a hill in that same field. You are actually looking at a disguised dog.

We may agree, for argument's sake, that your belief is Gettiered – it is true, it is justified, and there is a relevantly abnormal circumstance – while also failing to be knowledge. Why, though, is it not knowledge? Can we explicate – understand epistemologically – this complex state of affairs? Can we do so Gettieristically – that is, by pointing illuminatingly to your belief's being Gettiered as the reason why it is not knowledge?

Many epistemologists would currently be tempted to do so by talking along the following lines – that is, by calling upon some concept of epistemic luck:[16]

---

[15] Anti-luck epistemology (as it is usually called) is a current favorite among epistemologists, thanks mainly to Duncan Pritchard (e.g. 2005). For detailed discussion of such an approach, see Hetherington (2016a, ch. 3). I will comment only briefly on it in this section.

[16] See Pritchard (2005) on different forms that epistemic luck might take. On whether knowledge in general can admit of being lucky in some such way, see the debate between Pritchard (2013) and Hetherington (2013).

Your belief is only luckily true, relative to your evidence and to the line of thought that you have used in reaching your belief on the basis of that evidence. After all, the evidence concerns only the animal in front of you (the disguised dog), not the animal (elsewhere in the field, hidden from you) in virtue of which your final belief – your Gettiered belief – is actually true. In one respect, the fact that the field contains a sheep of which you are wholly unaware is fortunate for you as a believer, in that it makes your belief true. But that fact (of the field containing that hidden-from-you sheep) has played no role in guiding you to form that belief, or indeed in shaping the content of the evidence on the basis of which you have formed that belief. If you had been using that same evidence (which in fact is provided by your looking at that disguised dog), and reaching that same belief in that same evidence-guided way, then you could easily have been reaching a false belief rather than the true one that – luckily – you have actually formed.

There is something natural in that thinking. Even so, it is fundamentally flawed: in particular, it could not be explicating your belief's failing, *in being Gettiered*, to be knowledge. The most that such thinking could be explicating – by calling upon the concept of epistemic luck as it does – is something like this:

> Focus again on belief B within Gettier case G. Grant for the sake of argument that B could easily fail to be knowledge, in that it could easily be – in other words, it could easily reappear – within a possible situation where it is false in spite of the same evidence being used to support it as is actually used for that purpose within G. But B's being false within that alternative possible situation entails that B is not Gettiered there: by the factivity of being Gettiered, one part of any belief's being Gettiered is its being true. In effect, therefore, all that we would have modeled, via that alternative possible situation, is the fact that the belief B – even the justified belief B – could easily be present or reappear within a *non-*Gettier situation (since, again, B would not be true within that alternative possible situation). So, even if we allow that, within G, *the belief B* – or even *the justified belief B* – has been formed in a way that could easily have failed to produce a true belief, this does not tell us that B has been formed in such a way as part of *its being Gettiered*.

The point is that even if there are possible worlds where (the justified) B is false, and even if there are worlds where (the justified) B is formed in the same way as it is within G, such worlds are not among those that we would consult when trying to understand what is involved *in a belief such as B's being Gettiered*. If we are to accomplish this in modal terms (a popular approach adopted, for argument's sake, in this discussion), we will be looking at possible worlds that include the state of affairs of B's being Gettiered – the same state of affairs that we are trying to understand Gettieristically, in its obtaining here in this world.[17] Yet none of those worlds envisaged by the would-be Gettieristic explicative thinking – calling as it does upon the concept of epistemic luck, for instance – do this. Instead, those worlds are ones where (along with various other details that the would-be Gettieristic account deems of explicative import) B is false.[18] Thus, to point to such worlds is to depart from the explicative aim of modeling Gettierism in some revealing way. Gettierism is a thesis that requires us always to consider specifically the state of affairs of *B's being Gettiered* – B's obtaining within G, say – as we ask what else (such as B's failing to be knowledge) is part of, or implied by, that state of affairs. Hence, to explicate Gettierism is never to examine B within what could not be G (as is automatically so, once we are considering a false B within that alternative situation).[19]

It is clear how this general interpretive constraint applies to the sheep-in-the-field case, say, along with the claim that the case can be explicated Gettieristically via a concept of epistemic luck. For argument's sake, we may again agree that it is clear, in the epistemologically relevant sense, what it means to say that a belief is true only luckily, given how it has been formed within the particular setting. Let us continue to grant, still for argument's sake, that forming a belief in such a way is not in general a way to be gaining

---

[17] By analogy, for example, think of how, in examining whether people are essentially embodied, we consider only possible worlds where there are people, before we investigate whether all of those people are embodied within those worlds.

[18] To this, someone might object as follows: "What if B had been a necessary truth – true in all relevant possible worlds? There could be a Gettiered belief like that. In which case, the would-be Gettieristic explication in terms of epistemic luck would say that the method of forming the belief, say, leads to false beliefs within too many relevant possible worlds – so much so as to be modeling the belief's being Gettiered and thereby not being knowledge, not merely its being formed fallibly." This objection does not affect the core of my argument. First, if the belief-forming method is described as including the outcome of one's forming the true (because Gettiered) belief, then we face the same problem, *mutatis mutandis*, that I am presenting now. Alternatively, if the belief-forming method is described so as not to include the outcome of one's forming the true (because Gettiered) belief, then we face a complementary problem – one that will be presented in Section 13.7. Basically, we will not have shown that the belief-forming method is failing, *due to being part of a Gettier case*, to be producing a belief that is knowledge; rather, we will have retreated to a *not-necessarily-Gettieristic* explication. For extended discussion of this problem, see Hetherington (2016a, secs 3.6, 3.7).

[19] For more on this issue of Gettierism and transworld identification of Gettier cases, see Hetherington (2017).

knowledge: that is, forming a belief luckily (in that sense) is not in general a way for a belief to be knowledge. However, what we have found just now is that the epistemologically interpretive situation is nonmonotonic in this respect, once Gettier cases are part of the story. That is, the interpretive situation has the following complexity:

> First, even if (as we are granting is possible, for argument's sake) it could be that *forming a belief luckily* is a reason why a resulting belief is not knowledge, the accompanying explication of why that belief is not knowledge cannot also be part of explicating how *forming a true belief luckily* is a reason why the resulting belief is not knowledge.

> Second, if we are to explicate a Gettier case in a Gettieristic way by calling on the idea of epistemic luck, then we need to be doing so by understanding how the case's central (Gettiered) belief fails to be knowledge, in virtue of being *formed epistemically luckily* – with this *including* the belief's being true (since it is being considered in its capacity *as* a Gettiered belief).

I am not saying that your luckily true belief that there is a sheep in the field is knowledge. Nor am I denying this. My point is meta-epistemological. I am saying that any purportedly explicative reasoning in support of a Gettieristic interpretation of the particular case must fail, insofar as (by calling upon the idea of epistemic luck) it is pointing to some possibility of falsity (perhaps along with more than this possibility). This is a limitation upon our capacity to *understand* why a Gettiered belief is not knowledge (if indeed it is not knowledge). Even if we grant (as I am doing, for argument's sake) that the anti-luck thinking supports (1), we have to concede that it does not support (2), which – unlike (1) – *is* an instantiation of Gettierism:

(1) *Forming a (justified) belief luckily* precludes the belief's being knowledge;

(2) *Forming a (justified) true belief luckily* precludes the belief's being knowledge.

  Again, the reason for that explicative disparity is simple, as follows.

  First, we evaluate (1) by considering instances of the description "forming a belief luckily." Presumably this requires our explication to encompass possible situations where one forms a true belief (such as in the Gettier case itself). However, it also requires our explication to encompass possible situations where one forms – presumably in the same way – a false belief (such as where all else, as far as possible, remains in place from the Gettier case, except for the belief's being false within those possible situations). This is because, no matter what else is part of forming a true belief luckily, some sort of possibility of forming a false belief (either the same one or a different one) is at least part of that.

Second, however, we evaluate (2) by considering only cases where one forms a true belief (such as in the Gettier case itself). For a (justified) true belief being formed luckily, along with a claimed consequence of this state of affairs, is what is supposedly being explicated. Accordingly, to evaluate (2) at all by considering possible cases or worlds where one forms a false belief is already a mistake of explicative focus. In effect, it is to confuse (2) with (1). Most importantly, it is not giving us a Gettieristic result: it is not explicating the Gettier case itself in a Gettieristic way, by maintaining a focus on possible situations where the case's Gettiered belief is still that case's Gettiered belief. Instead, it is – unwittingly, I suspect – amounting only to an explication of how, if one was in a situation very like a Gettier case – just like the sheep-in-the-field case, for example, except for changing the Gettier case's detail of one's belief (that there is a sheep in the field) being true – then one's belief would not be knowledge within that situation. Consequently, it is mistaken to assume or believe that, by adverting to possible situations like that one (in which one's belief is false), we are explicating a Gettieristic interpretation of the belief in question. Explicating someone's *forming a (justified) belief luckily* is not the same as explicating her *forming a (justified) true belief luckily*. And only the latter can be part of a Gettieristic explication.

13.7 How the Limitative Result Becomes a Problem

Is this chapter's limitative result also a *problem* for many post-Gettier theories of knowledge? Yes, it is. Section 13.6 indicated briefly how this would be so for at least one form that might be taken by an anti-luck epistemology, in particular. But other kinds of supposedly explicative epistemological theory are likewise vulnerable, *mutatis mutandis*. The problem outlined in Section 13.6 – for anti-luck attempts to explicate a Gettier case Gettieristically – can be applied more widely.

Consider, once more, any would-be Gettieristic explicator of some Gettier case, G. She directs our attention to F, some feature of the case – a feature that she describes in more, or in less, detail. Her correlative Gettieristic thinking then proceeds in this manner:

By being Gettiered within G, B is not knowledge. This is because, in being
Gettiered, B is F – and because being F precludes being knowledge.

In practice, our hypothesized explicator instantiates "F" with, perhaps, one of
the following epistemological favorites: "is formed in an intellectually unvir-
tuous way," "is such that there is an ultimate defeater of its being true or of its
being justified," "is caused aberrantly," "is not formed as a result of proper
cognitive functioning," etc. That is, our Gettieristic explicator might reach for
one of the many influential post-Gettier proposals that have been made by
epistemologists when seeking to understand what further circumstances need
to obtain if even a justified true belief, say, is to be knowledge.

However, the problem with using any of these ideas in this imagined
setting – where the aim is to understand Gettier cases, and thereby knowledge,
in a Gettieristic way – flows smoothly from our earlier limitative result,
developed so far for anti-luck Gettierism in particular. The problem can be
formulated in a general form, as the following dilemma.

The infallibilism alternative. Suppose that a given one of these specific
proposals (as to what is also required if a justified true belief, say, is to be
knowledge) is somehow – even if unwittingly – infallibilist in whatever
F-centered demand it places upon knowing. Then (from Section 13.2) we
may infer that the proposal's application to Gettier case G is methodologically
inadequate, at any rate for the particular epistemologist's Gettieristically
explicative ends. This application of what amounts to an infallibilist proposal
(even if, again, the standard being applied is only unwittingly infallibilist)
could not be interpreting G appropriately, given that a fallibilist conception of
knowledge is what Gettier was discussing. Thus, on this infallibilist alternative, a Gettieristic explication is not available, no matter with what further,
epistemologically enticing, details "F" is being instantiated.

The fallibilism alternative. Suppose, instead, that a given one of those
epistemological proposals is somehow fallibilist – again, it might be only
covertly or unwittingly so – in the F-centered demand that it places upon
knowing. Yet (from Sections 13.4 through 13.6) although this could be
a methodologically apt demand, its application to a Gettier case must
fail anyway: because F's applicability depends upon at least the (fallibilist)
possibility of the believer forming a false belief rather than the true belief that
she has actually formed within G, that fallibilist element in the hypothesized
attempt at Gettieristic explication is already enough to guarantee the applicability of this chapter's limitative result, regardless of however much else of
epistemic interest and significance is involved in satisfying the F-centered

demand issued by the proposed Gettieristic thinking. Thus, on this alternative also, a Gettieristic explication is not available, no matter with what further, epistemologically enticing, details "F" is being instantiated.

Consequently, a dilemma – outlined here only briefly – confronts anyone attempting to explicate a Gettier case in a Gettieristic way, anyone attempting to understand why a particular Gettiered belief fails to be knowledge. As it happens (and as I have explained elsewhere: 2016a, ch. 2), I believe that most post-Gettier epistemology has succumbed to the second horn of this dilemma.[20] That is why this chapter has emphasized the limitative result that pertains to fallibility in particular – the dilemma's second horn.

13.8 Conclusion

None of this entails that knowing is inexplicable. But we do have a result that limits how knowing could ever be explicated. And perhaps this is at least part of why post-Gettier epistemology has been so inconclusive for so many. Maybe (given Section 13.7) this limitative result has worrying implications for what has been a lengthy tradition of epistemological attempts to explicate Gettier cases in particular, and thereby to resolve the Gettier problem.

As it happens, I do believe that knowledge can be explicated, and that Gettier cases *can* help to shape the resulting epistemological account. Arguing for that optimistic view, however, is not this chapter's role.[21]

---

[20] But not all; there are some whose epistemological predilections render the dilemma's first alternative applicable to them, as I explain also (2016a, ch. 5).

[21] See Hetherington (2016a, ch. 7) for details of that optimistic view.

Bibliography

Adams, E. W. (1988). "Modus tollens revisited," *Analysis* 48: 122–8.

Adams, F. and Clarke, M. (2005). "Resurrecting the tracking theories," *Australasian Journal of Philosophy* 83: 207–21.

Adler, J. E. (2002). *Belief's Own Ethics.* Cambridge, MA: The MIT Press.

Almeder, R. (1974). "Truth and Evidence," *The Philosophical Quarterly* 24: 365–8.

Aloni, M. (2016). "Disjunction," in *The Stanford Encyclopedia of Philosophy* (Winter 2016 Edition), E. N. Zalta (ed.): https://plato.stanford.edu/archives/win2016 /entries/disjunction/

Alston, W. (2005). "Internalism and externalism in epistemology," in E. Craig (ed.), *The Shorter Routledge Encyclopedia of Philosophy.* Abingdon: Routledge, pp. 454–5.

Alvarez, M. (2010). *Kinds of Reasons: An Essay in the Philosophy of Action.* Oxford University Press.

Anderson, C. (unpublished manuscript). *Cartesian Infallibilism and Knowledge First Epistemology.*

Antognazza, M. R. (2015). "The benefit to philosophy of the study of its history," *British Journal for the History of Philosophy* 23: 161–84.

Armstrong, D. M. (1973). *Belief, Truth and Knowledge.* Cambridge University Press.

Armstrong, D. M. (2004). *Truth and Truthmakers.* Cambridge University Press.

Ayer, A. J. (1956). *The Problem of Knowledge.* London: Macmillan.

Baumann, P. (2012). "Nozick's defense of closure," in K. Becker and T. Black (eds.), *The Sensitivity Principle in Epistemology.* Cambridge University Press, pp. 11–27.

Bealer, G. (1998). "Intuition and the autonomy of philosophy," in M. DePaul and W. Ramsey (eds.), *The Psychology of Intuition and Its Role in Philosophical Inquiry.* Lanham: Rowman & Littlefield, pp. 201–40.

Beall, J. C. and Restall, G. (2006). *Logical Pluralism.* Oxford University Press.

Beaney, M. (2013). "What is analytic philosophy?" in M. Beaney (ed.), *The Oxford Handbook of The History of Analytic Philosophy.* Oxford University Press, pp. 3–29.

Beaney, M. (2016). "Analysis," *The Stanford Encyclopedia of Philosophy* (Summer 2016 Edition), E. N. Zalta (ed.): https://plato.stanford.edu/archives/sum2016 /entries/analysis/

Becker, K. (2006). "Is counterfactual reliabilism compatible with higher-level knowledge?" *Dialectica* 60: 79–84.

Becker, K. (2007). *Epistemology Modalized*. New York: Routledge.

Becker, K. (2012). "Methods and how to individuate them," in K. Becker and T. Black (eds.), *The Sensitivity Principle in Epistemology*. Cambridge University Press, pp. 81–97.

Becker, K. (2016). "Deductive closure principle," in *Routledge Encyclopedia of Philosophy*: www.rep.routledge.com/articles/thematic/deductive-closure-principle/v-2

Becker, K. and Black, T. (eds.) (2012). *The Sensitivity Principle in Epistemology*. Cambridge University Press.

Beebe, J. R. and Buckwalter, W. (2010). "The epistemic side-effect effect," *Mind & Language* 25: 1–25.

Beebe, J. R. and Jensen, M. (2012). "Surprising connections between knowledge and action: The robustness of the epistemic side-effect effect," *Philosophical Psychology*, 25(5): 689–715. http://doi.org/10.1080/09515089.2011.622439

Bengson, J. (2013). "Experimental attacks on intuitions and answers," *Philosophy and Phenomenological Research* 86: 495–532.

Bengson, J. (2014). "How philosophers use intuition and 'intuition,'" *Philosophical Studies* 171: 555–76.

Bennett, J. (2003). *A Philosophical Guide to Conditionals*. Oxford University Press.

Bird, A. (2004). "Is evidence non-inferential?" *The Philosophical Quarterly* 54: 252–65.

Bird, A. (2007). "Justified judging," *Philosophy and Phenomenological Research* 74: 81–110.

Blouw, P., Buckwalter, W., and Turri, J. (2018). "Gettier cases: A taxonomy," in R. Borges, C. de Almeida, and P. Klein (eds.), *Explaining Knowledge: New Essays on the Gettier Problem*. Oxford University Press, pp. 242–52.

BonJour, L. (1987). "Nozick, externalism, and skepticism," in S. Luper-Foy (ed.), *The Possibility of Knowledge: Nozick and His Critics*. Totowa: Rowman & Littlefield, pp. 297–313.

Borges, R. (2015). "On synchronic dogmatism," *Synthese* 192: 3677–93.

Borges, R. (2017). "Inferential knowledge and the Gettier conjecture," in R. Borges, C. de Almeida, and P. D. Klein (eds.), *Explaining Knowledge: New Essays on the Gettier Problem*. Oxford University Press, pp. 273–91.

Broncano-Berrocal, F. (2016). "Luck," *Internet Encyclopedia of Philosophy*: www.iep.utm.edu/luck/

Broncano-Berrocal F. and Carter, J. A. (2017). "Epistemic luck," in T. Crane (ed.), *Routledge Encyclopedia of Philosophy*. www.rep.routledge.com/articles/thematic/epistemic-luck/v-1

Brown, J. (2013). "Infallibilism, evidence, and pragmatics," *Analysis* 73: 626–35.

Buckwalter, W. (2014). "Gettier made ESEE," *Philosophical Psychology* 27: 363–83.

Buckwalter, W. and Stich, S. (2011). "Gender and the philosophy club," *The Philosophers' Magazine* 52: 60–5.

Burge, T. (2005). "Disjunctivism and perceptual psychology," *Philosophical Topics* 33: 1–78.

Burgess, J. P. (2005). "No requirement of relevance," in S. Shapiro (ed.), *The Oxford Handbook of Philosophy of Mathematics and Logic*. Oxford University Press, pp. 727–50.

Burgess, J. P. (2009). *Philosophical Logic*. Princeton University Press.

Cappelen, H. (2012). *Philosophy without Intuitions*. Oxford University Press.

Cappelen, H. (2014). "Replies to Weatherson, Chalmers, Weinberg, and Bengson," *Philosophical Studies* 171: 577–600.

Carnap, R. (1947). *Meaning and Necessity*. University of Chicago Press.

Cassam, Q. (2009). "Can the concept of knowledge be analysed?" in P. Greenough and D. Pritchard (eds.), *Williamson on Knowledge*. Oxford University Press, pp. 12–30.

Casullo, A. (2003). *A Priori Justification*. Oxford University Press.

Chalmers, D. J. and Jackson, F. (2001). "Conceptual analysis and reductive explanation," *The Philosophical Review* 110: 315–60.

Chisholm, R. M. (1957). *Perceiving: A Philosophical Study*. Cornell University Press.

Chisholm, R. M. (1966). *Theory of Knowledge*. Englewood Cliffs: Prentice-Hall.

Chisholm, R. M. (1977). *Theory of Knowledge*, 2nd edn. Englewood Cliffs: Prentice-Hall.

Chisholm, R. M. (1989). *Theory of Knowledge*, 3rd edn. Englewood Cliffs: Prentice Hall.

Chudnoff, E. (2013). *Intuition*. Oxford University Press.

Chudnoff, E. (2018). "The epistemic significance of perceptual learning," *Inquiry* 61, no. 5-6 (2018): 520–542.

Church, I. M. (2013). "Manifest failure failure: The Gettier problem revived," *Philosophia* 41: 171–7.

Cohen, S. (1988). "How to be a fallibilist," *Philosophical Perspectives* 2: 91–123.

Cohen, S. (1998). "Contextualist solutions to epistemological problems: Skepticism, Gettier, and the lottery," *Australasian Journal of Philosophy* 76: 289–306.

Cohen, S. (1999). "Contextualism, skepticism, and the structure of reasons," *Philosophical Perspectives* 13: 57–89.

Cohen, S. and Comesaña, J. (2013). "Williamson on Gettier Cases and Epistemic Logic," *Inquiry* 56(1): 15–29.

Colaćo, D., Buckwalter, W., Stich, S., and Machery, E. (2014). "Epistemic intuitions in fake-barn thought experiments," *Episteme* 11: 199–212.

Comesaña, J. (2005a). "Justified versus warranted perceptual belief: A case against disjunctivism," *Philosophy and Phenomenological Research* 71: 367–83.

Comesaña, J. (2005b). "We are (almost) all externalists now," *Philosophical Perspectives* 19: 59–76.

Comesaña, J. and Kantin, H. (2010). "Is evidence knowledge?" *Philosophy and Phenomenological Research* 80: 447–54.

Conee, E. (1988). "Why solve the Gettier problem?" in D. Austin (ed.) *Philosophical Analysis: A Defense by Example*. Dordrecht: Kluwer, pp. 55–8.

Conee, E. and Feldman, R. (2004). "Internalism defended," in *Evidentialism: Essays in Epistemology*. Oxford University Press, pp. 53–82.

Craig, E. J. (1990). *Knowledge and the State of Nature: An Essay in Conceptual Synthesis*. Oxford: Clarendon Press.

Cross, T. (2010). "Skeptical success," in T. Gendler and J. Hawthorne (eds.), *Oxford Studies in Epistemology*, vol. 3. Oxford University Press, pp. 35–62.

Cullen, S. (2010). "Survey-driven romanticism," *Review of Philosophy and Psychology* 1: 275–96.

Dancy, J. (1985). *Introduction to Contemporary Epistemology*. Malden: Blackwell.

David, M. and Warfield, T. A. (2008). "Knowledge-closure and skepticism," in Q. Smith (ed.), *Epistemology: New Essays*. Oxford University Press, pp. 137–87.

De Almeida, C. (2017). "Knowledge, benign falsehoods, and the Gettier Problem," in R. Borges, C. de Almeida, and P. Klein (eds.), *Explaining Knowledge: New Essays on the Gettier Problem*. Oxford University Press, pp. 292–311.

De Almeida, C. (forthcoming a). "Klein, skepticism, epistemic closure, and evidential underdetermination," in B. Fitelson, R. Borges, and C. Braden (eds.), *Knowledge, Scepticism, and Defeat: Themes from Klein*. Dordrecht: Springer.

De Almeida, C. (forthcoming b). "On our epistemological debt to Moore and Russell," in S. Hetherington and M. Valaris (eds.), *Knowledge in Contemporary Philosophy*. London: Bloomsbury.

DeRose, K. (1992). "Contextualism and knowledge attributions," *Philosophy and Phenomenological Research* 52: 913–29.

DeRose, K. (1995). "Solving the skeptical problem," *The Philosophical Review* 104: 1–52.

DeRose, K. (1996). "Knowledge, assertion and lotteries," *Australasian Journal of Philosophy* 74: 568–80.

DeRose, K. (1999). "Contextualism: An explanation and defense," in J. Greco and E. Sosa (eds.), *The Blackwell Guide to Epistemology*, Malden: Blackwell, pp. 185–203.

Descartes, R. (1991). *The Philosophical Writings of Descartes, Vol. 3: Correspondence*, trans. John G. Cottingham, Robert Stoothof, Dugald Murdoch, and Anthony Kenny. Cambridge University Press.

Descartes, R. (2008). *Meditations on First Philosophy: With Selections from the Objections and Replies*, (ed.) M. Moriarty. Oxford University Press.

Deutsch, M. (2010). "Intuitions, counter-examples, and experimental philosophy," *Review of Philosophy and Psychology* 1: 447–60.

Deutsch, M. (2015). *The Myth of the Intuitive: Experimental Philosophy and Philosophical Method*. Cambridge, MA: The MIT Press.

Deutsch, M. (2016). "Replies to commentators," *Inquiry* 60: 420–42.

Dougherty, T. (2011). "Fallibilism," in S. Bernecker and D. Pritchard (eds.), *The Routledge Companion to Epistemology*. New York: Routledge, pp. 131–43.

Dretske, F. I. (1970). "Epistemic operators," *The Journal of Philosophy* 67: 1007–23.

Dretske, F. I. (1971). "Conclusive reasons," *Australasian Journal of Philosophy*. 49: 1–22.

Dretske, F. I. (1981). *Knowledge and the Flow of Information*. Cambridge, MA: The MIT Press.

Dretske, F. I. (2005). "The case against closure," in M. Steup and E. Sosa (eds.), *Contemporary Debates in Epistemology*. Malden: Blackwell, pp. 13–25.

Dretske, F. I. (2014). "The case against closure," in M. Steup, J. Turri, and E. Sosa (eds.), *Contemporary Debates in Epistemology*, 2nd edn., Malden: Wiley-Blackwell, pp. 27–40.

Dutant, J. (2015). "The legend of the justified true belief analysis," *Philosophical Perspectives* 29: 95–145.

Earl, D. (n.d.). "The classical theory of concepts," *Internet Encyclopedia of Philosophy*: http://www.iep.utm.edu/conc-cl/

Feldman, R. (2003). *Epistemology*. Upper Saddle River: Prentice Hall.

Firth, R. (1978). "Are epistemic concepts reducible to ethical concepts?" in A. I. Goldman and J. Kim (eds.), *Values and Morals: Essays in Honor of William Frankena, Charles Stevenson, and Richard Brandt*. Dordrecht: D. Reidel, pp. 215–29.

Fodor, J. (1998). *Concepts: Where Cognitive Science Went Wrong*. Oxford University Press.

Fricker, E. (2009). "Is knowing a state of mind? The case against," in P. Greenough and D. Pritchard (eds.), *Williamson on Knowledge*. Oxford University Press, pp. 31–60.

Friedman, O. and Turri, J. (2015). "Is probabilistic evidence a source of knowledge?" *Cognitive Science* 39: 1062–80.

Gettier, E. L. (1963). "Is justified true belief knowledge?" *Analysis* 23: 121–3.

Ginsborg, H. (2006). "Reasons for belief," *Philosophy and Phenomenological Research* 72: 286–318.

Goldberg, S. (2007). *Anti-Individualism: Mind and Language, Knowledge and Justification*. Cambridge University Press.

Goldberg, S. (2010). *Relying on Others: An Essay in Epistemology*. Oxford University Press.

Goldberg, S. (2011). "The division of epistemic labour," *Episteme* 8: 112–25.

Goldman, A. I. (1967). "A causal theory of knowing," *The Journal of Philosophy* 64: 357–72.

Goldman, A. I. (1976). "Discrimination and perceptual knowledge," *The Journal of Philosophy* 73: 771–91.

Goldman, A. I. (1979). "What is justified belief?" in G. S. Pappas (ed.), *Justification and Knowledge: New Studies in Epistemology*. Dordrecht: D. Reidel, pp. 1–23.

Goldman, A. I. (1986). *Epistemology and Cognition*. Harvard University Press.

Goldman, A. I. (1993). *Philosophical Applications of Cognitive Science*. Boulder: Westview Press.

Goldman, A. I. (1999). "*A priori* warrant and naturalistic epistemology," *Philosophical Perspectives* 13: 1–28.

Goldman, A. I. (2005). "Kornblith's naturalistic epistemology," *Philosophy and Phenomenological Research*, 71: 403–10.

Goldman, A. I. (2007). "Philosophical intuitions: Their target, their source, and their epistemic status," *Grazer Philosophische Studien* 74: 1–26.

Goldman, A. I. (2009). "Williamson on knowledge and evidence," in P. Greenough and D. Pritchard (eds.), *Williamson on Knowledge*. Oxford University Press, pp. 73–92.

Goldman, A. I. (2011). Toward a synthesis of reliabilism and evidentialism? Or: Evidentialism's problems, reliabilism's rescue package," in T. Dougherty (ed.), *Evidentialism and Its Discontents*. Oxford University Press, pp. 254–80.

Goldman, A. I. (2015). "Review of Hilary Kornblith, *A Naturalistic Epistemology: Selected Papers*," Notre Dame Philosophical Reviews: http://ndpr.nd.edu /news/a-naturalistic-epistemology-selected-papers/

Goldman, A. I. and Pust, J. (1998). "Philosophical theory and intuitional evidence," in M. DePaul and W. Ramsey (eds.), *Rethinking Intuition: The Psychology of Intuition and Its Role in Philosophical Inquiry*. Lanham: Rowman and Littlefield, pp. 179–97.

Greco, J. (1994). "Review of Kvanvig (1992)," *Philosophy and Phenomenological Research* 54: 973–6.

Greco, J. (1999). "Agent reliabilism," *Philosophical Perspectives* 13: 273–96.

Greco, J. (2003). "Knowledge as credit for true belief," in M. DePaul and L. Zagzebski (eds.), *Intellectual Virtue: Perspectives from Ethics and Epistemology*. Oxford: Clarendon Press, pp. 111–34.

Greco, J. (2004). "A different sort of contextualism," *Erkenntnis* 61: 383–400.

Greco, J. (2007). "The nature of ability and the purpose of knowledge," *Philosophical Issues* 17: 57–69.

Greco, J. (2009). "Knowledge and success from ability," *Philosophical Studies* 142: 17–26.

Greco, J. (2010). *Achieving Knowledge: A Virtue-Theoretic Account of Epistemic Normativity*. Cambridge University Press.

Greco, J. (2012). "A (different) virtue epistemology," *Philosophy and Phenomenological Research* 85: 1–26.

Greco, J. (2013). "Knowledge, testimony, and action," in T. Henning and D. P. Schweikard (eds.), *Knowledge, Virtue, and Action: Essays on Putting Epistemic Virtues to Work*. New York: Routledge, pp. 15–29.

Greco, J. (2015). "Post-Gettier epistemology," *Veritas* 60: 421–37.

Greco, J. (forthcoming a). "The role of trust in testimonial knowledge," in K. Dormandy (ed.), *Trust in Epistemology*. New York: Routledge.

Greco, J. (forthcoming b). *The Transmission of Knowledge*.

Green, A. (2012). "Extending the credit theory of knowledge," *Philosophical Explorations* 15: 121–32.

Green, A. (2014). "Deficient testimony is deficient teamwork," *Episteme* 11: 213–27.

Green, A. (2017). *The Social Contexts of Intellectual Virtue: Knowledge as a Team Achievement*. New York: Routledge.

Greenough, P. and Pritchard, D. (eds.). (2009). *Williamson on Knowledge*. Oxford University Press.

Gundersen, L. (2012). "Knowledge, cognitive dispositions and conditionals," in K. Becker and T. Black (eds.), *The Sensitivity Principle in Epistemology*. Cambridge University Press, pp. 66–80.

Hacker, P. M. S. (2013). *The Intellectual Powers: A Study of Human Nature*. Malden: Wiley Blackwell.

Hahn, H. (1980). "The crisis in intuition," in his *Empiricism, Logic, and Mathematics: Philosophical Papers*, (ed.) B. McGuiness. Dordrecht: D. Reidel, pp. 73–102.

Harman, G. (1973). *Thought*. Princeton University Press.

Hawthorne, J. (2004). *Knowledge and Lotteries*. Oxford: Clarendon Press.

Hawthorne, J. (2014). "The case for closure," in M. Steup, J. Turri, and E. Sosa (eds.), *Contemporary Debates in Epistemology*, 2nd edn. Malden: Wiley-Blackwell, pp. 40–56.

Heller, M. (1999). "The proper role for contextualism in an anti-luck epistemology," *Philosophical Perspectives*, 13: 115–29.

Henderson, D. and Greco, J. (eds.) (2015). *Epistemic Evaluation: Purposeful Epistemology*. Oxford University Press.

Hetherington, S. (1992). *Epistemology's Paradox: Is a Theory of Knowledge Possible?* Savage: Rowman & Littlefield.

Hetherington, S. (1998). "Actually knowing," *The Philosophical Quarterly* 48: 453–69.

Hetherington, S. (1999). "Knowing failably," *The Journal of Philosophy* 96: 565–87.

Hetherington, S. (2001). *Good Knowledge, Bad Knowledge: On Two Dogmas of Epistemology*. Oxford: Clarendon Press.

Hetherington, S. (2005a). "Fallibilism," *The Internet Encyclopedia of Philosophy*, www.iep.utm.edu/f/fallibil.htm

Hetherington, S. (2005b). "Gettier problems," *Internet Encyclopedia of Philosophy*: www.iep.utm.edu/gettier/

Hetherington, S. (2006). "Knowledge that works: A tale of two conceptual models," in S. Hetherington (ed.) *Aspects of Knowing: Epistemological Essays*. Oxford: Elsevier, pp. 219–40.

Hetherington, S. (2010). "Elusive epistemological justification," *Synthese* 174: 315–30.

Hetherington, S. (2011a). *How To Know: A Practicalist Conception of Knowing*. Malden: Wiley Blackwell.

Hetherington, S. (2011b). "The Gettier Problem," in S. Bernecker and D. Pritchard (eds.), *The Routledge Companion to Epistemology*. New York: Routledge, pp. 119–30.

Hetherington, S. (2012). "The significance of fallibilism within Gettier's challenge: A case study," *Philosophia* 40: 539–47.

Hetherington, S. (2013). "Knowledge can be lucky," in M. Steup, J. Turri, and E. Sosa (eds.), *Contemporary Debates in Epistemology*, 2nd edn. Malden: Wiley Blackwell, pp. 164–76.

Hetherington, S. (2016a). *Knowledge and the Gettier Problem*. Cambridge University Press.

Hetherington, S. (2016b). "Gettier Problem," *Routledge Encyclopedia of Philosophy*. www.rep.routledge.com/articles/thematic/gettier-problems/v-2.

Hetherington, S. (2016c). "Understanding fallible warrant and fallible knowledge: Three proposals," *Pacific Philosophical Quarterly* 97: 270–82.

Hetherington, S. (2017). "Gettier cases: Transworld identity and counterparts," in R. Borges, C. de Almeida, and P. Klein (eds.), *Explaining Knowledge: New Essays on the Gettier Problem*. Oxford University Press, pp. 366–83.

Hetherington, S. (2018). "Skepticism and fallibilism," in D. Machuca and B. Reed (eds.), *Skepticism: From Antiquity to the Present*. London: Bloomsbury, pp. 609–19.

Hetherington, S. (forthcoming). "The redundancy problem: From knowledge-infallibilism to knowledge-minimalism," *Synthese.*

Hill, T. E. (1961). *Contemporary Theories of Knowledge.* New York: The Ronald Press Company.

Hilpinen, R. (2017). "Sed ubi Socrates currit? On the Gettier Problem before Gettier," in R. Borges, C. de Almeida, and P. D. Klein (eds.), *Explaining Knowledge: New Essays on the Gettier Problem.* Oxford University Press, pp. 135–51.

Hoffman, W. E. (1975). "Almeder on truth and evidence," *The Philosophical Quarterly* 25: 59–61.

Hofman, F. (2014). "Gettier for justification," *Episteme* 11: 305–18.

Horvath, J. and Wiegmann, A. (2016). "Intuitive expertise and intuitions about knowledge," *Philosophical Studies* 173: 2701–26.

Howard-Snyder, D., Howard-Snyder, F., and Feit, N. (2003). "Infallibilism and Gettier's legacy," *Philosophy and Phenomenological Research* 66: 304–27.

Hughes, N. (2014). "Is knowledge the ability to φ for the reason that *p*?" *Episteme* 11: 457–62.

Hyman, J. (1999). "How knowledge works," *The Philosophical Quarterly*.49: 433–51.

Ichikawa, J. J. and Jarvis, B. W. (2013). *The Rules of Thought.* Oxford University Press.

Ichikawa, J. J. and Jenkins, C. S. I. (forthcoming). "On putting knowledge 'first,'" in J. A. Carter, E. C. Gordon, and B. Jarvis (eds.), *Knowledge First: Approaches to Epistemology and Mind.* Oxford University Press.

Ichikawa, J. J. and Steup, M. (2014). "The analysis of knowledge," *The Stanford Encyclopedia of Philosophy*, (Spring 2014 Edition), E. N. Zalta (ed.): http://plato.stanford.edu/archives/spr2014/entries/knowledge-analysis/

Ichikawa, J. J. and Steup, M. (2018). "The analysis of knowledge," *The Stanford Encyclopedia of Philosophy*, (Summer 2018 Edition), E. N. Zalta (ed.): https://plato.stanford.edu/archives/sum2018/entries/knowledge-analysis/

Jackson, F. (1987). *Conditionals.* Oxford: Basil Blackwell.

Jackson, F. (1998). *From Metaphysics to Ethics: A Defence of Conceptual Analysis.* Oxford: Clarendon Press.

Jackson, F. (2011). "On Gettier holdouts," *Mind & Language* 26: 468–81.

Jacquette, D. (1996). "Is nondefectively justified true belief knowledge?" *Ratio* 9: 115–27.

Jenkins, C. S. I. (2014). "'Intuition,' intuition, concepts and the a priori," in A. R. Booth and D. P. Rowbottom (eds.), *Intuitions.* Oxford University Press, pp. 91–115.

Johnston, M. (2004). "The obscure object of hallucination," *Philosophical Studies* 120: 113–83.

Kallestrup, J. and Pritchard, D. (2011). "Virtue epistemology and epistemic Twin Earth," *European Journal of Philosophy* 22: 335–57.

Kallestrup, J. and Pritchard, D. (2012). "Robust virtue epistemology and epistemic anti-individualism," *Pacific Philosophical Quarterly* 93: 84–103.

Kaplan, M. (1985). "It's not what you know that counts," *The Journal of Philosophy* 82: 350–63.

Kauppinen, A. (2007). "The rise and fall of experimental philosophy," *Philosophical Explorations* 10: 95–118.

Kearns, S. (2007). "In praise of folly: A reply to Blome-Tillmann," *Analysis* 67: 219–22.

Kelp, C. (2013). "Extended cognition and robust virtue epistemology," *Erkenntnis* 78: 245–52.

Kelp, C. (2016). "Justified belief: Knowledge first-style," *Philosophy and Phenomenological Research* 93: 79–100.

Kelp. C. (forthcoming). "Knowledge first virtue epistemology," in J. A. Carter, E. Gordon, and B. Jarvis (eds.), *Knowledge First: Approaches in Epistemology and Mind*. Oxford University Press.

Kim, M. and Yuan, Y. (2015). "No cross-cultural differences in the Gettier car case intuition: A replication study of Weinberg et al. 2001," *Episteme* 12: 355–61.

Klein, P. D. (1981). *Certainty: A Refutation of Scepticism*. Minneapolis: University of Minnesota Press.

Klein, P. D. (2002). "Skepticism," in P. K. Moser (ed.), *The Oxford Handbook of Epistemology*. Oxford University Press, pp. 336–61.

Klein, P. D. (2015). "Skepticism," in *The Stanford Encyclopedia of Philosophy* (Summer 2015 Edition), E. N. Zalta (ed.): https://plato.stanford.edu/archives /sum2015/entries/skepticism/

Klein, P. D. (2017). "The nature of knowledge," in R. Borges, C. de Almeida, and P. D. Klein (eds.), *Explaining Knowledge: New Essays on the Gettier Problem*. Oxford University Press, pp. 35–56.

Koksvik, O. (2013). "Intuition and conscious reasoning," *The Philosophical Quarterly* 63: 709–15.

Kornblith, H. (2002). *Knowledge and Its Place in Nature*. Oxford: Clarendon Press.

Kornblith, H. (2007). "Naturalism and intuitions," *Grazer Philosophische Studien* 74: 27–49.

Kripke, S. A. (1980). *Naming and Necessity*. Harvard University Press.

Kvanvig, J. L. (1992). *The Intellectual Virtues and the Life of the Mind*, Savage: Rowman & Littlefield.

Kvanvig, J. L. (2005). "The closure mess," in J. L. Kvanvig (ed.), Certain Doubts. http:// certaindoubts.com/the-closure-mess/

Kvanvig, J. L. (2006). "Closure principles," *Philosophy Compass* 3: 256–67.

Kvanvig, J. L. (2008). "Epistemic luck," *Philosophy and Phenomenological Research* 77: 272–81.

Kvanvig, J. L. (2017). "Lessons from Gettier," in R. Borges, C. de Almeida, and P. D. Klein (eds.), *Explaining Knowledge: New Essays on the Gettier Problem*. Oxford University Press, pp. 152–68.

Lackey, J. (2007). "Why we don't deserve credit for everything we know," *Synthese* 158: 345–61.

Lackey, J. (2009). "Knowledge and credit," *Philosophical Studies* 142: 27–42.

Laurence, S. and Margolis, E. (1999). "Concepts and Cognitive Science," in E. Margolis and S. Laurence (eds.), *Concepts: Core Readings*. Cambridge, MA: MIT Press, pp. 3–81.

Lehrer, K. (1965). "Knowledge, truth and evidence," *Analysis* 25: 168–75.

Lehrer, K. (1990). *Theory of Knowledge*. Boulder: Westview Press.

Lehrer, K. and Paxson, T. D. (1969). "Knowledge: Undefeated justified true belief," *The Journal of Philosophy* 66: 225–37.

Leite, A. (2005). "On Williamson's arguments that knowledge is a mental state," *Ratio* 18: 165–75.

Leite, A. (2010). "Fallibilism," in J. Dancy, E. Sosa, and M. Steup (eds.), *A Companion to Epistemology*, 2nd edn. Malden: Blackwell, pp. 370–5.

Le Morvan, P. (2016). "Knowledge and security," *Philosophy* 91: 411–30.

Lewis, D. (1973). *Counterfactuals*. Oxford: Blackwell.

Lewis, D. (1979). "Counterfactual dependence and time's arrow," *Noûs* 13: 455–76.

Lewis, D. (1996). "Elusive knowledge," *Australasian Journal of Philosophy* 74: 549–67.

Littlejohn, C. (2012). *Justification and the Truth-Connection*. Cambridge University Press.

Littlejohn, C. (2014). "Fake barns and false dilemmas," *Episteme* 11: 369–89.

Locke, D. (2015). "Knowledge, explanation, and motivating reasons," *American Philosophical Quarterly* 52: 215–32.

Lowy, C. (1978). "Gettier's notion of justification," *Mind* 87: 105–8.

Ludwig, K. (2007). "The epistemology of thought experiments: First person versus third person approaches," *Midwest Studies in Philosophy* 31: 128–59.

Luper-Foy, S. (1984). "The epistemic predicament: Knowledge, Nozickian tracking, and scepticism," *Australasian Journal of Philosophy* 62: 26–49.

Luper-Foy, S. (1987). "The possibility of skepticism," in S. Luper-Foy (ed.), *The Possibility of Knowledge: Nozick and His Critics*. Totowa: Rowman & Littlefield, pp. 219–41.

Luper, S. (2003). "Indiscernability skepticism," in S. Luper (ed.), *The Skeptics: Contemporary Essays*. Aldershot: Ashgate, pp. 183–202.

Luper, S. (2016). "Epistemic closure," in *The Stanford Encyclopedia of Philosophy* (Spring 2016 Edition), E. N. Zalta (ed.): https://plato.stanford.edu/entries/closure-epistemic/

Lycan, W. G. (2006). "On the Gettier Problem problem," in S. Hetherington (ed.), *Epistemology Futures*. Oxford: Clarendon Press, pp. 148–68.

Machery, E., Stich, S., Rose, D., Alai, M., Angelucci, A., Berniūnas, R., et al. (2017). "The Gettier intuition from South America to Asia," *Journal of the Indian Council of Philosophical Research*, 34: 517–41.

Machery, E., Stich, S., Rose, D., Chatterjee, A., Karasawa, K., Struchiner, N., et al. (2017). "Gettier across cultures," *Noûs* 51: 645–64.

MacIver, A. M. (1958). "Knowledge," *Proceedings of the Aristotelian Society*, Supp. Vol. 32: 1–24.

Madison, B. J. C. (2011). "Combating anti anti-luck epistemology," *Australasian Journal of Philosophy* 89: 47–58.

Malmgren, A.-S. (2011). "Rationalism and the content of intuitive judgements," *Mind* 120: 263–327.

Mandelbrot, B. B. (1983). *The Fractal Geometry of Nature*. New York: W. H. Freeman.

Mares, E. D. (2004). *Relevant Logic: A Philosophical Interpretation*. Cambridge University Press.

Mares, E. D. (2005). "Relevance logic," in D. Jacquette (ed.), *A Companion to Philosophical Logic*. Oxford: Blackwell, pp. 609–27.

Mares, E. D. and Meyer, R. K. (2001). "Relevant logic," in L. Goble (ed.), *The Blackwell Guide to Philosophical Logic*. Oxford: Blackwell, pp. 280–308.

Marion, M. (2016). "John Cook Wilson," *The Stanford Encyclopedia of Philosophy* (Spring 2016 Edition), E. N. Zalta (ed.): https://plato.stanford.edu/archives /spr2016/entries/wilson/

Matilal, B. K. (1986). *Perception: An Essay on Classical Indian Theories of Knowledge*. Oxford: Clarendon Press.

McDowell, J. (1998). *Meaning, Knowledge, and Reality*. Harvard University Press.

McDowell, J. (2010). "Tyler Burge on disjunctivism," *Philosophical Explorations* 13: 243–55.

McGee, V. (1985). "A counterexample to modus ponens," *The Journal of Philosophy* 82: 462–71.

McGinn, M. (2012). "Non-inferential knowledge," *Proceedings of the Aristotelian Society* 112: 1–28.

McGlynn, A. (2014). *Knowledge First?* Houndmills: Palgrave Macmillan.

McMyler, B. (2012). "Responsibility for testimonial belief," *Erkenntnis* 76: 337–52.

Melchior, G. (manuscript [book]) *Knowing and Checking*.

Merricks, T. (1995). "Warrant entails truth," *Philosophy and Phenomenological Research* 55: 841–55.

Millar, A. (2010). "Knowledge and recognition," in D. Pritchard, A. Millar, and A. Haddock, *The Nature and Value of Knowledge: Three Investigations*. Oxford University Press, pp. 89–188.

Miracchi, L. (2015). "Competence to know," *Philosophical Studies* 172: 29–56.

Mitova, V. (2015). "Truthy psychologism about evidence," *Philosophical Studies* 172: 1105–26.

Montminy, M. (2014). "Knowledge despite falsehood," *Pacific Philosophical Quarterly* 44: 463–75.

Moon, A. (2013). "Warrant does entail truth," *Synthese* 184: 287–97.

Murphy, G L. (2002). *The Big Book of Concepts*. Cambridge, MA: The MIT Press.

Murphy, P. and Black, T. (2012). "Sensitivity meets explanation: An improved counterfactual condition on knowledge," in K. Becker and T. Black (eds.), *The Sensitivity Principle in Epistemology*. Cambridge University Press, pp. 28–42.

Nado, J. (2014). "Philosophical expertise," *Philosophy Compass* 9: 631–41.

Nagel, J. (2012). "Intuitions and experiments: A defense of the case method in epistemology," *Philosophy and Phenomenological Research* 85: 495–527.

Nagel, J., San Juan, V., and Mar, R. A. (2013). "Lay denial of knowledge for justified true beliefs," *Cognition* 129: 652–61.

Neta, R. (2002). "S Knows that P," *Noûs* 36: 663–81.

Neta, R. (2003). "Contextualism and the problem of the external world," *Philosophy and Phenomenological Research* 66: 1–31.

Neta, R. (2008). "What evidence do you have?" *The British Journal for the Philosophy of Science* 59: 89–119.

Neta, R. and Rohrbaugh, G. (2004). "Luminosity and the safety of knowledge," *Pacific Philosophical Quarterly* 85: 396–406.

Nolan, D. (1997). "Impossible worlds: A modest approach," *Notre Dame Journal of Formal Logic* 38: 535–72.

Nozick, R. (1981). *Philosophical Explanations*. Harvard University Press.

Olsson, E. J. (2015). "Gettier and the method of explication: A 60 year old solution to a 50 year old problem," *Philosophical Studies* 172(1): 57–72.

Pappas, G. S. and Swain, M. (eds.) (1978). *Essays on Knowledge and Justification*. Cornell University Press.

Plantinga, A. (1993a). *Warrant: The Current Debate*. Oxford University Press.

Plantinga, A. (1993b). *Warrant and Proper Function*. Oxford University Press.

Powell, D., Horne, Z., Pinillos, A., and Holyoak, K. (2013). "Justified true belief triggers false recall of knowing," *Proceedings of the 35th Annual Conference of the Cognitive Science Society*. Austin: Cognitive Science Society, pp. 1151–6.

Pritchard, D. (2002). "Resurrecting the Moorean Response to the Sceptic," *International Journal of Philosophical Studies* 10: 283–307.

Pritchard, D. (2005). *Epistemic Luck*. Oxford: Clarendon Press.

Pritchard, D. (2007). "Anti-luck epistemology," *Synthese* 158: 277–97.

Pritchard, D. (2008). "Sensitivity, safety, and anti-luck epistemology," in J. Greco (ed.), *The Oxford Handbook of Scepticism*, Oxford University Press, pp. 437–55.

Pritchard, D. (2009). *Knowledge*. Basingstoke: Palgrave Macmillan.

Pritchard, D. (2010). "Knowledge and understanding," in D. Pritchard, A. Millar, and A. Haddock, *The Nature and Value of Knowledge: Three Investigations*. Oxford University Press, pp. 1–88.

Pritchard, D. (2012). "Anti-luck virtue epistemology," *The Journal of Philosophy* 109: 247–79.

Pritchard, D. (2013). "Knowledge cannot be lucky," in M. Steup, J. Turri, and E. Sosa (eds.), *Contemporary Debates in Epistemology*, 2nd edn. Malden: Wiley Blackwell, pp. 152–64.

Pritchard, D. (2014). "The modal account of luck," *Metaphilosophy* 45: 594–619.

Pritchard, D. (2015a). "Anti-luck epistemology and the Gettier Problem," *Philosophical Studies* 172: 93–111.

Pritchard, D. (2015b). "Risk," *Metaphilosophy* 46: 436–61.

Pritchard, D. (2016a). *Epistemic Angst: Radical Skepticism and the Groundlessness of our Believing*. Princeton University Press.

Pritchard, D. (2016b). "Epistemic risk," *The Journal of Philosophy* 113: 550–71.

Pritchard, D. (2017). "Knowledge, luck and virtue: Resolving the Gettier Problem," in R. Borges, C. de Almeida, and P. Klein, (eds.), *Explaining Knowledge: New Essays on the Gettier Problem*. Oxford University Press, pp. 57–73.

Pritchard, D. (forthcoming). "Anti-risk epistemology and negative epistemic dependence," *Synthese*.

Pritchard, D., Millar, A., and Haddock, A. (2010). *The Nature and Value of Knowledge: Three Investigations*. Oxford University Press.

Pritchard, D. and Whittington, L. (eds.) (2015). *The Philosophy of Luck*. Malden: Wiley Blackwell.

Rabinowitz, D. (2011). "The safety condition for knowledge," *Internet Encyclopedia of Philosophy*: www.iep.utm.edu/safety-c/

Ramsey, W. (1992). "Prototypes and conceptual analysis," *Topoi* 11: 59–70.

Read, S. (1988). *Relevant Logic: A Philosophical Examination of Inference*. Oxford: Basil Blackwell.

Read, S. (1995). *Thinking about Logic: An Introduction to the Philosophy of Logic*. Oxford University Press.

Riggs, W. D. (2002). "Reliability and the value of knowledge," *Philosophy and Phenomenological Research* 64: 79–96.

Riggs, W. D. (2007), "Why epistemologists are so down on their luck," *Synthese* 158: 329–44.

Riggs, W. D. (2009). "Two problems of easy credit," *Synthese* 169: 201–16.

Roth, M. D. and Galis, L. (eds.) (1970). *Knowing: Essays in the Analysis of Knowledge*. New York: Random House.

Roush, S. (2006). *Tracking Truth: Knowledge, Evidence, and Science*. Oxford: Clarendon Press.

Russell, B. (1948). *Human Knowledge: Its Scope and Limits*. London: George Allen & Unwin.

Ryan, S. (1996). "Does warrant entail truth?" *Philosophy and Phenomenological Research* 56: 183–92.

Ryle, G. (1949). *The Concept of Mind*. London: Hutchinson.

Ryle, G. (1971 [1946]). "Knowing how and knowing that," in his *Collected Papers*, Vol. II. London: Hutchinson, pp. 212–25.

Sainsbury, R. M. (1997). "Easy possibilities," *Philosophy and Phenomenological Research* 57: 907–19.

Sanford, D. H. (2003). *If P, Then Q: Conditionals and the Foundations of Reasoning*, 2nd edn. London: Routledge.

Schaffer, J. (2004). "From contextualism to contrastivism," *Philosophical Studies* 119: 73–104.

Schaffer, J. (2005). "Contrastive knowledge," *Oxford Studies in Epistemology* 1: 235–71.

Schellenberg, S. (2017). "Perceptual capacities, knowledge, and Gettier cases," in C. de Almeida, R. Borges, and P. Klein (eds.), *Explaining Knowledge: New Essays on the Gettier Problem*. Oxford University Press, pp. 74–95.

Schnee, I. (2015). "There is no knowledge from falsehood," *Episteme* 12: 53–74.

Seligman, M. E. P. (2002). *Authentic Happiness: Using the New Positive Psychology to Realize Your Potential for Lasting Fulfillment*. New York: Free Press.

Seyedsayamdost, H. (2015). "On normativity and epistemic intuitions: Failure of replication," *Episteme* 12: 95–116.

Shapiro, S. (2014). *Varieties of Logic*. Oxford University Press.

Shope, R. K. (1983). *The Analysis of Knowing: A Decade of Research*. Princeton University Press.

Shope, R. K. (1984). "Cognitive abilities, conditionals, and knowledge: A response to Nozick," *The Journal of Philosophy* 81: 29–48.

Shope, R. K. (2004). "The analysis of knowing," in I. Niiniluoto, M. Sintonen, and J. Wolenski (eds.). *Handbook of Epistemology*. Dordrecht: Kluwer, pp. 283–329.

Siegel, S. (2011). *The Contents of Visual Experience*. Oxford University Press.

Sinnott-Armstrong, W., Moor, J., and Fogelin, R. (1990). "A defence of modus tollens," *Analysis* 50: 9–16.

Smith, E. E. and Medin, D. L. (1981). *Categories and Concepts*. Harvard University Press.

Sorensen, R. A. (1987). "The vagueness of knowledge," *Canadian Journal of Philosophy* 17: 767–804.

Sorensen, R. A. (1988). "Dogmatism, junk knowledge, and conditionals," *The Philosophical Quarterly* 38: 433–54.

Sosa, E. (1980). "The raft and the pyramid: Coherence versus foundations in the theory of knowledge," *Midwest Studies in Philosophy*, 5: 3–25. (Reprinted in E. Sosa, [1991]. *Knowledge in Perspective: Selected Essays in Epistemology*. Cambridge University Press.)

Sosa, E. (1988). "Beyond skepticism, to the best of our knowledge," *Mind* 97: 153–89.

Sosa, E. (1991). *Knowledge in Perspective: Selected Essays in Epistemology*. Cambridge University Press.

Sosa, E. (1999a). "How must knowledge be modally related to what is known?" *Philosophical Topics* 26: 373–84.

Sosa, E. (1999b). "How to defeat opposition to Moore," *Philosophical Perspectives* 13: 141–53.

Sosa, E. (2003). "The place of truth in epistemology," in M. DePaul and L. Zagzebski (eds.), *Intellectual virtues: Perspectives from Ethics and Epistemology*. Oxford: Clarendon Press, pp. 155–79.

Sosa, E. (2007a). *A Virtue Epistemology: Apt Belief And Reflective Knowledge, Vol. 1*. Oxford: Clarendon Press.

Sosa, E. (2007b). "Experimental philosophy and philosophical intuition," *Philosophical Studies* 132: 99–107.

Sosa, E. (2009). *Reflective Knowledge: Apt Belief and Reflective Knowledge, Vol. II*. Oxford University Press.

Sosa, E. (2011). *Knowing Full Well*. Princeton University Press.

Sosa, E. (2015). *Judgement and Agency*. Oxford University Press.

Sosa, E. (2017). *Epistemology*. Princeton University Press.

Sosa, E. (forthcoming). *Epistemic Explanations: A Theory of Telic Normativity, and What It Explains*.

Spinoza, B. (1992). *Ethics*, (trans.) Samuel Shirley, (ed.) Seymour Feldman. Indianapolis: Hackett.

Stalnaker, R. C. (1968). "A theory of conditionals," in N. Rescher (ed.), *Studies in Logical Theory*. Oxford: Blackwell, pp. 98–112.

Stalnaker, R. C. (1975). "Indicative conditionals," reprinted in F. Jackson (ed.), *Conditionals*. Oxford University Press (1991), pp. 136–54.

Stanley, J. (2005). *Knowledge and Practical Interests*. Oxford: Clarendon Press.

Stanley, J. and Williamson, T. (2001). "Knowing how," *The Journal of Philosophy* 98: 411–44.

Starmans, C. and Friedman, O. (2012). "The folk conception of knowledge," *Cognition* 124: 272–83.

Starmans, C. and Friedman, O. (2013). "Taking 'know' for an answer: A reply to Nagel, San Juan, and Mar," *Cognition* 129: 662–5.

Stich, S. (1992). "What is a theory of mental representation?" *Mind* 101: 243–61.

Strawson, P. F. (1992). *Analysis and Metaphysics: An Introduction to Philosophy.* Oxford University Press.

Sutton, J. (2007). *Without Justification.* Cambridge, MA: The MIT Press.

Swain, S., Alexander, J., and Weinberg, J. M. (2008). "The instability of philosophical intuitions: Running hot and cold on Truetemp," *Philosophy and Phenomenological Research* 76: 138–55.

Travis, C. (2013). *Perception: Essays after Frege.* Oxford University Press.

Turri, J. (2010). "Contingent a priori knowledge," *Philosophy and Phenomenological Research* 82: 327–44.

Turri, J. (2011). "Manifest failure: The Gettier Problem solved," *Philosophers' Imprint* 11: 1–11.

Turri, J. (2012a). "In Gettier's wake," in S. Hetherington (ed.), *Epistemology: The Key Thinkers.* London: Continuum, pp. 214–29.

Turri, J. (2012b). "Is knowledge justified true belief?" *Synthese* 184: 247–59.

Turri, J. (2013). "A conspicuous art: Putting Gettier to the test," *Philosophers' Imprint* 13: 1–16.

Turri, J. (2014). "The problem of ESEE knowledge," *Ergo* 1: 101–27.

Turri, J. (2015a). "An open and shut case: Epistemic closure in the manifest image," *Philosophers' Imprint* 15: 1–18.

Turri, J. (2015b). "From virtue epistemology to abilism: Theoretical and empirical developments," in C. B. Miller, M. R. Furr, A. Knobel, and W. Fleeson (eds.), *Character: New Directions from Philosophy, Psychology, and Theology.* Oxford University Press, pp. 315–30.

Turri, J. (2015c). "Skeptical appeal: The source-content bias," *Cognitive Science* 39: 307–24.

Turri, J. (2015d). "Unreliable knowledge," *Philosophy and Phenomenological Research,* 90: 529–45.

Turri, J. (2016a). "Knowledge judgments in 'Gettier' cases," in J. Sytsma and W. Buckwalter (eds.), *A Companion to Experimental Philosophy.* Malden: Wiley-Blackwell, pp. 337–48.

Turri, J. (2016b). "Knowledge and assertion in 'Gettier' cases," *Philosophical Psychology* 29: 759–75.

Turri, J. (2016c). "Vision, knowledge, and assertion," *Consciousness and Cognition* 41: 41–9.

Turri, J. (2016d). "A new paradigm for epistemology: From reliabilism to abilism," *Ergo* 3: 189–231.

Turri, J. (2017a). "Experimental, cross-cultural, and classical Indian epistemology," *Journal of Indian Council of Philosophical Research* 34: 501–16.

Turri, J. (2017b). "Knowledge attributions in iterated fake barn cases," *Analysis* 77: 104–15.

Turri, J. (manuscript [unpublished paper]). "A peculiar and perpetual tendency: An asymmetry in knowledge attribution for affirmations and negations."

Turri, J. (in press). "Knowledge attributions and lottery cases: A review and new evidence."

Turri, J. and Buckwalter, W. (2017). "Descartes's schism, Locke's reunion: Completing the pragmatic turn in epistemology," *American Philosophical Quarterly* 54: 25–46.

Turri, J., Buckwalter, W., and Blouw, P. (2014). "Knowledge and luck," *Proceedings of the 36th Annual Conference of the Cognitive Science Society*. Austin: Cognitive Science Society, pp. 1958–63.

Turri, J., Buckwalter, W., and Blouw, P. (2015). "Knowledge and luck," *Psychonomic Bulletin & Review* 22: 378–90.

Turri, J., Buckwalter, W., and Rose, D. (2016). "Actionability judgments cause knowledge judgments," *Thought* 5: 212–22.

Turri, J. and Friedman, O. (2014). "Winners and losers in the folk epistemology of lotteries," in J. R. Beebe (ed.), *Advances in Experimental Epistemology*. London: Bloomsbury, pp. 45–69.

Unger, P. (1975). *Ignorance: A Case for Scepticism*. Oxford: Clarendon Press.

Vaesen, K. (2011). "Knowledge without credit, exhibit 4: Extended cognition," *Synthese* 181: 515–29.

Van Cleve, J. (2004). "Externalism and disjunctivism," in R. Schantz (ed.), *The Externalist Challenge*. Berlin: De Gruyter, pp. 481–95.

Vogel, J. (1987). "Tracking, closure, and inductive knowledge," in S. Luper-Foy (ed.), *The Possibility of Knowledge: Nozick and His Critics*. Totowa: Rowman & Littlefield, pp. 197–215.

Vogel, J. (1990). "Are there counterexamples to the closure principle?" in M. Roth and G. Ross (eds.), *Doubting: Contemporary Perspectives on Skepticism*. Dordrecht: Kluwer, pp. 13–29.

Vogel, J. (2000). "Reliabilism leveled," *The Journal of Philosophy* 97: 602–23.

Vogel, J. (2007). "Subjunctivitis," *Philosophical Studies* 134: 73–88.

Warfield, T. A. (2005). "Knowledge from falsehood," *Philosophical Perspectives* 19: 405–16.

Weatherson, B. (2003). "What good are counterexamples?" *Philosophical Studies* 115: 1–31.

Weinberg, J. M. (2007). "How to challenge intuitions empirically without risking skepticism," *Midwest Studies in Philosophy* 31: 318–43.

Weinberg, J. M. and Alexander, J. (2014). "The challenge of sticking with intuitions through thick and thin," in A. R. Booth and D. P. Rowbottom (eds.), *Intuitions*. Oxford University Press, pp. 187–212.

Weinberg, J., Nichols, S., and Stich, S. (2001). "Normativity and epistemic intuitions," *Philosophical Topics* 29: 429–60.

Williams, M. (1978). "Inference, justification, and the analysis of knowledge," *The Journal of Philosophy* 75: 249–63.

Williams, M. (2015). "What's so special about human knowledge?" *Episteme* 12: 249–68.

Williamson, T. (2000). *Knowledge and Its Limits*. Oxford: Clarendon Press.

Williamson, T. (2004). "Philosophical 'intuitions' and scepticism about judgement," *Dialectica* 58: 109–53.

Williamson, T. (2008). *The Philosophy of Philosophy*, Malden: Blackwell.

Williamson, T. (2009). "Replies to critics," in P. Greenough and D. Pritchard (eds.), *Williamson on Knowledge*. Oxford University Press, pp. 279–384.

Williamson, T. (2011). "Knowledge first epistemology," in S. Bernecker and D. Pritchard (eds.), *The Routledge Companion to Epistemology*. New York: Routledge, pp. 208–18.

Williamson, T. (2013). "How deep is the distinction between a priori and a posteriori knowledge? The a priori in philosophy," in A. Casullo and J. C. Thurow (eds.), *The A Priori in Philosophy*. Oxford University Press, pp. 291–312.

Wittgenstein, L. (1969). *On Certainty*. Oxford: Blackwell.

Woods, M. (1997). *Conditionals*. Oxford: Clarendon Press.

Wright, J. C. (2010). "On intuitional stability: The clear, the strong, and the paradigmatic," *Cognition* 115: 491–503.

Zagzebski, L. T. (1994). "The inescapability of Gettier problems," *The Philosophical Quarterly* 44: 65–73.

Zagzebski, L. T (1996). *Virtues of the Mind: An Inquiry into the Nature of Virtue and the Ethical Foundations of Knowledge*. Cambridge University Press.

Zagzebski, L. T. (1999). "What is knowledge?" in J. Greco and E. Sosa (eds.), *The Blackwell Guide to Epistemology*. Oxford: Blackwell, pp. 92–116.

Zagzebski, L. T. (2000). "From reliabilism to virtue epistemology," *The Proceedings of the Twentieth World Congress of Philosophy* 5: 173–9.

Zagzebski, L. T. (2009). *On Epistemology*. Belmont: Wadsworth.

Index

ability intuition, 105, 106
Adams, E.W., 35, 36, 44
Adams, F., 74
Adler, J., 57
Alai, M., 205, 206
Alexander, J., 211–12
Almeder, R., 14
Aloni, M., 43
Alston, W.P., 69
Alvarez, M., 64
animal knowledge, 131, 137, 142, 151–2, *See also*
    Sosa, E.
anti-luck intuition, 85, 96, 97–9, 105–6, *See also*
    epistemic luck
anti-luck platitude, 96, *See also* anti-luck
    intuition
anti-luck virtue epistemology. *See also*
    Pritchard, D., and virtue epistemology
Antognazza, M.R., 163
Aristotle, 27, 125
Armstrong, D.M., 44, 72, 222
Ayer, A.J., 2, 3, 13, 66

Baumann, P., 123
Bealer, G., 179
Beall, Jc., 46
Beaney, M., 162, 164, 172, 174
Becker, K., 9, 30, 102
Beebe, J., 210
Bengson, J., 179, 180, 190
Bennett, J., 35
Bird, A., 53, 55, 64, 167
Black, T., 122
Blouw, P., 208–11
BonJour, L., 38
Borges, R., 9, 45
Broncano-Berrocal, F., 84
Brown, J., 43, 63
Buckwalter, W., 172, 209, 210, 211, 212

Burge, T., 61, 177
Burgess, J., 35, 42, 47

Cappelen, H., 179, 181–2, 188–90, 192, 197
Carnap, R., 173
Carter, J.A., 84
Cassam, Q., 174
causality. *See also* Goldman, A.I., and causal
    theory
  and contextualism, 91–4
  and knowledge, 109, 130, 163, 173
  and knowledge as performance, 18, 128–9,
    133, 140, 147, 154
Chalmers, D.J., 172
Chatterjee, A., 205, 206
Chisholm, R.M., 2, 3, 5, 13, 48, 66, 102, 128,
    201, 228
Chudnoff, E., 10
Church, I., 202
Clarke, M., 74
Cohen, S., 21, 78, 82, 83, 87–8, 89, 169
Colaćo, D., 212
Comesaña, J., 54, 61, 72, 169
Conee, E., 70–1, 164
Contextualism, 9, 95, *See also* Cohen, S.;
    DeRose, K.; Lewis, D., and contextualism;
    Lewis, D., and Gettier cases
  and lottery cases, 83
  and luck, 89–91, 94–5
contrastivism, 9, 81–2
Cook Wilson, J., 166
Craig, E., 139, 172–5
Cross, T., 121
Cullen, S., 206

Dancy, J., 201
David, M., 30
DeRose, K., 78, 82, 83, 123
Descartes, R., 70, 182–3, 187, 193

Deutsch, M., 179, 181–2, 188–90, 192, 197
Dougherty, T., 219
Dretske, F., 108
    and closure, 16, 27, 28–30, 38–9, 122
    and conclusive reasons, 57
    and epistemic sensitivity, 57, 102, 108,
        111
    and relevant alternatives, 78, 111
    and reliabilism, 72
    and skepticism, 44–5
Dutant, J., 5, 13, 51, 96, 163, 201

Earl, D., 161, 167, 168
epistemic closure, 27, 30, 31, 43, 44, 45–6, See also
        Dretske, F., and closure; epistemic safety,
        and closure; fallibilism, and closure;
        Hawthorne, J., and closure; justified-true-
        belief definition of knowledge, and closure;
        Klein, P., and closure; Nozick, R., and
        closure; Pritchard, D., and closure;
        skepticism, and closure; Sosa, E., and
        closure; Williamson, T., and closure
    and epistemic sensitivity, 111, 122–3
    and Gettier problem, 8, 12, 15, 17, 50–1, 67
epistemic externalism, 13, 23, 68, 69, 71–2, 74, 76
        See also reliabilism
epistemic internalism, 13, 68, 69–70, 71, 114
epistemic luck, 91, 92, 93, 132, 163, 187, See also
        anti-luck intuition; contextualism, and luck;
        epistemic safety, and luck; epistemic
        sensitivity, and luck; Hetherington, S., and
        luck; lottery cases; Pritchard, D., and luck;
        virtue epistemology, and Gettier cases;
        virtue epistemology, and luck in
        performance; Zagzebski, L., and conceptual
        analysis; Zagzebski, L., and Gettier cases
    and Gettier cases, 14, 52, 53–4, 57, 61, 82, 95,
        109, 127–8, 149
    and Gettier problem, 51–2, 96–7, 107, 126,
        144, 192, 216, 229–33
epistemic normativity, 128, 129, 144, See also
        Greco, J.; Sosa, E., and knowledge as
        performance; Turri, J., and knowledge as
        performance
epistemic risk, 97, 101
epistemic safety, 9, 24, 163, See also Sosa, E., and
        epistemic safety; Williamson, T., and
        epistemic safety
    and closure, 123

    and Gettier cases, 102–4
    and luck, 102–4, 141
epistemic sensitivity, 9, 57, 74, 109, 123, 163, See
        also Dretske, F., and epistemic sensitivity;
        epistemic closure, and epistemic sensitivity;
        Sosa, E., and epistemic sensitivity; Vogel, J;
        Williamson, T., and epistemic sensitivity
    and Goldman, 109–10, 122
    and luck, 105–6
    and Nozick, 57, 102, 108, 111–17, 120–1,
        122–3
Ewing, A.C., 174
experimental philosophy, 10, 172, 175, 179–82,
        194, 196, 204, 212–14, 215, 216–17, See also
        intuition; Sosa, E., and experimental
        philosophy; Turri, J.

fallibilism, 21–2, 50, 63, 219, See also epistemic
        luck; Hetherington, S., and fallibilism;
        Lewis, D., and fallibilism; skepticism, and
        fallibilism; Turri, J., and fallibilism; warrant,
        and truth; Williamson, T., and luminosity;
        Zagzebski, L., and Gettier cases
    and closure, 15–16, 17, 51
    and conceptions of knowledge, 5–6, 17
    and Gettier problem, 8, 11–12, 14–15, 17, 67,
        219–21, 222, 223, 226–8, 233–4
Feldman, R., 70–1, 203
Firth, R., 31
Fodor, J., 167, 168
Fogelin, R., 44
Fricker, E., 168
Friedman, O., 205, 207, 208, 211

Gettier case, 2, 4, 9, 10, 82, 85, 89, 90, 108, 133–4,
        138, 141, 215, 221–3, 228, See also causality,
        and knowledge as performance; epistemic
        luck, and Gettier cases; Gettierism; Gettier
        problem; intuition, and Gettier cases;
        justified-true-belief definition of
        knowledge; Lewis, D., and Gettier cases;
        virtue epistemology, and Gettier cases;
        Zagzebski, L., and Gettier cases
    fake barns case, 18–19, 24, 79, 82, 86–7, 89,
        91–2, 94, 95, 109, 124, 129–31, 134, 136,
        137–8, 139, 140, 153, See also Goldman, A.I.,
        and fake barns case
    job/coins case, 24, 49, 56, 67–8, 75, 109, 110,
        112, 178, 186, 189

Gettier case (cont.)
  Nogot/Havit case, 80–1, 87, 88, 91, 92, 94, 113,
    127, 137, 201
  sheep in the field case, 5, 102, 103, 127, 129,
    228–9, 230–1, 232
  stopped-clock case, 79, 85, 86, 89, 91, 92, 93, 94
Gettier intuition, 68, 94, *See also* intuition
Gettier problem, 6–10, 123, 151–2, 214–17,
    218–19, *See also* epistemic luck, and Gettier
    problem; fallibilism, and Gettier problem;
    Gettier case; intuition, and Gettier problem;
    justified-true-belief definition of
    knowledge; post-Gettier epistemology;
    pre-Gettier epistemology; Nozick, R., and
    truth-tracking; reliabilism, and Gettier
    cases; Williamson, T., and conceptual
    analysis
  and conceptual analysis, 66, 104, 106, 159,
    163–6, 167, 172–3, 176
  and contextualism, 84, 95
  and explication, 173, 224–6, 227, 230, 232–4,
    See also Craig, E.
Gettier, E., 1, *See also* Gettier case; Gettier
    intuition; Gettierism; Gettier problem;
    justified-true-belief definition of
    knowledge; post-Gettier epistemology;
    pre-Gettier epistemology
Gettierism, 223, 230, *See also* Gettier problem,
    and explication
Ginet, C., 52, 109, 130
Ginsborg, H., 60
Goldberg, S., 130, 131, 134
Goldman, A.I., 175, 201, 210, *See also* epistemic
    sensitivity, and Goldman
  and causal theory, 57, 109, 110
  and concepts, 162, 165, 168–9, 171–2
  and experimental philosophy, 179
  and fake barns case, 52, 79, 110–11, 130, 152,
    211
  and justification, 30–1
  and relevant alternatives, 78, 110
  and reliabilism, 30, 71, 72, 73, 110
Greco, J., 9, 18, 25, 87, 92, 93, 107, 164, 174–5,
    210
Green, A., 132, 134, 142
Gundersen, L.B., 124

Hacker, P., 162, 168, 174
Haddock, A., 104, 107

Hahn, H., 195
Harman, G., 113
Hawthorne, J.
  and closure, 16, 29, 30, 31, 39, 41, 45,
    122, 123
  and lottery cases, 79, 83
Heller, M., 78, 88, 89
Henderson, D., 175
Hetherington, S., 109, 162, 165, 200, 215, *See also*
    Gettier problem, and explication
  and fallibilism, 11, 15, 17, 19, 24
  and Gettier cases, 17
  and luck, 52, 94, 96, 97
Hill, T., 1
Hilpinen, R., 43, 66
Hoffmann, W.E., 14
Hofman, F., 54
Holyoak, K., 208
Horne, Z., 208
Horvath, J., 214
Howard-Snyder, D., 12, 15, 16
Hughes, N., 54
Hyman, J., 53

Ichikawa, J., 161, 162, 165, 166, 167, 170
infallibilism. *See also* fallibilism; skepticism, and
    infallibilism
intuition, 172, 191, 194, *See also* ability intuition;
    anti-luck intuition; Cappelen, H.;
    Deutsch, M.; experimental philosophy;
    Gettier intuition; Goldman, A.I., and
    concepts; justified-true-belief definition of
    knowledge, and intuition; Williamson, T.,
    and intuition
  about skepticism, 123
  and Gettier cases, 8, 24, 51, 52, 53, 54,
    56, 89, 93, 113, 121, 134, 138, 152,
    200, 205
  and Gettier problem, 174–5, 192–3, 195–6,
    200
  experience, 182–3, 190, 195, 196
  philosophical, 109, 196–8, 214, 216

Jackson, F., 36, 37, 45, 161, 162, 168, 171, 172,
    177, 200, 201
Jacquette, D., 201, 203
Jarvis, B., 162
Jenkins, C., 162, 166, 167, 171
Johnston, M., 185

justified-true-belief definition of knowledge, 3–5, 17, 20, 68, 102, *See also* Gettier case; Gettier problem; lottery cases; pre-Gettier epistemology; Zagzebski, L., and Gettier cases
  and closure, 28, 67
  and intuition, 68, 178, 187–8, 189, 195, 200–1
  as JTB, 7, 13, 15, 16, 21, 48, 54, 65, 159, 163, 173, 189, 201, 215
  Gettier's question, 1, 11, 15, 16, 26, 66, 97, 108, 159, 177, 178, 199, 220–1

Kallestrup, J., 131, 136–7, 140, 142
Kantin, H., 54
Kaplan, M., 5, 163, 201
Kauppinen, A., 181
Kearns, S., 20
Kelp, C., 134, 141, 167, 169
Kim, M., 172, 205
Klein, P., 66
  and closure, 32, 38–9
  and skepticism, 41, 44
knowledge-first epistemology, 10, 21, 58, 141–2, 166–8, 169–70, 175, *See also* Williamson, T.
Koksvik, O., 190
Kornblith, H., 162, 165, 167, 168, 169–70
Kripke, S.A., 70, 177, 196
Kvanvig, J.L., 28, 30, 44, 125, 161, 211

Lackey, J., 131–4, 135, 137, 139–40, 142
Laurence, S., 167, 168
Le Morvan, P., 5
Lehrer, K., 57, 113, 127, 161, 164, 166, 201
Leite, A., 165, 168
Lewis, D., 120
  and contextualism, 78, 79–82, 87, 88
  and fallibilism, 21, 79–80
  and Gettier cases, 81–2, 84, 95
  and lottery cases, 79, 81, 82–4
  and possible words, 100
  and subjunctive conditionals, 112, 120–1
Littlejohn, C., 9, 53, 64, 130, 140
Locke, D., 54
Locke, J., 161
lottery cases, 13, 73, 79, 85, 89, 95, 98–103, *See also* contextualism, and lottery cases; Hawthorne, J., and lottery cases; Lewis, D., and lottery cases; Pritchard, D., and lottery cases

lottery problem, 83, *See also* lottery cases
Lowy, C., 51
Ludwig, K., 179, 180, 181
Luper, S., 29, 31, 38, 57, 116, 119
Lycan, W., 2, 7, 10, 15, 109, 160, 164, 168, 172, 201, 216, 218, 219

Machery, E., 172, 205, 206, 212
MacIver, A.M., 162, 163, 171
Madison, B.J.C., 52
Malmgren, A-S., 184
Mandelbrot, B., 195
Mar, R.A., 206, 208
Mares, E., 33–4, 38
Margolis, E., 167, 168
Marion, M., 167
Matilal, B.K., 201
McDowell, J., 58–62, 63, 65
McGee, V., 35, 37, 40
McGinn, M., 60
McGlynn, A., 166, 167, 169
McMyler, B., 132, 142
Medin, D.L., 167
Melchior, G., 109
Merricks, T., 12, 15, 16
Meyer, R.K., 33
Millar, A., 104, 107, 130, 140, 141–2
Miracchi, L., 141
Mitova, V., 54
Montminy, M., 75
Moon, A., 12
Murphy, G.L., 168
Murphy, P., 122

Nado, J., 181
Nagel, J., 172, 179, 180, 206, 208
Neta, R., 53, 78, 161, 211
Nichols, S., 10, 204–5
Nolan, D., 112
Nozick, R., 38, 108, 119, 120, *See also* epistemic sensitivity, and Nozick
  and closure, 38, 39
  and truth-tracking, 74–6

Olsson, E., 173

Pappas, G., 2, 50–2
Paxson, T.D., 57, 113
Pinillos, A., 208

Plantinga, A., 52, 172, 201
Plato, 2, 3, 5, 13, 66, 94, 151–2, 160, 162,
    167, 177
post-Gettier epistemology, 1–2, 7–8, 9, 10, 56,
    109, 167, 173, 218, 223, 226, 234
Powell, D., 208
pre-Gettier epistemology, 1
Pritchard, D., 9, 131, 210, 211, See also ability
    intuition; anti-luck intuition
    and closure, 29
    and conceptual analysis, 68
    and lottery cases, 85–6
    and luck, 84–6, 129, 130, 134–6, 228
    and virtue epistemology, 125, 126, 131, 134–7,
        140–1, 142
Pust, J., 162, 171, 179
Putnam, H., 177

Rabinowitz, D., 84
Ramsey, W., 167
Read, S., 33, 34, 45
reflective knowledge, 137, 151, 152, See also Sosa, E.
relevant alternatives, 153, See also Dretske, F.,
    and relevant alternatives; Goldman, A.I.,
    and relevant alternatives
reliabilism, 18, 72–3, 74, 76, 114, 163, 173, See
    also Dretske, F., and reliabilism; Goldman,
    A.I., and reliabilism
    and ability, 138, 150
    and Gettier cases, 66, 69, 73–4
Restall, G., 46
Riggs, W., 126, 129, 132
Rohrbaugh, G., 211
Rose, D., 205, 206
Roush, S., 57, 122
Russell, B., 79, See also Gettier case,
    stopped-clock case
Ryan, S., 12, 15, 16
Ryle, G., 3, 174
Rysiew, P., 10

Sainsbury, R.M., 103
San Juan, V., 206, 208
Sanford, D., 35, 36
Schaffer, J., 81–2
Schellenberg, S., 62
Schnee, I., 75
Seligman, M., 221
Seyedsayamdost, H., 172, 205

Shapiro, S., 46
Shope, R.K., 4, 10, 15, 97, 117, 162,
    163, 219
Siegel, S., 60
Skepticism, 14, 44, 164, See also Dretske, F. and
    skepticism; Klein, P., and skepticism;
    Lewis, D., and contextualism
    and closure, 30
    and fallibilism, 21, 25
    and infallibilism, 21, 23, 25
Smith, E.E., 167
Socrates, 160, 163, 242
Sorensen, R., 37, 39–42, 45, 165
Sosa, E., 9, 103, 128, 137, See also animal
    knowledge; reflective knowledge
    and closure, 38
    and epistemic safety, 57
    and epistemic sensitivity, 103, 119
    and experimental philosophy, 179, 180,
        181
    and Gettier cases, 130, 131,
        210, 211
    and knowledge as performance, 18, 20
    and virtue epistemology, 76, 107, 125, 126,
        127, 129, 132, 137, 142
Spinoza, B., 193–4, 197, 248
Stalnaker, R.C., 35, 100
Stanley, J., 3
Starmans, C., 205, 207, 208
Steup, M., 161, 162, 165, 170
Stich, S., 10, 160, 172,
    204–6, 212
Strawson, P.F., 174, 175
Sutton, J., 65
Swain, M., 2, 50–2
Swain, S., 172, 179, 180, 211–12

testimonial knowledge, 126, 132, 135, 137, 142–3,
    See also Lackey, J.
Thomson, J.J., 177
Travis, C., 61
truthmaking, 222
truth-tracking, 38, 66, 69, 76, 108, 173, See also
    Nozick, R., and truth-tracking
Turri, J., 10, 140
    and a priori knowledge, 70
    and fallibilism, 20, 21, 23–6
    and knowledge as performance, 18–20, 129,
        137–9

Unger, P., 53

Vaesen, K., 134
value of knowledge, 128, 142, 151, 164, 175, *See also* Sosa, E.; Williamson, T., and value of knowledge
virtue epistemology, 106, 107, 125, 134, 136, 137, 141, 149, *See also* Greco, J.; Pritchard, D.; Sosa, E.; Zagzebski, L.
  and Gettier cases, 125–8, 129–31, 134, 137, 142, 143
  and luck in performance, 145, 155
Vogel, J., 83, 117–20, 123

Warfield, T., 30, 75
warrant, 53, 54
  and knowledge, 13, 16, 49, 56
  and truth, 12, 24, 31, 52–3
Weatherson, B., 162, 168, 171, 173
Weinberg, J., 10, 172, 180, 197, 204–5, 211–12
Whittington, L., 99
Wiegmann, A., 214
Williams, M., 164, 165
Williamson, T., 58, 161, 182

and closure, 122
and conceptual analysis, 15, 68–9, 161
and epistemic safety, 57, 103, 170
and epistemic sensitivity, 116
and evidence, 53, 63–5
and intuition, 179, 182, 183
and knowledge-first epistemology, 10, 21, 71, 106, 141, 142, 166–7, 169–70, 174
and knowledge-how, 3
and luminosity, 21, 22
and methodology, 183–8, 197
and value of knowledge, 164
wisdom. *See also* Sosa, E.
Wittgenstein, L., 152, 153
Woods, M., 35, 36
Wright, J.C., 212

Yuan, Y., 172, 205

Zagzebski, L., 14, 169
  and conceptual analysis, 161, 162, 164–5, 172
  and Gettier cases, 11, 14, 43, 126, 203, 210, 219
  and virtue epistemology, 76, 107, 125, 129